Greek Dramas
Æschylus—Sophocles
Euripides—Aristophanes

The World's Great Books

Committee of Selection

Thomas B. Reed
Speaker of the House
of Representatives

William R. Harper
President of the
University of Chicago

Edward Everett Hale
Author of The Man
Without a Country

Ainsworth R. Spofford
Of the Congressional
Library

Rossiter Johnson
Editor of Little Classics and Editor-in-Chief of this Series

Édition de Grand Luxe

INTERIOR OF A GREEK THEATRE.

Photogravure from a drawing of a restoration of a small theatre
in Athens, in which some of the plays of Aristophanes
and Euripides were presented.

Greek Dramas

By
Æschylus, Sophocles, Euripides,
and Aristophanes

With Biographical Notes and a Critical Introduction
by Bernadotte Perrin

Illustrated

New York
D. Appleton and Company
1900

THE GREEK DRAMA

———▸◆◂———

FREQUENT experiments have shown that Greek dramas, in English version, or even in the original Greek, still have power to hold and impress a modern English-speaking audience. But these dramas gain in power, whether acted or read, as hearer or reader succeeds in realizing the peculiar conditions under which they were originally produced. And it is not enough to remind the modern hearer or reader of the merely external features of dramatic representation at Athens—of the vast open-air theatre, the national audiences, the competition for state recognition after state support, of the masks, costumes, and other accessories that distinguish ancient from modern dramatic art. The modern hearer or reader of an ancient Greek play must, above all else, press back to as full a realization as possible of the religious origin and the abiding religious associations of Greek tragedy and comedy. Even after the sense of the religious origin and significance of the drama became vague in the Athenian mind, the representations were part of a fixed religious festival of annual recurrence. In the great days of Athenian drama, when the plays included in this volume were first brought out, there was no such thing as a play having a "run." Indeed, repetition of a successful play was rare. It was given once for all, as a religious offering at an annual religious celebration. The spectator was more or less consciously a worshipper. The theatre adjoined a temple, and was within the temple precinct. The Oberammergau passion-play is a helpful modern parallel;

iii

but no such parallel can be more than slightly suggestive of the ancient conditions. To construct one that is really helpful would require large play of imagination. Suppose that the Roman Catholic Church, out of whose bosom, out of whose liturgy, with its epic and choral elements, the modern drama sprang, had succeeded in retaining that complete control of the religious drama which it had down to the thirteenth century, and that the secular drama also had developed under such control; suppose the Roman Catholic to be a state religion in a small but independent city-state of the size of Hartford or New Haven, the sole capital, the focus, the "eye" of a territory smaller than Rhode Island, in which there were more than a hundred rural Roman Catholic churches, all recognising a central cathedral leader and head; suppose the rural churches conducted religious plays for their respective communities at annual harvest festivals, and that the great cathedral head-church gave at Christmas and Easter a series of plays by three poets who had surpassed all competitors, and who then contended for first, second, and third rank before immense audiences comprising most of the male citizens of the city-state and many visitors from all parts of the United States—suppose all this, and we have only a reasonably adequate modern parallel.

The Greek drama was such an integral part of the religion and cultus of Dionysus. This god was not a genius of vines and wines merely, though even in that case the scope of the personification would be no less broad and dignified than that of Demeter. For the Greek, the grape and wine were just as truly gifts of God as grain and bread, just as intimately associated with daily and yearly human toil, weariness, and refreshment. But Dionysus represents far more than this. He is originally the germinal or male principle in universal life, that principle which, in spite of the universal law of decay and death, keeps the universe teeming with exuberant

life. He is the Father-principle in the universe, as Demeter is the Mother-principle. These two great principles, aided by the principle of light and heat personated
in Apollo, wage perpetual warfare against the principles
of darkness and death. Death triumphs for the winter
season, but Life triumphs in the great resurrection of
spring. Here is the basis for the exquisite myth of Demeter and Persephone. But Dionysus also, as life-principle, has his passion, death, and resurrection, and on
these themes early Greek folk-song expressed itself in
tones of sympathy, despair, and triumph. The strains of
such song would naturally sweep the whole range of human emotion.

According to Herodotus, Dionysus is comparatively a
late god in the Hellenic pantheon. His cultus was introduced from the Orient by way of Phrygia and Thrace.
Like the life-principle which the god personated, his
cultus was aggressive, struggling, often temporarily defeated, but finally victorious. The desperate conflicts of
the new religion with older religions also gave themes
for the choral songs of its votaries. Homer knows Dionysus only as this aggressive new religious principle, refused admittance by Lycurgus, king of the Thracian
Edonians, and bringing down on his enemy blindness and
death. His cultus fought its way from Thrace to Thebes,
and the awful myth of Pentheus, torn by his own mother
in an ecstasy of the Dionysiac inspiration, embodies the
cruelties of religious war, where a man's foes are they of
his own household.

As Lord of Life, subject to death in life and life after
death, Dionysus is closely associated with the souls of
the departed and their worship; with prophecy as based
on communion with departed spirits; with Apollo and
Demeter at Delphi and Eleusis. Under the name Za-
greus he is almost blended with Hades, Lord of Death.
As great Inspirer, he is closely associated with the cultus
of the Muses. He is, therefore, to be thought of as the

source of every aspiration and inspiration, higher and lower—of battle rage, madness, joyful song and dance, mysterious nightly revels, ecstasies, rhapsodies, visions, unutterable longings and fancies. His office might in no irreverent spirit be compared to that of the Holy Spirit in the belief of the primitive Christian Church. St. Paul's first letter to the Corinthians shows plainly that the supposed gifts of the Spirit—prophecy, tongues, healing—were often abused and allowed to run into orgiastic excesses.

The impulse to give expression to strong feeling in song or dance or imitative action, or combinations of these, is universal. Choral song and dance flourished long among Greek country people before city poets developed and perfected them. Rude folk-songs may be heard to-day among the peasantry or labouring classes of all lands. The choral folk-songs in honour of Dionysus were most naturally sung at the vintage festivals in autumn, and one may hear such rude vintage songs now among the Swabians or the Bavarians. The Dionysiac vintage hymns were rude, turbulent, passionate, but rich in tragic contents; for the great Giver and Inspirer was soon to succumb to the law of ever-recurring death. As in the Christian mass, so here in rude folk version was an Incarnatus movement, a Passus et sepultus est. There was not wanting an attendant sacrifice of propitiation. Such deep themes combined, of course, with the lower excesses naturally attendant on a popular vintage festival.

Popular choral hymns to Apollo, on the other hand, the god of light, warmth, and victory, were joyful, and less charged with deep passion. The Apollinic choral was more intellectual and less emotional than the Dionysiac. Both styles of poetry were especially cultivated by the Dorians of Peloponnesus. It was poetry to be sung by masses of singers, in distinction from lyric or epic poetry intended for solo performers. The early tyrants therefore favoured it as a popular diversion. Court poets elaborated its structure. Into the wild and turbulent measures of the Dionysiac choral they infused the purer and more intellectual features of Apollinic song. The resurrection motive in the myth was emphasized more, and the literary, as distinguished from the folk Dionysiac dithyramb, was the result. This was a hymn in praise of Dionysus for a trained chorus of fifty voices, composed with elaborate responsive structure of strophe and antistrophe by a trained and successful poet for the spring festival of the god. According to the best Greek tradition, it was perfected at Corinth, a Dorian city, toward the end of the seventh century B.C., by Arion the Lesbian—

> "Arion, whose melodic soul
> Taught the dithyramb to roll."

This Dorian origin of the Dionysiac dithyramb accounts for the persistence of Doric dialectic forms in the choral parts of Athenian drama, though composed by Ionian poets. These dialectic forms—broad, long a-sounds, welcome to singers—can not be represented in translation.

Meanwhile the cultus of Dionysus had made its way from Thebes in Bœotia down into Attica, where the little mountain hamlet of Icaria seems to have been its first conquest—no peaceful conquest either, as the sad myth of Icarius indicates. Here it was that the Dionysiac dithyramb slowly developed into tragedy.

Guided by the best Greek tradition, and by careful and chronological analysis of extant Greek dramas, one may trace the successive steps in this remarkable evolution with reasonable certainty. The Dionysiac choral had from the very start, and always retained, mimetic or imitative germs—latent drama. And the evolution of the drama of Hellas was from this lyric form with latent drama to dramatic form with lingering lyric features. In other words, the choral songs of a Greek play are not musical interludes put between original dialogues, but the original nucleus out of which the dialogues grew.

Moreover, the origin of the drama was distinctly rural. The city ultimately adopted it from the country, but never succeeded in refining away all traces of this rustic origin. The rustic singers, untrained and of irregular number, who sang rude chorals in praise of Dionysus at vintage festivals, were from the start imitative to a certain extent, in that they assumed the rôle of satyrs, or rustic attendants on the vegetation genius Dionysus. As satyrs they wore goat skins, and were called *tragoi;* their song *tragoidia*, the song of goat-skin wearers.

At Icaria, a secluded hill town halfway between Athens and Marathon, this rustic tragedy, first brought to high lyric level, no doubt, by influences from Corinth, the home of the artistic dithyramb, budded into drama. Here excavations of the American School at Athens, conducted by the late Professor Merriam, of Columbia, in the spring of 1888, brought to light sure traces of an active and persistent worship of Dionysus, closely associated with dramatic performances under state support. "The scenery," says Professor Merriam, in his Annual Report, "is in harmony with the twofold side of the worship of Dionysus—the gay and joyous, the sad and mournful—and aptly fitted to inspire a Thespis and a Susarion to further advances on the trodden path." Here we may imagine rustic tragedy—i. e., Dionysiac choral song, becoming more and more mimetic as the singers, impersonating satyrs, threw themselves more and more into their rôles. The art of Dionysiac choral song may have become patrial in the place—handed down from generation to generation in certain families—like the rôles in the great passion-play at Oberammergau. A local chorus of fifty voices, the conventional number for the literary form, would soon establish a style, to be handed on and improved. As the local art became famous, visitors would be attracted—lay visitors and poets. And so tradition has it—and good tradition, as Greek tradition goes—that Susarion of Megara, the father of Greek comedy, visited Icaria about the middle of the sixth century. He may have come to be seen and heard, as well as to see and hear. He found a local artist there under whose name—and he is little more than a name—we place the two most important steps in the evolution of the drama out of lyric song. This artist was Thespis, and the two great inventions that justify us in calling him the father of Greek tragedy were the *rhesis* or recital-part, and the impersonating actor.

Even a choral song by fifty voices can be dramatic as the singers lose themselves more and more in their themes. Divide the chorus, and the antiphonal effect, so prominent in the Hebrew psalms, and in itself so dramatic, is secured. Let one of the choreutæ or *tragoi*, say the leader, sing, in recitative solo, the goodness, joys, or sufferings of Dionysus, while the rest of the chorus, either all together or in groups, respond in choral song to these recitals, and a dramatic result is obtained as vivid, certainly, as that produced by modern oratorio. Of this recital-rôle, with good reason attributed to Thespis, the great narrative rôles of extant Greek drama are a logical development and survival. The history of civilization which Æschylus puts into the mouth of his Prometheus, the story of Io's wanderings in the same play, the narratives of Guard and Messenger in the "Antigone" of Sophocles, of Nurse and Messenger in the "Medea" of Euripides, of the Servants, male and female, in his "Alcestis," are features due, in the first instance, to this advance of Thespis.

Without further step a simple drama is possible. The second step, however, was still more fruitful. Delegating the recital-rôle to a second member of the chorus, the leader now personated Dionysus, pretended to be Dionysus himself, acted out his joys and sufferings, while the reciter still told of others, and the chorus sang response to both actor and reciter. With one member of the chorus to relate thus certain episodes of joy or sorrow in the god's career, and the leader of the chorus to act out related episodes, and with the dialogue naturally developing between reciter, actor, and chorus, a definite plot, with beginning, culmination, and ending, could readily have been presented. And when, next, both reciter and actor assumed two or more rôles, both dialogue and action would be diversified and enriched. All the personages of the Dionysiac story could be brought into the action—the relatives, friends, and foes of the god—and dialogue would come more and more to the fore, while the lyric parts of the play would recede.

Soon the theme of tragedy was widened as its resources increased. The actor passed from personations of Dionysus or his relatives, friends, and foes, to those of any gods or heroes whatever. For there were seeds of drama in many other myths and cults besides those of Dionysus, and Herodotus tells us (v, 67) of tragic choruses that sang the sufferings of Adrastus. This advance threw open the whole domain of heroic and sacred legend for dramatic representation, though the drama's special relation to Dionysus never entirely disappeared from popular consciousness, and the priest of Dionysus had the place of honour in theatres of later centuries.

We may fairly suppose that the visit of Susarion to Icaria quickened the invention of Thespis. As a result of his improvements in the local Icarian drama, it attracted the notice of artists and statesmen at Athens. Solon is said to have gone to see Thespis acting in his own play, and Pisistratus the tyrant, anxious to enrich the literary atmosphere of his court at Athens, induced him to bring his dramas for representation to the city. Here they secured state patronage, and the Parian Marble assigns the first competitive victory of Thespis to the year 536 B. C. One of the four titles of plays thus brought out at Athens by Thespis was "Pentheus," wherein the story of Dionysus was still material for tragic plot, but other titles betoken that emancipation from purely Dionysiac themes alluded to above. At last the drama is a prominent part of a brilliant city's great annual festivals.

To trace the growth of the Greek drama further does not require so much imagination, for tradition becomes surer, and authentic titles of plays presented more numerous and suggestive. No play of Phrynichus, the successor of Thespis, has come down to us, but he is said to have written nine tragedies, and among them an "Alcestis." Of course competition, in the careers of Thespis and Phrynichus, means that they had rivals, and sometimes victorious rivals. But for purposes of brief introduction only the greater names and surer traditions need to be reviewed. Phrynichus worked with the dramatic apparatus that he inherited from Thespis, though sundry innovations are ascribed to him, such as the female part carried by male singers or actors. In the nature of things, the dialogue was continually developing at the expense of the choral parts, and yet the lyric songs of Phrynichus are extolled almost beyond measure by so great a master of song as Aristophanes. They were the elderly Athenian's favourites even after a Sophocles had arisen.

But the most startling innovation made by Phrynichus was his selection of recent historical events for dramatization. His first dramatic victory is set at 512 B. C., and no later than 494 the great city of Miletus—daughter city of Athens, according to tradition, and encouraged by her to withstand the Persian might—was abandoned to an awful destruction. "The Athenians," says Herodotus (vi, 21), "showed themselves beyond measure afflicted at the fall of Miletus, in many ways expressing their sympathy, and especially by their treatment of Phrynichus. For when this poet brought out his drama of the capture of Miletus, the whole theatre burst into tears, and the people sentenced him to pay a fine of a thousand drachmas for recalling to them their own misfortunes. They likewise made a law that no one should ever again exhibit that piece." Whatever the æsthetic bearing and value of this famous sentence, it is clear that Phrynichus changed his method of handling contemporary history, if we may trust an item of dramatic information preserved by Plutarch in his "Themistocles." Four years after the glorious victory of Salamis, Themistocles defrayed the expenses of representing a play of Phrynichus. This play was probably the "Phœnician Women," and its theme was the victory of Salamis, for which Themistocles won the greatest credit. The title shows the composition of the chorus of the play, and that makes it plain that the scene was transferred to the enemy's country, where the necessary idealization could be better secured, and that the grief of the enemy was depicted in order to enhance the triumph of the victor. An inspiring instead of a rebuking theme, an ideal instead of a familiar scene, made the play a success—so much of a success that Æschylus, the great follower of Phrynichus, tried to secure for his favourite Aristides a larger credit for Salamis than the popularity of Themistocles allowed. This correction of popular sentiment Æschylus attempted in his "Persians," which celebrated Salamis, and was brought out in 472. To make the story of dramatic and political rivalry complete, Aristides should have defrayed the expenses of this controversial play of Æschylus; but so attractive a conclusion has no definite authority, though Plutarch plainly shows, in the opening chapter of his "Aristides," that there was plenty of dubious tradition about plays produced at the charges of that ardent rival of Themistocles.

Fortunately, the "Persians" has come down to us, and a brief description of its action and structure will best show the development now reached by the drama, and also serve as a transition to the briefer account of the careers of the four Greek dramatists of whose work we have entire specimens—briefer, because the specimens tell their own story. The play was given by two actors, and a chorus with its leader or representative. One of the two actors took the parts of Atossa, widowed queen-mother of Xerxes, and also of Xerxes, for mother and son are not brought together in the action; the other actor took the parts of the messenger, and of the Darius-ghost. The scene is in front of the royal palace at Susa, the tomb of Darius being in the foreground. The action, to give the barest outline, moves as follows: Enter chorus of Persian elders, singing their anxious solicitude for the great hosts of Xerxes in their distant campaign; enter Atossa, who shares her own forebodings of disaster with the chorus, till both are overwhelmed by the announcement of an in-rushing messenger that the whole Persian host has perished; choral lamentations at the messenger's brief announcements; Atossa hears the detailed story of the messenger (description of Salamis); choral hymn of lament; Atossa invokes with offerings the spirit of Darius, the chorus joining with an invocation hymn; the ghost of Darius appears with rebukes for Persian pride and prophecies of further disaster (Platæa); choral lament; enter Xerxes, a fugitive, who with the chorus responsively bewails his doom, and is at last escorted into the palace, where Atossa had gone after the vision of Darius. With this simple scheme, all the swelling exultations over Marathon, Salamis, and Platæa are given voice, and in the long description of the battle of Salamis, where Æschylus was an eyewitness, Aristides is given his due meed of praise.

The play is, of course, full of wars and fightings, as is even to greater degree the same poet's "Seven against Thebes," which, as Aristophanes testifies, made every hearer long to go out to battle. Æschylus is a warrior poet, Miltonic in style, Cromwellian in military spirit. His first dramatic victory falls in 485, halfway between Marathon and Salamis, at both of which he fought. His life, from 525 to 456 B. C., covers the militant upward career of Athens, and has no lessons of defeat and humiliation, except as he saw political principles which he disliked coming into control, and the dramatic tastes of the city where he had been easily supreme inclining toward the new ideals of a younger rival in the field.

A dramatic defeat by Sophocles may have disappointed Æschylus, but need not have embittered him, in spite of the romantic story given by Plutarch in his "Cimon." It was the national fame of Æschylus that took him to the brilliant courts of Sicily, from which he returned to Athens to vanquish Sophocles with his incomparable Orestes plays, whither he returned again, and where, as fate would have it, he died.

The " Prometheus Bound " was perhaps brought out in Athens shortly after the poet's return from Sicily, while the impressions of an eruption of Mount Ætna were still fresh in men's minds (page 18). Only two actors were at this time assigned by the state, and the play conforms to this restriction in a manner that makes one forget the restriction entirely. The first actor took the parts of Hephæstus and Prometheus, the silent Titan being represented by a huge effigy during the first part of the prologue, and the second actor the parts of Kratos (Strength), Oceanus, Io, and Hermes, the choral songs giving this apparently overburdened actor time for rest and change of costumes. The chorus of twelve Ocean nymphs makes a most spectacular entry in their winged car, as does their Father Oceanus on his winged quadruped. The scene is laid among desolate cliffs of Scythia, and after the narrative and prophecy of Prometheus have carried the imagination of the audience through the manifold fascinations of unknown geographies, the play closes with a convulsion of nature. Its theme is sublime—the conflict between a noble but short-sighted beneficence, and a beneficence that is omniscient and in league with destiny. The disastrous conflict alone is presented in this play, the reconciliation by atonement in the play that followed, the "Prometheus Loosed," of

which only significant fragments are preserved, and the
glorious reward of suffering after penitence in the final
play of the trilogy, the " Prometheus Fire-bearer." Of
this play hardly more than the name has reached us, but
we imagine it to have been a great cultus-drama, like the
extant "Eumenides." Still a fourth play followed immediately in the original representation, a satyr-play, probably some grotesque mythical farce. In such groups of
four were the dramas of Æschylus presented, organic
tetralogies, four dramatic chapters of a single myth.

Sophocles also presented his tragedies in groups of
four, but freed himself from the restriction of a single
myth for all. Each play was independent of the other
three. The tetralogy was inorganic. Hence each play
of Sophocles is larger and more complete in its unity
than any single play of Æschylus. His resources, too,
were increased by the state. He had three actors at
his disposition, at least in all his plays that have come
down to us. This made it possible for him to enrich his
characterizations, enliven his dialogues, and quicken his
action. It is thus we get such delicate character-foils as
Ismene to Antigone, Chrysothemis to Electra, with ini-
tial stages of a secondary plot. The state also enlarged
the chorus for Sophocles to fifteen, a decided gain in
musical and spectacular resources. All these resources
Æschylus also enjoyed in his later contests with his
rivals, but he was unable to emancipate himself from
the influences of the old restrictions.

Sophocles is the poet-laureate of the Athenian empire,
of the golden Periclean age. He celebrated Salamis as a
youth of sixteen and died two years before the fall of
Athens. We get distinct glimpses of his pre-eminence
in physical vigour and beauty, in wealth and culture, in
state finance, diplomacy, and legislation; while the record of his dramatic victories is long—almost unbroken.
At his death a contemporary comic poet—and the comic
poets spared not Pericles—passed this encomium on him:

B

"Blessed Sophocles! He lived out a long life, a prosperous, fortunate, and gifted man; he wrote many beautiful tragedies, he died a beautiful death, and he never had a sorrow." From a career so rich and tranquil we may well expect to get a rich and tranquil, well-poised art, and we are not disappointed. His themes may not be so grand, nor his diction so grandiose, as those of Æschylus; but he brings the great heroic strifes and figures down from a superhuman to a beautifully idealized human level. "The impression of unity conveyed by one of his plays is prodigious. Probably no other dramatist in any age has been able to move a tragedy forward with such unswerving ethical relentlessness."

As in the still greater tragedy of "Œdipus the King" its author is not to be held accountable for the savage and bloody features of the myth, so in the "Antigone." It is a myth crowded with ghastly features. "Its horrors reach their height in the special subject of the present play, the indignities offered to a dead body." But back of all gruesome detail, the sure mark of popular legend, lies the constant human element, the struggle between the higher and the lower impulses of the individual human soul. For Antigone the question is: Shall I allow the lower impulses of retributive vengeance, even when sanctioned by the formal authority of the state, to triumph over the higher impulses of brotherly love, implanted in the soul by Heaven? She answers in the nobler way, and pays her life for the privilege.

From the playwright's point of view the play differs from the "Prometheus" not only in its deeper psychology, its increase in action and vivacious dialogue, its greater subordination of the epic and lyric elements, but also in its greatest oratorical feature, the forensic scene— the high debate on the issue at stake between father and son, king and lover. This marks the advent of an element of public debate in public life, which was unknown in the career of Æschylus. In just so far as the poet

allows his work to mirror the peculiar and transitory features of the life of his day he ceases to be the perfect
artist for all times, though he has "brought the afflictive
and fatalistic elements of the story into such exquisite
balance with the heroic and intentional as most fully to
hold the reader's interest, admiration, and awe."

The plays of Euripides are much more a reflex of the
spiritual, social, and political upheavals and perplexities
of his generation, a generation later than that of Sophocles, although much of their lives coincided. Sophocles
represents the poise and full glory of Athenian power
and culture; Euripides their disintegration and confusion.
Himself a restless, introspective, unhappy, but fearlessly
inquiring spirit, his plays reflect the unrest and the forebodings of a changing order of things. For this reason
he comes nearer to the modern heart than either of his
great predecessors — "Euripides the Human, with his
droppings of warm tears." He has infused into the old
mythical framework of his dramas the hot, human passions of himself and his fellow-men, with no shielding
cloak of idealism. An ancient verdict clearly declares
that the heroes and heroines of Sophocles are men and
women as they should be; those of Euripides, men and
women as they are.

His "Medea" conforms in story and in construction
to tradition, but the jealous wife in this "Medea," to
which she sacrifices mother love, and the mother love
that struggles with jealousy, are no more Athenian than
English, no more Asiatic than Athenian. Mother love
succumbs in "Medea," but wife love triumphs over
mother love and death in the "Alcestis," "that strangest,
saddest, sweetest song of his." Self-sacrifice submits to
death to save selfishness (Admetus); selfishness is converted by this death, and then self-sacrifice is restored to
life by the great self-sacrificer (Heracles), and bestowed
once more upon converted selfishness. As Euripides infused into the skeleton of the old legend all the warmth

and pathos of the lives of loving women and selfish men about him, so Browning infuses into the drama of Euripides the richer warmth and deeper pathos of modern lives. His paraphrase of the "Alcestis," in "Balaustion's Adventure," is shining testimony to the increasing dignity and depth of human life.

All these great plays are constructed on this general scheme: I. Prologue; II. Chorus Entry; III. Episode (dialogue); IV. Choral Song; V. Episode; VI. Choral Song; VII. Episode; VIII. Choral Song; IX. Exodus. There may be slight variations in the number of the divisions, the lyric element may be increased by duetts between actor and chorus, or by solos from the actors, but the general scheme remains the same, the very nomenclature testifying to the original predominance of the chorus.

In this original choral element there was much mimicry and mummery. There were also excesses in the original rustic worship of Dionysus, which found representation in the satyr-play or farce that once closed the tetralogy. As the satyr-play disappears from the tragic tetralogy, we find comedy coming into prominence, and at last, long after its elder sister, receiving state support. It had remained a country festival of the vintage long after tragedy had been made a city rite. It slowly conquered its way up to state recognition as it took on more and more artistic form. And it was the form of the reigning tragedy, naturally, which imposed itself on the somewhat chaotic materials for artistic comedy that were latent in every vintage festival all over Hellas, though a more distinct impulse toward artistic form seems to have come from Sicily. So much Aristotle knew, but not who gave comedy its distinct artistic being. Before men were aware of her claim to distinct and beautiful personality, Thalia stood full grown by the side of grave Melpomene.

About 460 B. C. comedy had its first chorus assigned it by the state, and the years 460–430 knew the work of the

comic artists who made Aristophanes possible. He himself gives us their names and artistic traits and poetic
careers in the marvellous "parabasis" of the "Knights."
The parabasis is the dramatic feature that most distin-
guishes comedy from tragedy. The rest of a comedy of
Aristophanes—and we must judge of old Athenian comedy almost solely by him—can easily be brought under
the prevalent form of tragedy. The choral parts are
more freely distributed, and are, of course, in lighter vein,
often in the lightest vein of personal satire or jolly con-
ceit; but the ruling form, after all, is: Prologue, chorus,
episode, chorus, alternating episodes and choruses, exodus. The material of the dialogue is an indiscriminate
blending of caricature, personal satire, broad farce, and
genuine character-comedy, though the last element is
scarce. Athens was a great city, but a city-state, and
a city where everybody knew everybody else. Comedy dramatized that city's morals, politics, arts, and letters. Comedies were political and social pamphlets, always in opposition to the new because it was new, and
always giving full contrasts between old and new;
whence the value of these comedies for the study of the
life of their day.

But the parabasis is so distinct a feature of the old
Athenian comedy that it needs to be fully described and
understood. In its performance all dramatic illusion is
boldly abandoned or deftly played with, and yet in its
formal structure the original germs from which the whole
organism of the comedy grew are plainly to be seen.
The parabasis of the "Clouds" lacks one of the seven
technical divisions that go to make up the full structure
as elsewhere seen, but otherwise it is an admirable speci-
men of its kind. After the actors have been carefully
taken from the scene by the natural progress of the
action, the coryphæus or leader of the chorus of twenty-
four female shapes, fantastically draped to represent
clouds, chants an accompaniment to their departure,

wishing them success in their undertaking (p. 312, l. 15–18). This division is called the *Kommation*. Then, the chorus wheeling about and advancing to face the audience, whence the name parabasis, the coryphæus chants what may be called the Poet's Manifesto (p. 312, l. 20–p. 313, l. 32). The poet himself was the coryphæus. He complains bitterly of the audience because when the "Clouds" was presented first they did not award it the first prize. He now presents it in an improved shape, and counts on its complete success. This division is technically named the *Parabasis* (proper), and usually ends in a series of short verses to be recited all in one breath, the *Pnigos*, or choker-passage, omitted here for metrical reasons. The thought never is specialized in it. It is merely a bit of metrical and elocutional farce. Then the chorus unite in singing a lyric invocation to sundry gods—Zeus, Poseidon, and, very appropriately for clouds, Æther and Helios (air and sun). This is technically the Ode, a relic of the original choral song, from which both tragedy and comedy sprang (p. 313, l. 33–37). Then follows, chanted or recited by the coryphæus, the *Epirrhema*, or Address, a manifesto of the chorus as such—i. e., as clouds, directed at the audience. The Athenians make bad return for the kindly attentions of the clouds to them, since they have elected the rascally Cleon to military office (p. 314, l. 3–24). Then the Responsive Ode (p. 314, l. 25–32) is sung by the united chorus, invoking Apollo, Artemis, Athena, and Dionysus to come to the great dramatic function, once a purely religious service. Last comes the Responsive Address, the *Antepirrhema*, a second manifesto of the Clouds as such (p. 314, l. 33–p. 315, l. 17). The Clouds bring an aggrieved message to the Athenians from the Moon, who met them as they were getting ready to go to Athens. She says the Athenian calendar is all topsy-turvy.

After this singular mixture of personal appeal, religious song, political and social protest and satire, the

actors reappear and the burlesque resumes its sway. It
is surely a high tribute to the artistic sense of the Athenian public that the rude, comic elements of cultus hymn
and travelling gibe and satire should have to assume
such elaborate structural dress as this in order to win
public support and favour. It is perhaps also a tribute
to the keen discernment of the same public that it refused
to confound Socrates with the common run of formal
rhetoricians or Sophists, as Aristophanes wilfully or ig-
norantly did in his coarse caricature of the great teacher;
at least the comedy in which he did so, by its failure,
broke the poet's long line of brilliant successes, and
apparently almost broke the poet's heart.

As the choral hymns of tragedy by their relative
prominence are a sure index of the age of the play, so is
the parabasis in comedy. A complete parabasis in the
first part of the play, and a short parabasis in the second
part, mark the earlier work of the poet; a single parabasis, even incomplete, his later manner; and the absence
of any parabasis at all his latest. And his latest manner,
represented by the "Plutus," is an entirely new manner.
The Athens of 388 B. C. is no longer an imperial centre,
but, politically, a provincial city. Character-types take
the place of flesh-and-blood politicians; social evils the
place of great national policies. It is wealth now, not
imperial sway, which needs fresh allotment under the
comic lash. The comedy of character-types, Middle
Comedy as it is called for convenience, soon and readily
passes into New Comedy, the comedy of manners. But
in the Greek original time has spared us complete specimens only of Old and Middle Comedy.

For all the plays here presented no stage was needed.
That, with permanent stone theatre and stage structures,
came in far later times. Actors issue from a typical structure or scene, temporarily brought to adjoin the circular
orchestra, into the orchestra itself, where they mingle
freely with the chorus, and where the coryphæus takes

part in the action. The chorus and actors, as circumstances require, enter and leave the orchestra by passages on either side the central scene. The orchestra is almost surrounded by the rising tiers of rude and temporary seats for the spectators.

BERNADOTTE PERRIN.

FAMOUS AND UNIQUE MANUSCRIPT AND BOOK ILLUSTRATIONS.

A series of fac-similes, showing the development of manuscript and book illustrating during four thousand years.

FRAGMENT OF A MANUSCRIPT OF TERENCE.

Fac-simile of a miniature in a manuscript copy of the plays of Terence in the Library of the Vatican.

GETA SERVVS· DEMEA SENEX

Geta seruus domini sui alloquit se ipsu advmonturalis ... *iudicio* *evocone*

GET · era ego huic ad hoc pulsam qua mox virgine accersant · sed eccu demea·salmisses es
DEM · oh quin vare · GET geta · DEM geta homine maximi pretii esse · hodie indicavi am-
mo meo · nam is mihi est pfecto seruus spectatus satis · cui dominus curae est · ita ut tibi sensi
geta · & tibi ob eam rem · si quid usus uenerit lubens bene facim · mecti ro esse ad sabilis & bene
precht · GET bonus es cu haec is tumas · DEM paulatim plebo primolum facio meam·

AESCHINVS   DEMEA SENEX· GETA SERVVS SERVVS SERVVS
ADVLESCENS

AES occidunt me quidem dum nimis sanctas nuptias student facere · inapparando totu con-
sumunt diem · DEM quid agitur aeschine AES ehem pater mi · tun hic eras · DEM tuus
hercle uero · & animo · & natura pater quite amat plus qua hosce oculos · sed cur non domu
uxorem quaeso accersis AES cupio uero hoc mihi mora est · tibi cinaetirmena cum
qui canat · DEM eho uin tu huic seni auscultare · AES quid · DEM missa haec face · turbá

On lit a la Fin du Manuscrit

MRODGARIVS   SCRIPSIT

CONTENTS

ILLUSTRATIONS

ÆSCHYLUS.

Photogravure from an engraving after an antique bust.

THE PROMETHEUS BOUND
OF ÆSCHYLUS

TRANSLATED BY

ELIZABETH BARRETT BROWNING

ÆSCHYLUS, the first in time and strength of the three great Greek tragedians, was born in Eleusis, Attica, in 525 B. C. His father, Euphorion, is supposed to have been a priest in the old temple of Demeter, which was destroyed by the Persians, 484 B. C.; and the son was undoubtedly an initiate into the famous mysteries of his native town, and was accused before the council of the Areopagus (468 B. C.), according to some authorities, for having revealed them in one of his plays. The latter part of his life was lived in the stirring days of the Persian wars, and when thirty-five years old he fought with distinction and was wounded at the battle of Marathon. He was also at Salamis and Platea, and appears himself to have been prouder of his record as a soldier than of his reputation as a writer. Fable relates that when Æschylus was a boy he fell asleep while watching a vineyard, and Dionysus came to him in a dream and told him to write tragedy. He awoke and wrote his first verses. He was twenty-five years old when he made his first appearance as a writer of tragedy at Athens; but it was not until he was forty-one that he stood first in the competition. He wrote more than seventy plays, seven of which have come down to us in their entirety: "The Supplicants," "The Persians," "The Seven against Thebes," "Prometheus Bound," and the trilogy known as the "Oresteia," including "Agamemnon," "The Choephori," and "The Eumenides." He was fifty-three when he produced the trilogy of which "The Persians" was the first member and is the only surviving one. It is probably also the earliest of his works that we possess. In 468 B. C. he was defeated in the competition by his young rival, Sophocles. Soon afterward, either from chagrin at this defeat or under banishment by the Areopagus, he went to the court of Hiero of Syracuse, where he again produced "The Persians." In 467 B. C. Hiero died, and nine years later Æschylus returned to Athens to put the "Oresteia" on the stage. An unpopular chorus in "The Eumenides" again forced him to leave Athens, to die, two years afterward (456 B. C.), at Gela, in Sicily. An oracle had foretold that Æschylus should die by a blow from heaven, and the prediction was in a manner fulfilled by the way in which he met his death. An eagle, wishing to crack the shell of a tortoise, carried it high in the air, and mistaking the bald head of the poet for a stone, dropped it upon that. Æschylus wrote three tragedies on the subject of Prometheus; the first pictured him carrying the gift of fire to men; the second chained to Caucasus; the third delivered from his chains. The second is the only one that has survived. Many translations of "Prometheus Bound" have been made. Mrs. Browning's is the best, being a great English poem as well as a translation of a great Greek tragedy.

DRAMATIS PERSONÆ

PROMETHEUS.
OCEANUS.
HERMES.
HEPHÆSTUS.
STRENGTH and FORCE.
IO, daughter of Inachus.
CHORUS of Ocean Nymphs.

SCENE—AT THE ROCKS

PROMETHEUS BOUND

———▸•◂•◂———

STRENGTH and FORCE, HEPHÆSTUS and PROMETHEUS

STRENGTH. We reach the utmost limit of the
earth—
The Scythian track, the desert without man.
And now, Hephæstus, thou must needs fulfil
The mandate of our Father, and with links
Indissoluble of adamantine chains
Fasten against this beetling precipice
This guilty god.   Because he filched away
Thine own bright flower, the glory of plastic fire,
And gifted mortals with it—such a sin
It doth behoove he expiate to the gods,
Learning to accept the empery of Zeus,
And leave off his old trick of loving man.
 Hephæstus. O Strength and Force, for you our Zeus's
  will
Presents a deed for doing, no more!—But I,
I lack your daring, up this storm-rent chasm
To fix with violent hands a kindred god,
Howbeit necessity compels me so
That I must dare it, and our Zeus commands
With a most inevitable word.   Ho, thou!
High-thoughted son of Themis, who is sage!
Thee loath, I loath must rivet fast in chains
Against this rocky height unclomb by man,

5

Where never human voice nor face shall find
Out thee who lov'st them ; and thy beauty's flower,
Scorched in the sun's clear heat, shall fade away.
Night shall come up with garniture of stars
To comfort thee with shadow, and the sun
Disperse with retrickt beams the morning-frosts ;
But through all changes, sense of present woe
Shall vex thee sore, because with none of them
There comes a hand to free. Such fruit is plucked
From love of man! And in that thou, a god,
Didst brave the wrath of gods, and give away
Undue respect to mortals, for that crime
Thou art adjudged to guard this joyless rock,
Erect, unslumbering, bending not the knee,
And many a cry and unavailing moan
To utter on the air. For Zeus is stern,
And new-made kings are cruel.

   Strength.   Be it so.
Why loiter in vain pity? Why not hate
A god the gods hate?—one, too, who betrayed
Thy glory unto men?

   Hephæstus.   An awful thing
Is kinship joined to friendship.

   Strength.   Grant it be :
Is disobedience to the Father's word
A possible thing? Dost quail not more for that?

   Hephæstus. Thou, at least, art a stern one, ever bold.

   Strength. Why, if I wept, it were no remedy ;
And do not thou spend labour on the air
To bootless uses.

   Hephæstus.   Cursed handicraft!
I curse and hate thee, O my craft!

   Strength.   Why hate
Thy craft most plainly innocent of all
These pending ills?

   Hephæstus. I would some other hand
Were here to work it!

Strength. All work hath its pain,
Except to rule the gods. There is none free
Except King Zeus.

Hephæstus. I know it very well;
I argue not against it.

Strength. Why not, then,
Make haste and lock the fetters over him,
Lest Zeus behold thee lagging?

Hephæstus. Here be chains.
Zeus may behold these.

Strength. Seize him; strike amain;
Strike with the hammer on each side his hands;
Rivet him to the rock.

Hephæstus. The work is done,
And thoroughly done.

Strength. Still faster grapple him;
Wedge him in deeper; leave no inch to stir.
He's terrible for finding a way out
From the irremediable.

Hephæstus. Here's an arm, at least,
Grappled past freeing.

Strength. Now, then, buckle me
The other securely. Let this wise one learn
He's duller than our Zeus.

Hephæstus. Oh, none but he
Accuse me justly.

Strength. Now, straight through the chest,
Take him and bite him with the clinching tooth
Of the adamantine wedge, and rivet him.

Hephæstus. Alas! Prometheus, what thou sufferest here
I sorrow over.

Strength. Dost thou flinch again,
And breathe groans for the enemies of Zeus?
Beware lest thine own pity find thee out.

Hephæstus. Thou dost behold a spectacle that turns
The sight o' the eyes to pity.

Strength. I behold

A sinner suffer his sin's penalty.
But lash the thongs about his sides.
    Hephæstus.   So much
I must do.   Urge no further than I must.
    Strength. Ay, but I will urge! and, with shout on
        shout,
Will hound thee at this quarry.   Get thee down,
And ring amain the iron round his legs.
    Hephæstus. That work was not long doing.
    Strength.   Heavily now
Let fall the strokes upon the perforant gyves ;
For he who rates the work has a heavy hand.
    Hephæstus. Thy speech is savage as thy shape.
    Strength.   Be thou
Gentle and tender, but revile not me
For the firm will and the untruckling hate.
    Hephæstus. Let us go.   He is netted round with chains.
    Strength. Here, now, taunt on! and, having spoiled the
        gods
Of honours, crown withal thy mortal men
Who live a whole day out.   Why, how could they
Draw off from thee one single of thy griefs?
Methinks the Dæmons gave thee a wrong name,
Prometheus, which means Providence, because
Thou dost thyself need providence to see
Thy roll and ruin from the top of doom.
    Prometheus. (*alone*) O holy Æther, and swift-wingèd
        Winds,
And River-wells, and Laughter innumerous
Of yon sea-waves !   Earth, mother of us all,
And all-viewing cyclic Sun, I cry on you—
Behold me a god, what I endure from gods !
      Behold, with throe on throe,
        How, wasted by this woe,
    I wrestle down the myriad years of time !
      Behold how, fast around me,
The new King of the happy ones sublime

Has flung the chain he forged, has shamed and
    bound me!
Woe, woe! to-day's woe and the coming morrow's
I cover with one groan. And where is found me
        A limit to these sorrows?
And yet what word do I say? I have foreknown
Clearly all things that should be; nothing done
Comes sudden to my soul; and I must bear
What is ordained with patience, being aware
Necessity doth front the universe
With an invincible gesture. Yet this curse
Which strikes me now I find it hard to brave
In silence or in speech. Because I gave
Honour to mortals, I have yoked my soul
To this compelling fate. Because I stole
The secret fount of fire, whose bubbles went
Over the ferule's brim, and manward sent
Art's mighty means and perfect rudiment,
That sin I expiate in this agony,
Hung here in fetters, 'neath the blanching sky.
        Ah, ah me! what a sound!
What a fragrance sweeps up from a pinion unseen
Of a god, or a mortal, or Nature between,
Sweeping up to this rock where the Earth has her
    bound,
To have sight of my pangs, or some guerdon obtain.
Lo, a god in the anguish, a god in the chain!
        The god Zeus hateth sore,
        And his gods hate again,
As many as tread on his glorified floor,
Because I love mortals too much evermore.
Alas me! what a murmur and motion I hear,
        As of birds flying near!
        And the air undersings
        The light stroke of their wings,
And all life that approaches I wait for in fear.

CHORUS *of Sea-nymphs, 1st strophe*

Fear nothing ! our troop
Floats lovingly up
With a quick-oaring stroke
Of wings steered to the rock,
Having softened the soul of our father below.
For the gales of swift-bearing have sent me a sound,
And the clank of the iron, the malleted blow,
Smote down the profound
Of my caverns of old,
And struck the red light in a blush from my brow,
Till I sprang up unsandalled, in haste to behold,
And rushed forth on my chariot of wings manifold.

Prometheus. Alas me ! alas me !
Ye offspring of Tethys, who bore at her breast
Many children, and eke of Oceanus, he,
Coiling still around earth with perpetual unrest !
Behold me and see
How transfixed with the fang
Of a fetter I hang
On the high-jutting rocks of this fissure, and keep
An uncoveted watch o'er the world and the deep.

CHORUS, *1st antistrophe*

I behold thee, Prometheus ; yet now, yet now,
A terrible cloud whose rain is tears
Sweeps over mine eyes that witness how
Thy body appears
Hung awaste on the rocks by infrangible chains ;
For new is the hand, new the rudder, that steers
The ship of Olympus through surge and wind,
And of old things passed, no track is behind.

Prometheus. Under earth, under Hades,
Where the home of the shade is,
All into the deep, deep Tartarus,

I would he had hurled me adown.
I would he had plunged me, fastened thus
In the knotted chain, with the savage clang,
All into the dark, where there should be none,
Neither god nor another, to laugh and see.
　　But now the winds sing through and shake
　　The hurtling chains wherein I hang,
　　And I in my naked sorrows make
　　　Much mirth for my enemy.

CHORUS, *2d strophe*

Nay! who of the gods hath a heart so stern
　　As to use thy woe for a mock and mirth?
Who would not turn more mild to learn
　　Thy sorrows? who of the heaven and earth
　　　　Save Zeus? But he
　　　　Right wrathfully
Bears on his sceptral soul unbent,
And rules thereby the heavenly seed,
Nor will he pause till he content
His thirsty heart in a finished deed,
Or till Another shall appear,
To win by fraud, to seize by fear,
The hard-to-be-captured government.

Prometheus. Yet even of me he shall have need,
　　That monarch of the blessed seed—
　　Of me, of me who now am cursed
　　　By his fetters dire—
　　To wring my secret out withal,
　　　And learn by whom his sceptre shall
Be filched from him, as was at first
　　His heavenly fire.
　　But he never shall enchant me
　　　With his honey-lipped persuasion;
　　Never, never, shall he daunt me,
　　With the oath and threat of passion,

Into speaking as they want me,
Till he loose this savage chain,
   And accept the expiation
Of my sorrow in his pain.

CHORUS, *2d antistrophe*
Thou art, sooth, a brave god,
   And, for all thou hast borne
From the stroke of the rod,
   Naught relaxest from scorn.
But thou speakest unto me
   Too free and unworn;
And a terror strikes through me
   And festers my soul,
   And I fear, in the roll
Of the storm, for thy fate
   In the ship far from shore;
Since the son of Saturnus is hard in his hate,
   And unmoved in his heart evermore.

Prometheus. I know that Zeus is stern;
I know he metes his justice by his will;
And yet his soul shall learn
More softness when once broken by this ill;
And, curbing his unconquerable vaunt,
He shall rush on in fear to meet with me
Who rush to meet with him in agony,
To issues of harmonious covenant.
   Chorus. Remove the veil from all things, and relate
The story to us—of what crime accused,
Zeus smites thee with dishonourable pangs,
Speak, if to teach us do not grieve thyself.
   Prometheus. The utterance of these things is torture
         to me,
But so, too, is their silence : each way lies
Woe strong as fate.
               When gods began with wrath,

And war rose up between their starry brows,
Some choosing to cast Chronos from his throne
That Zeus might king it there, and some in haste
With opposite oaths, that they would have no Zeus
To rule the gods forever—I, who brought
The counsel I thought meetest, could not move
The Titans, children of the Heaven and Earth,
What time, disdaining in their rugged souls
My subtle machinations, they assumed
It was an easy thing for force to take
The mastery of fate. My mother, then,
Who is called not only Themis, but Earth too
(Her single beauty joys in many names),
Did teach me with reiterant prophecy
What future should be, and how conquering gods
Should not prevail by strength and violence,
But by guile only. When I told them so,
They would not deign to contemplate the truth
On all sides round; whereat I deemed it best
To lead my willing mother upwardly,
And set my Themis face to face with Zeus
As willing to receive her. Tartarus,
With its abysmal cloister of the Dark,
Because I gave that counsel, covers up
The antique Chronos and his siding hosts,
And, by that counsel helped, the king of gods
Hath recompensed me with these bitter pangs;
For kingship wears a cancer at the heart—
Distrust in friendship. Do ye also ask
What crime it is for which he tortures me?
That shall be clear before you. When at first
He filled his father's throne, he instantly
Made various gifts of glory to the gods,
And dealt the empire out. Alone of men,
Of miserable men, he took no count,
But yearned to sweep their track off from the world,
And plant a newer race there. Not a god

Resisted such desire, except myself.
I dared it! I drew mortals back to light,
From meditated ruin deep as hell!
For which wrong I am bent down in these pangs
Dreadful to suffer, mournful to behold,
And I who pitied man am thought myself
Unworthy of pity; while I render out
Deep rhythms of anguish 'neath the harping hand
That strikes me thus—a sight to shame your Zeus!

Chorus. Hard as thy chains, and cold as all these rocks,
Is he, Prometheus, who withholds his heart
From joining in thy woe. I yearned before
To fly this sight; and, now I gaze on it,
I sicken inward.

Prometheus. To my friends, indeed,
I must be a sad sight.

Chorus. And didst thou sin
No more than so?

Prometheus. I did restrain besides
My mortals from premeditating death.

Chorus. How didst thou medicine the plague-fear of
death?

Prometheus. I set blind Hopes to inhabit in their house.

Chorus. By that gift thou didst help thy mortals well.

Prometheus. I gave them also fire.

Chorus. And have they now,
Those creatures of a day, the red-eyed fire?

Prometheus. They have, and shall learn by it many arts.

Chorus. And truly for such sins Zeus tortures thee,
And will remit no anguish? Is there set
No limit before thee to thine agony?

Prometheus. No other—only what seems good to him.

Chorus. And how will it seem good? what hope remains?
Seest thou not that thou hast sinned? But that thou hast
sinned
It glads me not to speak of, and grieves thee;

Then let it pass from both, and seek thyself
Some outlet from distress.
  Prometheus.   It is in truth
An easy thing to stand aloof from pain,
And lavish exhortation and advice
On one vexed sorely by it. I have known
All in prevision. By my choice, my choice,
I freely sinned—I will confess my sin—
And, helping mortals, found mine own despair.
I did not think indeed that I should pine
Beneath such pangs against such skyey rocks,
Doomed to this drear hill, and no neighbouring
Of any life. But mourn not ye for griefs
I bear to-day: hear rather, dropping down
To the plain, how other woes creep on to me,
And learn the consummation of my doom.
Beseech you, nymphs, beseech you, grieve for me
Who now am grieving; for Grief walks the earth,
And sits down at the foot of each by turns.
 Chorus. We hear the deep clash of thy words,
  Prometheus, and obey.
  And I spring with a rapid foot away
   From the rushing car and the holy air,
    The track of birds;
  And I drop to the rugged ground, and there
  Await the tale of thy despair.

OCEANUS *enters*

Oceanus. I reach the bourne of my weary road
  Where I may see and answer thee,
  Prometheus, in thine agony.
 On the back of the quick-winged bird I glode,
  And I bridled him in
  With the will of a god.
 Behold, thy sorrow aches in me
  Constrained by the force of kin.
 Nay, though that tie were all undone,

For the life of none beneath the sun
Would I seek a larger benison
   Than I seek for thine.
And thou shalt learn my words are truth,
That no fair parlance of the mouth
   Grows falsely out of mine.
Now give me a deed to prove my faith;
For no faster friend is named in breath
   Than I, Oceanus, am thine.

Prometheus. Ha! what has brought thee? Hast thou
   also come
To look upon my woe? How hast thou dared
To leave the depths called after thee? the caves
Self-hewn, and self-roofed with spontaneous rock,
To visit Earth, the mother of my chain?
Hast come, indeed, to view my doom, and mourn
That I should sorrow thus? Gaze on, and see
How I, the fast friend of your Zeus—how I
The erector of the empire in his hand,
Am bent beneath that hand in this despair.

Oceanus. Prometheus, I behold; and I would fain
Exhort thee, though already subtle enough,
To a better wisdom. Titan, know thyself,
And take new softness to thy manners, since
A new king rules the gods. If words like these,
Harsh words and trenchant, thou wilt fling abroad,
Zeus haply, though he sit so far and high,
May hear thee do it, and so this wrath of his,
Which now affects thee fiercely, shall appear
A mere child's sport at vengeance. Wretched god,
Rather dismiss the passion which thou hast,
And seek a change from grief. Perhaps I seem
To address thee with old saws and outworn sense;
Yet such a curse, Prometheus, surely waits
On lips that speak too proudly: thou, meantime,
Art none the meeker, nor dost yield a jot
To evil circumstance, preparing still

To swell the account of grief with other griefs
Than what are borne.   Beseech thee, use me, then,
For counsel: do not spurn against the pricks,
Seeing that who reigns, reigns by cruelty
Instead of right.   And now I go from hence,
And will endeavour if a power of mine
Can break thy fetters through.   For thee—be calm,
And smooth thy words from passion.   Knowest thou not
Of perfect knowledge, thou who knowest too much,
That, where the tongue wags, ruin never lags?
    Prometheus.   I gratulate thee who hast shared and dared
All things with me, except their penalty.
Enough so! leave these thoughts.   It can not be
That thou shouldst move him.   He may not be moved;
And thou, beware of sorrow on this road.
    Oceanus.   Ay! ever wiser for another's use
Than thine.   The event, and not the prophecy,
Attests it to me.   Yet, where now I rush,
Thy wisdom hath no power to drag me back.
Because I glory, glory, to go hence,
And win for thee deliverance from thy pangs,
As a free gift from Zeus.
    Prometheus.   Why there, again,
I give thee gratulation and applause.
Thou lackest no good-will.   But, as for deeds,
Do naught! 'twere all done vainly, helping naught,
Whatever thou wouldst do.   Rather take rest,
And keep thyself from evil.   If I grieve,
I do not therefore wish to multiply
The griefs of others.   Verily, not so!
For still my brother's doom doth vex my soul—
My brother Atlas, standing in the west,
Shouldering the column of the heaven and earth,
A difficult burden!   I have also seen,
And pitied as I saw, the earth-born one,
The inhabitant of old Cilician caves,
The great war-monster of the hundred heads

  2

(All taken and bowed beneath the violent Hand),
Typhon the fierce, who did resist the gods,
And, hissing slaughter from his dreadful jaws,
Flash out ferocious glory from his eyes
As if to storm the throne of Zeus. Whereat,
The sleepless arrow of Zeus flew straight at him,
The headlong bolt of thunder-breathing flame,
And struck him downward from his eminence
Of exultation; through the very soul
It struck him, and his strength was withered up
To ashes, thunder-blasted. Now he lies,
A helpless trunk, supinely, at full-length
Beside the strait of ocean, spurred into
By roots of Ætna, high upon whose tops
Hephæstus sits, and strikes the flashing ore.
From thence the rivers of fire shall burst away
Hereafter, and devour with savage jaws
The equal plains of fruitful Sicily,
Such passion he shall boil back in hot darts
Of an insatiate fury and sough of flame,
Fallen Typhon, howsoever struck and charred
By Zeus's bolted thunder. But for thee,
Thou art not so unlearned as to need
My teaching; let thy knowledge save thyself.
I quaff the full cup of a present doom,
And wait till Zeus hath quenched his will in wrath.

 Oceanus. Prometheus, art thou ignorant of this,
That words do medicine anger?
 Prometheus.   If the word
With seasonable softness touch the soul,
And, where the parts are ulcerous, sear them not
By any rudeness.
 Oceanus.   With a noble aim
To dare as nobly—is there harm in that?
Dost thou discern it? Teach me.
 Prometheus.   I discern
Vain aspiration, unresultive work.

Oceanus. Then suffer me to bear the brunt of this,
Since it is profitable that one who is wise
Should seem not wise at all.
    Prometheus.   And such would seem
My very crime.
    Oceanus.   In truth thine argument
Sends me back home.
    Prometheus.   Lest any lament for me
Should cast thee down to hate.
    Oceanus.   The hate of him
Who sits a new king on the absolute throne?
    Prometheus. Beware of him, lest thine heart grieve by
      him.
    Oceanus. Thy doom, Prometheus, be my teacher!
    Prometheus.   Go!
Depart! Beware! And keep the mind thou hast.
    Oceanus. Thy words drive after, as I rush before.
Lo, my four-footed bird sweeps smooth and wide
The flats of air with balanced pinions, glad
To bend his knee at home in the ocean-stall.

                        [OCEANUS *departs.*

CHORUS, *1st strophe*

I moan thy fate, I moan for thee,
  Prometheus! From my eyes too tender
Drop after drop incessantly
  The tears of my heart's pity render
My cheeks wet from their fountains free;
Because that Zeus, the stern and cold,
  Whose law is taken from his breast,
  Uplifts his sceptre manifest
    Over the gods of old.

1st antistrophe

All the land is moaning
With a murmured plaint to-day;
  All the mortal nations
  Having habitations

In the holy Asia
  Are a dirge entoning
For thine honour and thy brothers',
  Once-majestic beyond others
    In the old belief—
Now are groaning in the groaning
  Of thy deep-voiced grief.

2d strophe

Mourn the maids inhabitant
  Of the Colchian land,
Who with white, calm bosoms stand
  In the battle's roar:
Mourn the Scythian tribes that haunt
  The verge of earth, Mæotis' shore.

2d antistrophe

Yea! Arabia's battle crown,
And dwellers in the beetling town
  Mount Caucasus sublimely nears—
An iron squadron, thundering down
  With the sharp-prowed spears.

But one other before have I seen to remain
  By invincible pain,
Bound and vanquished—one Titan! 'twas Atlas, who
    bears
In a curse from the gods, by that strength of his own
  Which he evermore wears,
The weight of the heaven on his shoulder alone,
  While he sighs up the stars;
And the tides of the ocean wail, bursting their bars;
  Murmurs still the profound,
And black Hades roars up through the chasm of the
    ground,
And the fountains of pure-running rivers moan low
  In a pathos of woe.

Prometheus. Beseech you, think not I am silent thus
Through pride or scorn. I only gnaw my heart
With meditation, seeing myself so wronged.
For see—their honours to these new-made gods,
What other gave but I, and dealt them out
With distribution? Ay! but here I am dumb;
For here I should repeat your knowledge to you,
If I spake aught. List rather to the deeds
I did for mortals; how, being fools before,
I made them wise and true in aim of soul.
And let me tell you—not as taunting men,
But teaching you the intention of my gifts—
How, first beholding, they beheld in vain,
And, hearing, heard not, but, like shapes in dreams,
Mixed all things wildly down the tedious time,
Nor knew to build a house against the sun
With wicketed sides, nor any woodcraft knew,
But lived, like silly ants, beneath the ground
In hollow caves unsunned. There came to them
No steadfast sign of winter, nor of spring
Flower-perfumed, nor of summer full of fruit,
But blindly and lawlessly they did all things,
Until I taught them how the stars do rise
And set in mystery, and devised for them
Number, the inducer of philosophies,
The synthesis of letters, and, beside,
The artificer of all things, memory,
That sweet muse-mother. I was first to yoke
The servile beasts in couples, carrying
An heirdom of man's burdens on their backs.
I joined to chariots, steeds, that love the bit
They champ at—the chief pomp of golden ease.
And none but I originated ships,
The seaman's chariots, wanderings on the brine
With linen wings. And I—oh, miserable!—
Who did devise for mortals all these arts,
Have no device left now to save myself

From the woe I suffer.

Chorus.   Most unseemly woe
Thou sufferest, and dost stagger from the sense
Bewildered! Like a bad leech falling sick,
Thou art faint at soul, and canst not find the drugs
Required to save thyself.

Prometheus.   Hearken the rest,
And marvel further, what more arts and means
I did invent—this, greatest : if a man
Fell sick, there was no cure, nor esculent
Nor chrism nor liquid, but for lack of drugs
Men pined and wasted, till I showed them all
Those mixtures of emollient remedies
Whereby they might be rescued from disease.
I fixed the various rules of mantic art,
Discerned the vision from the common dream,
Instructed them in vocal auguries
Hard to interpret, and defined as plain
The wayside omens—flights of crook-clawed birds—
Showed which are by their nature fortunate,
And which not so, and what the food of each,
And what the hates, affections, social needs
Of all to one another—taught what sign
Of visceral lightness, colored to a shade,
May charm the genial gods, and what fair spots
Commend the lung and liver. Burning so
The limbs incased in fat, and the long chine,
I led my mortals on to an art abstruse,
And cleared their eyes to the image in the fire,
Erst filmed in dark. Enough said now of this.
For the other helps of man hid underground,
The iron and the brass, silver and gold,
Can any dare affirm he found them out
Before me? None, I know! unless he choose
To lie in his vaunt. In one word learn the whole—
That all arts came to mortals from Prometheus.

Chorus. Give mortals now no inexpedient help,

Neglecting thine own sorrow? I have hope still
To see thee, breaking from the fetter here,
Stand up as strong as Zeus.
    Prometheus.   This ends not thus,
The oracular fate ordains. I must be bowed
By infinite woes and pangs to escape this chain.
Necessity is stronger than mine art.
    Chorus. Who holds the helm of that Necessity?
    Prometheus. The threefold Fates and the unforgetting
           Furies.
    Chorus. Is Zeus less absolute than these are?
    Prometheus.   Yea,
And therefore can not fly what is ordained.
    Chorus. What is ordained for Zeus, except to be
A king forever?
    Prometheus. 'Tis too early yet
For thee to learn it: ask no more.
    Chorus.   Perhaps
Thy secret may be something holy?
    Prometheus.   Turn
To another matter: this, it is not time
To speak abroad, but utterly to veil
In silence. For by that same secret kept,
I 'scape this chain's dishonour, and its woe.

CHORUS, *1st strophe*

Never, oh, never,
May Zeus, the all-giver,
Wrestle down from his throne
In that might of his own
To antagonize mine!
Nor let me delay
As I bend on my way
Toward the gods of the shrine
Where the altar is full
Of the blood of the bull,
Near the tossing brine

Of Ocean my father.
May no sin be sped in the word that is said,
But my vow be rather
Consummated,
Nor evermore fail, nor evermore pine.

1st antistrophe

'Tis sweet to have
Life lengthened out
With hopes proved brave
By the very doubt,
Till the spirit infold
Those manifest joys which were foretold.
But I thrill to behold
Thee, victim doomed,
By the countless cares
And the drear despairs
Forever consumed—
And all because thou, who art fearless now
Of Zeus above,
Didst overflow for mankind below
With a free-souled, reverent love.

Ah, friend, behold and see!
What's all the beauty of humanity?
Can it be fair?
What's all the strength?   Is it strong?
And what hope can they bear,
These dying livers, living one day long?
Ah, seest thou not, my friend,
How feeble and slow,
And like a dream, doth go
This poor blind manhood, drifted from its end?
And how no mortal wranglings can confuse
The harmony of Zeus?

Prometheus, I have learned these things
From the sorrow in thy face.

Another song did fold its wings
Upon my lips in other days,
When round the bath and round the bed
The hymeneal chant instead
 I sang for thee, and smiled,
And thou didst lead, with gifts and vows,
 Hesione, my father's child,
To be thy wedded spouse.

Io *enters*

Io. What land is this? what people is here?
And who is he that writhes, I see,
 In the rock-hung chain?
Now what is the crime that hath brought thee to pain?
Now what is the land—make answer free—
Which I wander through in my wrong and fear?
 Ah, ah, ah me!
The gad-fly stingeth to agony!
O Earth, keep off that phantasm pale
Of earth-born Argus!—ah! I quail
 When my soul descries
That herdsman with the myriad eyes
Which seem, as he comes, one crafty eye.
Graves hide him not, though he should die;
But he doggeth me in my misery
From the roots of death, on high, on high;
And along the sands of the siding deep,
All famine-worn, he follows me,
And his waxen reed doth undersound
 The waters round,
And giveth a measure that giveth sleep.

Woe, woe, woe!
Where shall my weary course be done?
What wouldst thou with me, Saturn's son?
And in what have I sinned, that I should go
Thus yoked to grief by thine hand forever?

Ah, ah! dost vex me so
   That I madden and shiver
   Stung through with dread?
      Flash the fire down to burn me!
      Heave the earth up to cover me!
Plunge me in the deep, with the salt waves over me,
   That the sea-beasts may be fed!
   O king, do not spurn me
      In my prayer!
For this wandering everlonger, evermore,
   Hath overworn me,
And I know not on what shore
I may rest from my despair.

Chorus. Hearest thou what the ox-horned maiden saith?

Prometheus. How could I choose but hearken what she
      saith,
The frenzied maiden?—Inachus's child?—
Who love-warms Zeus's heart, and now is lashed
By Heré's hate along the unending ways?
   Io. Who taught thee to articulate that name—
      My father's? Speak to his child
      By grief and shame defiled!
Who art thou, victim, thou who dost acclaim
Mine anguish in true words on the wide air,
And callest, too, by name the curse that came
      From Heré unaware,
To waste and pierce me with its maddening goad?
      Ah, ah, I leap
With the pang of the hungry; I bound on the road;
      I am driven by my doom;
      I am overcome
By the wrath of an enemy strong and deep!
Are any of those who have tasted pain,
      Alas! as wretched as I?
Now tell me plain, doth aught remain

For my soul to endure beneath the sky?
Is there any help to be holpen by?
If knowledge be in thee, let it be said!
      Cry aloud—cry
To the wandering, woful maid.

   Prometheus. Whatever thou wouldst learn, I will declare;
No riddle upon my lips, but such straight words
As friends should use to each other when they talk.
Thou seest Prometheus, who gave mortals fire.
   Io. O common help of all men, known of all,
O miserable Prometheus, for what cause
Dost thou endure thus?
   Prometheus.   I have done with wail
For my own griefs but lately.
   Io.   Wilt thou not
Vouchsafe the boon to me?
   Prometheus.   Say what thou wilt,
For I vouchsafe all.
   Io.   Speak, then, and reveal
Who shut thee in this chasm.
   Prometheus.   The will of Zeus,
The hand of his Hephæstus.
   Io.   And what crime
Dost expiate so?
   Prometheus.   Enough for thee I have told
In so much only.
   Io.   Nay, but show besides
The limit of my wandering, and the time
Which yet is lacking to fulfil my grief.
   Prometheus. Why, not to know were better than to know
      know
For such as thou.
   Io.   Beseech thee, blind me not
To that which I must suffer.
   Prometheus.   If I do,

The reason is not that I grudge a boon.

    Io. What reason, then, prevents thy speaking out?

    Prometheus. No grudging, but a fear to break thine
      heart.

    Io. Less care for me, I pray thee. Certainty
I count for advantage.

    Prometheus.   Thou wilt have it so,
And therefore I must speak. Now hear—

    Chorus.   Not yet.
Give half the guerdon my way. Let us learn
First what the curse is that befell the maid,
Her own voice telling her own wasting woes :
The sequence of that anguish shall await
The teaching of thy lips.

    Prometheus.   It doth behoove
That thou, maid Io, shouldst vouchsafe to these
The grace they pray—the more, because they are called
Thy father's sisters ; since to open out
And mourn out grief, where it is possible
To draw a tear from the audience, is a work
That pays its own price well.

    Io.   I can not choose
But trust you, nymphs, and tell you all ye ask,
In clear words, though I sob amid my speech
In speaking of the storm-curse sent from Zeus,
And of my beauty, from which height it took
Its swoop on me, poor wretch ! left thus deformed
And monstrous to your eyes. For evermore
Around my virgin-chamber, wandering went
The nightly visions which entreated me
With syllabled smooth sweetness : " Blessed maid,
Why lengthen out thy maiden hours, when fate
Permits the noblest spousal in the world ?
When Zeus burns with the arrow of thy love,
And fain would touch thy beauty ? Maiden, thou
Despise not Zeus ! depart to Lerné's mead
That's green around thy father's flocks and stalls,

Until the passion of the heavenly Eye
Be quenched in sight." Such dreams did all night long
Constrain me—me, unhappy!—till I dared
To tell my father how they trod the dark
With visionary steps. Whereat he sent
His frequent heralds to the Pythian fane,
And also to Dodona, and inquired
How best, by act or speech, to please the gods.
The same returning brought back oracles
Of doubtful sense, indefinite response,
Dark to interpret; but at last there came
To Inachus an answer that was clear,
Thrown straight as any bolt, and spoken out—
This: " He should drive me from my home and land,
And bid me wander to the extreme verge
Of all the earth; or, if he willed it not,
Should have a thunder with a fiery eye
Leap straight from Zeus to burn up all his race
To the last root of it." By which Loxian word
Subdued, he drove me forth, and shut me out,
He loath, me loath; but Zeus's violent bit
Compelled him to the deed: when instantly
My body and soul were changèd and distraught,
And, hornèd as ye see, and spurred along
By the fanged insect, with a maniac leap
I rushed on to Cenchrea's limpid stream,
And Lerné's fountain-water. There, the earth-born,
The herdsman Argus, most immitigable
Of wrath, did find me out, and track me out
With countless eyes set staring at my steps;
And though an unexpected sudden doom
Drew him from life, I, curse-tormented still,
Am driven from land to land before the scourge
The gods hold o'er me. So thou hast heard the past;
And, if a bitter future thou canst tell,
Speak on. I charge thee, do not flatter me,
Through pity, with false words; for in my mind
Deceiving works more shame than torturing doth.

CHORUS

Ah, silence here!
Nevermore, nevermore,
Would I languish for
The stranger's word
To thrill in mine ear—
Nevermore for the wrong and the woe and the fear
So hard to behold,
So cruel to bear,
Piercing my soul with a double-edged sword
Of a sliding cold.
Ah, Fate! ah, me!
I shudder to see
This wandering maid in her agony.

Prometheus. Grief is too quick in thee, and fear too full;
Be patient till thou hast learned the rest.
Chorus. Speak: teach,
To those who are sad already, it seems sweet,
By clear foreknowledge to make perfect, pain.
Prometheus. The boon ye asked me first was lightly
won;
For first ye asked the story of this maid's grief,
As her own lips might tell it. Now remains
To list what other sorrows she so young
Must bear from Heré. Inachus's child,
O thou! drop down thy soul my weighty words,
And measure out the landmarks which are set
To end thy wandering. Toward the orient sun
First turn thy face from mine, and journey on
Along the desert-flats till thou shalt come
Where Scythia's shepherd-peoples dwell aloft,
Perched in wheeled wagons under woven roofs,
And twang the rapid arrow past the bow.
Approach them not, but, siding in thy course
The rugged shore-rocks resonant to the sea,
Depart that country. On the left hand dwell
The iron-workers, called the Chalybes,

Of whom beware, for certes they are uncouth,
And nowise bland to strangers. Reaching so
The stream Hybristes (well the scorner called),
Attempt no passage—it is hard to pass—
Or ere thou come to Caucasus itself,
That highest of mountains, where the river leaps
The precipice in his strength. Thou must toil up
Those mountain-tops that neighbour with the stars,
And tread the south way, and draw near, at last,
The Amazonian host that hateth man,
Inhabitants of Themiscyra, close
Upon Thermodon, where the sea's rough jaw
Doth gnash at Salmydessa, and provide
A cruel host to seamen, and to ships
A stepdame. They, with unreluctant hand,
Shall lead thee on and on till thou arrive
Just where the ocean-gates show narrowest
On the Cimmerian isthmus. Leaving which,
Behooves thee swim with fortitude of soul
The strait Mæotis. Ay, and evermore
That traverse shall be famous on men's lips,
That strait called Bosporus, the horned one's road,
So named because of thee, who so wilt pass
From Europe's plain to Asia's continent.
How think ye, nymphs? the king of gods appears
Impartial in ferocious deeds? Behold!
The god desirous of this mortal's love
Hath cursed her with these wanderings. Ah, fair child,
Thou hast met a bitter groom for bridal troth!
For all thou yet hast heard can only prove
The incompleted prelude of thy doom.
    Io. Ah, ah!
    Prometheus. Is't thy turn now to shriek and moan?
How wilt thou, when thou hast hearkened what remains?
    Chorus. Besides the grief thou hast told, can aught
      remain?
    Prometheus. A sea of foredoomed evil worked to storm.

Io. What boots my life, then? why not cast myself
Down headlong from this miserable rock,
That, dashed against the flats, I may redeem
My soul from sorrow? Better once to die
Than day by day to suffer.

Prometheus.   Verily,
It would be hard for thee to bear my woe
For whom it is appointed not to die.
Death frees from woe; but I before me see
In all my far prevision not a bound
To all I suffer, ere that Zeus shall fall
From being a king.

Io.   And can it ever be
That Zeus shall fall from empire?

Prometheus.   Thou, methinks,
Wouldst take some joy to see it.

Io.   Could I choose?
I who endure such pangs now, by that god!

Prometheus. Learn from me, therefore, that the event
     shall be.

Io. By whom shall his imperial sceptred hand
Be emptied so?

Prometheus.   Himself shall spoil himself,
Through his idiotic counsels.

Io.   How? declare,
Unless the word bring evil.

Prometheus.   He shall wed,
And in the marriage-bond be joined to grief.

Io. A heavenly bride, or human? Speak it out,
If it be utterable.

Prometheus.   Why should I say which?
It ought not to be uttered, verily.

Io.   Then
It is his wife shall tear him from his throne?

Prometheus. It is his wife shall bear a son to him
More mighty than the father.

Io.   From this doom

Hath he no refuge?

Prometheus.   None : or ere that I
Loosed from these fetters—

Io.   Yea : but who shall loose
While Zeus is adverse?

Prometheus.   One who is born of thee :
It is ordained so.

Io.   What is this thou sayest?
A son of mine shall liberate thee from woe?

Prometheus. After ten generations count three more,
And find him in the third.

Io.   The oracle
Remains obscure.

Prometheus.   And search it not to learn
Thine own griefs from it.

Io.   Point me not to a good
To leave me straight bereaved.

Prometheus.   I am prepared
To grant thee one of two things.

Io.   But which two?
Set them before me ; grant me power to choose.

Prometheus. I grant it ; choose now! Shall I name
     aloud
What griefs remain to wound thee, or what hand
Shall save me out of mine?

Chorus.   Vouchsafe, O god,
The one grace of the twain to her who prays,
The next to me, and turn back neither prayer
Dishonoured by denial.   To herself
Recount the future wandering of her feet ;
Then point me to the looser of thy chain,
Because I yearn to know him.

Prometheus.   Since ye will,
Of absolute will, this knowledge, I will set
No contrary against it, nor keep back
A word of all ye ask for.   Io, first
To thee I must relate thy wandering course

3

Far winding. As I tell it, write it down
In thy soul's book of memories. When thou hast passed
The refluent bound that parts two continents,
Track on the footsteps of the orient sun
In his own fire across the roar of seas—
Fly till thou hast reached the Gorgonæan flats
Beside Cisthené. There the Phorcides,
Three ancient maidens, live, with shape of swan,
One tooth between them, and one common eye,
On whom the sun doth never look at all
With all his rays, nor evermore the moon
When she looks through the night. Anear to whom
Are the Gorgon sisters three, enclothed with wings,
With twisted snakes for ringlets, man-abhorred:
There is no mortal gazes in their face,
And gazing can breathe on. I speak of such
To guard thee from their horror. Ay, and list
Another tale of a dreadful sight: beware
The Griffins, those unbarking dogs of Zeus,
Those sharp-mouthed dogs!—and the Arimaspian host
Of one-eyed horsemen, habiting beside
The river of Pluto that runs bright with gold:
Approach them not, beseech thee. Presently
Thou'lt come to a distant land, a dusky tribe
Of dwellers at the fountain of the Sun,
Whence flows the River Æthiops; wind along
Its banks, and turn off at the cataracts,
Just as the Nile pours from the Bybline hills
His holy and sweet wave: his course shall guide
Thine own to that triangular Nile-ground
Where, Io, is ordained for thee and thine
A lengthened exile. Have I said in this
Aught darkly or incompletely?—now repeat
The question, make the knowledge fuller! Lo,
I have more leisure than I covet here.

 Chorus. If thou canst tell us aught that's left untold,
Or loosely told, of her most dreary flight,

Declare it straight; but, if thou hast uttered all,
Grant us that latter grace for which we prayed,
Remembering how we prayed it.
    Prometheus.   She has heard
The uttermost of her wandering. There it ends.
But, that she may be certain not to have heard
All vainly, I will speak what she endured
Ere coming hither, and invoke the past
To prove my prescience true. And so—to leave
A multitude of words, and pass at once
To the subject of thy course—when thou hadst gone
To those Molossian plains which sweep around
Dodona shouldering Heaven, whereby the fane
Of Zeus Thesprotian keepeth oracle,
And, wonder past belief, where oaks do wave
Articulate adjurations—(ay, the same
Saluted thee in no perplexèd phrase,
But clear with glory, noble wife of Zeus
That shouldst be, there some sweetness took thy sense!)
Thou didst rush farther onward, stung along
The ocean-shore, toward Rhea's mighty bay,
And, tossed back from it, wast tossed to it again
In stormy evolution: and know well,
In coming time that hollow of the sea
Shall bear the name Ionian, and present
A monument of Io's passage through,
Unto all mortals. Be these words the signs
Of my soul's power to look beyond the veil
Of visible things. The rest to you and her
I will declare in common audience, nymphs,
Returning thither where my speech brake off.
There is a town, Canobus, built upon
The earth's fair margin, at the mouth of the Nile,
And on the mound washed up by it: Io, there
Shall Zeus give back to thee thy perfect mind,
And only by the pressure and the touch   ,
Of a hand not terrible; and thou to Zeus

Shalt bear a dusky son who shall be called
Thence Epaphus, *Touched*. That son shall pluck the fruit
Of all that land wide-watered by the flow
Of Nile ; but after him, when counting out
As far as the fifth full generation, then
Full fifty maidens, a fair woman-race,
Shall back to Argos turn reluctantly,
To fly the proffered nuptials of their kin,
Their father's brothers. These being passion-struck,
Like falcons bearing hard on flying doves,
Shall follow hunting at a quarry of love
They should not hunt ; till envious Heaven maintain
A curse betwixt that beauty and their desire,
And Greece receive them, to be overcome
In murtherous woman-war by fierce red hands
Kept savage by the night. For every wife
Shall slay a husband, dyeing deep in blood
The sword of a double edge—(I wish indeed
As fair a marriage-joy to all my foes !)
One bride alone shall fail to smite to death
The head upon her pillow, touched with love
Made impotent of purpose, and impelled
To choose the lesser evil—shame on her cheeks,
Than blood-guilt on her hands ; which bride shall bear
A royal race in Argos. Tedious speech
Were needed to relate particulars
Of these things ; 'tis enough that from her seed
Shall spring the strong He, famous with the bow,
Whose arm shall break my fetters off. Behold,
My mother Themis, that old Titaness,
Delivered to me such an oracle ;
But how and when, I should be long to speak,
And thou, in hearing, wouldst not gain at all.

    Io.   Eleleu, eleleu !
          How the spasm and the pain,
          And the fire on the brain,
             Strike, burning me through !

How the sting of the curse, all aflame as it flew,
  Pricks me onward again!
How my heart in its terror is spurning my breast,
And my eyes like the wheels of a chariot roll round!
I am whirled from my course, to the east, to the west,
In the whirlwind of frenzy all madly inwound;
And my mouth is unbridled for anguish and hate,
And my words beat in vain, in wild storms of unrest,
  On the sea of my desolate fate.

[Io rushes out.

C<small>HORUS</small>—strophe

Oh, wise was he, oh, wise was he,
Who first within his spirit knew,
And with his tongue declared it true,
That love comes best that comes unto
    The equal of degree!
And that the poor and that the low
Should seek no love from those above,
Whose souls are fluttered with the flow
Of airs about their golden height,
Or proud because they see arow
  Ancestral crowns of light.

Antistrophe

Oh, never, never, may ye, Fates,
  Behold me with your awful eyes
  Lift mine too fondly up the skies
Where Zeus upon the purple waits!
  Nor let me step too near, too near,
To any suitor bright from heaven;
  Because I see, because I fear,
This loveless maiden vexed and laden
By this fell curse of Heré, driven
  On wanderings dread and drear.

Epode

Nay, grant an equal troth instead
  Of nuptial love, to bind me by!

It will not hurt, I shall not dread
  To meet it in reply.
But let not love from those above
Revert and fix me, as I said,
  With that inevitable Eye !
I have no sword to fight that fight,
I have no strength to tread that path,
I know not if my nature hath
The power to bear, I can not see
Whither from Zeus's infinite
I have the power to flee.

Prometheus. Yet Zeus, albeit most absolute of will,
Shall turn to meekness—such a marriage-rite
He holds in preparation, which anon
Shall thrust him headlong from his gerent seat
Adown the abysmal void; and so the curse
His father Chronos muttered in his fall,
As he fell from his ancient throne and cursed,
Shall be accomplished wholly.   No escape
From all that ruin shall the filial Zeus
Find granted to him from any of his gods
Unless I teach him.   I the refuge know,
And I, the means.   Now, therefore, let him sit
And brave the imminent doom, and fix his faith
On his supernal noises hurtling on
With restless hand the bolt that breathes out fire ;
For these things shall not help him, none of them,
Nor hinder his perdition when he falls
To shame, and lower than patience : such a foe
He doth himself prepare against himself,
A wonder of unconquerable hate,
An organizer of sublimer fire
Than glares in lightnings, and of grander sound
Than aught the thunder rolls, out-thundering it,
With power to shatter in Poseidon's fist
The trident-spear, which, while it plagues the sea,

Doth shake the shores around it.   Ay, and Zeus,
Precipitated thus, shall learn at length
The difference betwixt rule and servitude.
 Chorus. Thou makest threats for Zeus of thy desires.
 Prometheus. I tell you all these things shall be fulfilled
Even so as I desire them.
 Chorus.   Must we, then,
Look out for one shall come to master Zeus?
 Prometheus. These chains weigh lighter than his sor-
  rows shall.
 Chorus. How art thou not afraid to utter such words?
 Prometheus. What should I fear, who can not die?
 Chorus.   But he
Can visit thee with dreader woe than death's.
 Prometheus. Why, let him do it!   I am here, prepared
For all things and their pangs.
 Chorus.   · The wise are they
Who reverence Adrasteia.
 Prometheus.   Reverence thou,
Adore thou, flatter thou, whomever reigns,
Whenever reigning!   But for me, your Zeus
Is less than nothing.   Let him act and reign
His brief hour out according to his will:
He will not, therefore, rule the gods too long.
But lo! I see that courier-god of Zeus,
That new-made menial of the new-crowned king:
He, doubtless, comes to announce to us something new.

HERMES *enters*

 Hermes. I speak to thee, the sophist, the talker-down
Of scorn by scorn, the sinner against gods,
The reverencer of men, the thief of fire—
I speak to thee and adjure thee: Zeus requires
Thy declaration of what marriage-rite
Thus moves thy vaunt, and shall hereafter cause
His fall from empire.   Do not wrap thy speech
In riddles, but speak clearly.   Never cast

Ambiguous paths, Prometheus, for my feet,
Since Zeus, thou mayst perceive, is scarcely won
To mercy by such means.
  Prometheus.   A speech well-mouthed
In the utterance, and full-minded in the sense,
As doth befit a servant of the gods!
New gods, ye newly reign, and think, forsooth,
Ye dwell in towers too high for any dart
To carry a wound there! Have I not stood by
While two kings fell from thence? and shall I not
Behold the third, the same who rules you now,
Fall, shamed to sudden ruin? Do I seem
To tremble and quail before your modern gods?
Far be it from me! For thyself depart;
Retread thy steps in haste. To all thou hast asked
I answer nothing.
  Hermes.   Such a wind of pride
Impelled thee of yore full sail upon these rocks.
  Prometheus. I would not barter—learn thou soothly
   that !—
My suffering for thy service. I maintain
It is a nobler thing to serve these rocks
Than live a faithful slave to Father Zeus.
Thus upon scorners I retort their scorn.
  Hermes. It seems that thou dost glory in thy despair.
  Prometheus. I glory? Would my foes did glory so,
And I stood by to see them !—naming whom,
Thou art not unremembered.
  Hermes.   Dost thou charge
Me also with the blame of thy mischance?
  Prometheus. I tell thee I loathe the universal gods,
Who, for the good I gave them, rendered back
The ill of their injustice.
  Hermes. Thou art mad,
Thou art raving, Titan, at the fever-height.
  Prometheus. If it be madness to abhor my foes,
May I be mad !

PROMETHEUS BOUND.

Photogravure from a painting by Gustav Graef.

Hermes.   If thou wert prosperous,
Thou wouldst be unendurable.
    Prometheus.   Alas !
    Hermes. Zeus knows not that word.
    Prometheus.   But maturing Time
Teaches all things.
    Hermes.   Howbeit, thou hast not learned
The wisdom yet, thou needest.
    Prometheus.   If I had,
I should not talk thus with a slave like thee.
    Hermes. No answer thou vouchsafest, I believe,
To the great Sire's requirement.
    Prometheus.   Verily
I owe him grateful service, and should pay it.
    Hermes. Why, thou dost mock me, Titan, as I stood
A child before thy face.
    Prometheus.   No child, forsooth,
But yet more foolish than a foolish child,
If thou expect that I should answer aught
Thy Zeus can ask. No torture from his hand,
Nor any machination in the world,
Shall force mine utterance ere he loose, himself,
These cankerous fetters from me. For the rest,
Let him now hurl his blanching lightnings down,
And with his white-winged snows, and mutterings deep
Of subterranean thunders, mix all things,
Confound them in disorder. None of this
Shall bend my sturdy will, and make me speak
The name of his dethroner who shall come.
    Hermes. Can this avail thee ? Look to it !
    Prometheus.   Long ago
It was looked forward to, precounselled of.
    Hermes. Vain god, take righteous courage ! Dare for
        once
To apprehend and front thine agonies
With a just prudence.
    Prometheus.   Vainly dost thou chafe

My soul with exhortation, as yonder sea
Goes beating on the rock. Oh! think no more
That I, fear-struck by Zeus to a woman's mind,
Will supplicate him, loathed as he is,
With feminine upliftings of my hands,
To break these chains. Far from me be the thought!
  Hermes. I have, indeed, methinks, said much in vain,
For still thy heart beneath my showers of prayers
Lies dry and hard, nay, leaps like a young horse
Who bites against the new bit in his teeth,
And tugs and struggles against the new-tried rein,
Still fiercest in the feeblest thing of all,
Which sophism is; since absolute will disjoined
From perfect mind is worse than weak. Behold,
Unless my words persuade thee, what a blast
And whirlwind of inevitable woe
Must sweep persuasion through thee! For at first
The Father will split up this jut of rock
With the great thunder and the bolted flame,
And hide thy body where a hinge of stone
Shall catch it like an arm; and when thou hast passed
A long black time within, thou shalt come out
To front the sun while Zeus's wingèd hound,
The strong, carnivorous eagle, shall wheel down
To meet thee, self-called to a daily feast,
And set his fierce beak in thee, and tear off
The long rags of thy flesh, and batten deep
Upon thy dusky liver. Do not look
For any end, moreover, to this curse,
Or ere some god appear to accept thy pangs
On his own head vicarious, and descend
With unreluctant step the darks of hell
And gloomy abysses around Tartarus.
Then ponder this—this threat is not a growth
Of vain invention; it is spoken and meant:
King Zeus's mouth is impotent to lie,
Consummating the utterance by the act.

So, look to it, thou ! take heed, and nevermore
Forget good counsel to indulge self-will.
 Chorus. Our Hermes suits his reasons to the times,
At least I think so, since he bids thee drop
Self-will for prudent counsel. Yield to him !
When the wise err, their wisdom makes their shame.
 Prometheus. Unto me the foreknower, this mandate of
   power
  He cries, to reveal it.
What's strange in my fate, if I suffer from hate
  At the hour that I feel it ?
Let the locks of the lightning, all bristling and whitening,
  Flash, coiling me round,
While the ether goes surging 'neath thunder and
  scourging
  Of wild winds unbound !
Let the blast of the firmament whirl from its place
  The earth rooted below,
And the brine of the ocean, in rapid emotion,
  Be driven in the face
Of the stars up in heaven, as they walk to and fro !
Let him hurl me anon into Tartarus—on—
  To the blackest degree,
With Necessity's vortices strangling me down !
But he can not join death to a fate meant for me !
 Hermes. Why, the words that he speaks and the
   thoughts that he thinks
  Are maniacal !—add,
If the Fate who hath bound him should loose not the links,
  He were utterly mad.
  Then depart ye who groan with him,
  Leaving to moan with him ;
Go in haste ! lest the roar of the thunder anearing
Should blast you to idiocy, living and hearing.
 Chorus. Change thy speech for another, thy thought
  for a new,
  If to move me and teach me indeed be thy care ;

For thy words swerve so far from the loyal and true
    That the thunder of Zeus seems more easy to bear.
How! couldst teach me to venture such vileness? behold!
    I choose with this victim this anguish foretold!
I recoil from the traitor in haste and disdain,
And I know that the curse of the treason is worse
        Than the pang of the chain.
    Hermes. Then remember, O nymphs, what I tell you
      before,
    Nor, when pierced by the arrows that Até will throw
      you,
Cast blame on your fate, and declare evermore
    That Zeus thrust you on anguish he did not foreshow
      you.
Nay, verily, nay! for ye perish anon
    For your deed, by your choice. By no blindness of
      doubt,
No abruptness of doom, but by madness alone,
    In the great net of Até, whence none cometh out,
        Ye are wound and undone.
    Prometheus. Ay! in act now, in word now no more,
        Earth is rocking in space.
And the thunders crash up with a roar upon roar,
    And the eddying lightnings flash fire in my face,
And the whirlwinds are whirling the dust round and
    round,
    And the blasts of the winds universal leap free,
And blow each upon each with a passion of sound,
    And ether goes mingling in storm with the sea.
Such a curse on my head, in a manifest dread,
    From the hand of your Zeus has been hurtled along.
Oh, my mother's fair glory! O Æther, enringing
All eyes with the sweet common light of thy bringing!
    Dost see how I suffer this wrong?

THE AGAMEMNON OF
ÆSCHYLUS

TRANSLATED BY

ROBERT POTTER

DRAMATIS PERSONÆ

WATCHMAN.
CLYTEMNESTRA.
HERALD.
AGAMEMNON.
CASSANDRA.
ÆGISTHUS.
CHORUS OF ARGIVE SENATORS.

SCENE: Argos, before the Palace of Agamemnon

AGAMEMNON

———►◆◄———

THE WATCHMAN. Ye fav'ring gods, relieve me
    from this toil:
    Fixed, as a dog, on Agamemnon's roof
    I watch the livelong year, observing hence
The host of stars, that in the spangled skies
Take their bright stations, and to mortals bring
Winter and summer; radiant rulers, when
They set, or rising, glitter through the night.
Here now I watch, if haply I may see
The blazing torch, whose flame brings news from Troy,
The signal of its ruin: these high hopes
My royal mistress, thinking on her lord,
Feeds in her heart. Meanwhile the dews of night
Fall on my couch, unvisited by dreams;
For fear, lest sleep should close my eyes, repels
The soft intruder. When my spirits prompt me
To raise the song, or hum the sullen notes
Preventing slumber, then I sigh, and wail
The state of this unhappy house, no more
Well-ordered as of old. But may my toils
Be happily relieved! Blaze, thou bright flame,
Herald of joy, blaze through the gloomy shades—
And it does blaze. Hail, thou auspicious flame,
That streaming through the night denouncest joy,
Welcomed with many a festal dance in Argos!
In the queen's ear I'll holloa this, and rouse her

From her soft couch with speed, that she may teach
The royal dome to echo with the strains
Of choral warblings greeting this blest fire,
Bright sign that Troy is taken.　Nor shall I
Forbear the prelude to the dance before her:
For by this watch, so prosperously concluded,
I to my masters shall assure good fortune.
Shall I then see my king returned, once more
To grace this house? and shall this hand once more
Hang on his friendly hand?　I could unfold
A tale.　But, hush; my tongue is chained: these walls,
Could they but speak, would make discoveries.
There are who know this; and to them this hint
Were plain: to those that know it not, mysterious.

　　　　Chorus.　The tenth slow year rolls on, since great in
　　　　　　arms
The noble sons of Atreus, each exalted
To majesty and empire, royal brothers,
Led hence a thousand ships, the Argive fleet,
Big with the fate of Priam and of Troy;
A warlike preparation; their bold breasts
Breathing heroic ardour to high deeds;
Like vultures, which, their unplumed offspring lost,
Whirl many a rapid flight, for that their toil
To guard their young was vain: till some high power,
For they are dear to Phœbus, dear to Pan,
And Jove with pity hears their shrill-voiced grief,
And sends, though late, the fury to avenge
Their plundered nests on the unpitying spoilers.
So now the power of hospitable Jove
Arms against Paris, for th' oft-wedded dame,
The sons of Atreus, bent to plunge the hosts
Of Greece and Troy in all the toils, that sink
The body down, the firm knee bowed in dust,
And the strong spear, ere conquest crowns their helms,
Shivered in battle.　These are what they are,
And fate directs th' event: nor the bent knee,

Libation pure, or supplicating tear,
Can soothe the stern rage of those merciless powers
In whose cold shrine no hallowed flame ascends.
But we, our age-enfeebled limbs unfit
For martial toils, inglorious here remain,
The staff supporting our weak steps, like children:
For as the infant years have not attained
The military vigour, withered age
Crawls through the streets like helpless infancy,
And passes as a day-dream.   But what tidings,
What circumstances of fair event hath reached
Thy royal ears, daughter of Tyndarus,
Inducing thee to send the victims round?
The shrines of all the gods, whose guardian cares
Watch o'er this state, be they enthroned in heaven,
Or rule beneath the earth, blaze with thy presents;
And from th' imperial dome a lengthened line
Of torches shoot their lustre to the skies.
O tell me what is fit for me to know,
And prudence suffers to be told: speak peace
To this anxiety, which one while swells
Presaging ill, and one while from the victims
Catches a gleam of hope, whose cheering ray
Breaks through the gloom that darkens o'er my soul.

Strophe

It swells upon my soul: I feel the power
      To hail th' auspicious hour,
When, their brave hosts marching in firm array,
      The heroes led the way.
   The fire of youth glows in each vein,
And heaven-born confidence inspires the strain.
      Pleased the omen to record,
      That to Troy's ill-fated strand
      Led each monarch, mighty lord,
      Led the bold confederate band,
The strong spear quiv'ring in their vengeful hand.

Full in each royal chieftain's view,
 A royal eagle whirls his flight;
In plumage one of dusky hue,
 And one his dark wings edged with white;
Swift to th' imperial mansion take their way,
 And in their armèd talons bear,
 Seized in its flight, a pregnant hare,
And in those splendid seats enjoy their prey.

Sound high the strain, the swelling notes prolong,
Till conquest listens to the raptured song.

Antistrophe

The venerable seer, whose skill divine
 Knows what the Fates design,
On each bold chief, that for the battle burns,
 His glowing eyeball turns;
 And thus in high prophetic strains
The rav'ning eagles and their prey explains:
 " Priam's haughty town shall fall,
 Slow they roll, the destined hours,
 Fate and fury shake her wall,
 Vengeance wide the ruin pours,
And conquest seizes all her treasured stores.
 Ah! may no storm from th' angry sky
 Burst dreadful o'er this martial train,
 Nor check their ardour, flaming high
 To pour the war o'er Troy's proud plain!
Wrath kindles in the chaste Diana's breast:
 Gorged with the pregnant mother's blood,
 And, ere the birth, her hapless brood,
Hell-hounds of Jove, she hates your horrid feast.

Sound high the strain, the swelling notes prolong,
Till conquest listens to the raptured song.

Epode

" The virgin goddess of the chase,
Fair from the spangled dewdrops that adorn
  The breathing flowrets of the morn,
  Protectress of the infant race
  Of all that haunt the tangled grove,
  Or o'er the rugged mountains rove,
She, beauteous queen, commands me to declare
  What by the royal birds is shown,
  Signal of conquest, omen fair,
  But darkened by her awful frown.
  God of the distant-wounding bow,
Thee, Pæan, thee I call; hear us, and aid;
  Ah! may not the offended maid
  Give the sullen gales to blow,
  Adverse to this eager train,
  And bar th' unnavigable main;
  Nor other sacrifice demand,
At whose barbaric rites no feast is spread;
  But discord rears her horrid head,
  And calls around her murd'rous band:
  Leagued with hate, and fraud, and fear,
  Nor king, nor husband, they revere;
  Indignant o'er a daughter weep,
  And burn to stamp their vengeance deep?"
Prophetic thus the reverend Chalcas spoke,
  Marking th' imperial eagles' whirling wings;
From his rapt lips the joyful presage broke,
  Success and glory to th' embattled kings.

Sound high the strain, th' according notes prolong,
Till conquest listens to the raptured song.

Strophe I

O thou, that sitt'st supreme above,
  Whatever name thou deign'st to hear,
Unblamed may I pronounce thee Jove!

Immersed in deep and holy thought,
If rightly I conjecture aught,
    Thy power I must revere:
Else vainly tossed the anxious mind
Nor truth, nor calm repose, can find.
Feeble and helpless to the light
    The proudest of man's race arose,
Though now, exulting in his might,
    Dauntless he rushes on his foes;
Great as he is, in dust he lies;
He meets a greater, and he dies.

Antistrophe 1

He that, when conquest brightens round,
    Swells the triumphal strain to Jove,
Shall ever with success be crowned.
Yet often, when to wisdom's seat
Jove deigns to guide man's erring feet,
    His virtues to improve;
He to affliction gives command
To form him with her chastening hand:
The memory of her rigid lore,
    On the sad heart imprinted deep,
Attends him through day's active hour,
    Nor in the night forsakes his sleep.
Instructed thus thy grace we own,
O thou, that sittest on Heaven's high throne!

Strophe 2

When now in Aulis' rolling bay
    His course the refluent floods refused,
And sickening with inaction lay
In dead repose th' exhausted train,
Did the firm chief of chance complain?
    No prophet he accused;
His eyes toward Chalcis bent he stood,
And silent marked the surging flood.

Sullen the winds from Strymon sweep,
　Mischance and famine in the blast,
Ceaseless torment the angry deep,
　The cordage rend, the vessels waste,
With tedious and severe delay
Wear the fresh flower of Greece away.

Antistrophe 2

When, in Diana's name, the seer
　Pronounced the dreadful remedy
More than the stormy sea severe,
　Each chieftain stood in grief profound,
And smote his sceptre on the ground:
　Then with a rising sigh
The monarch, while the big tears roll,
Expressed the anguish of his soul:
" Dreadful the sentence: not t' obey,
　Vengeance and ruin close us round:
Shall then the sire his daughter slay,
　In youth's fresh bloom with beauty crowned?
Shall on these hands her warm blood flow?
Cruel alternative of woe!

Strophe 3

" This royal fleet, this martial host,
　The cause of Greece shall I betray,
The monarch in the father lost?
　To calm these winds, to smooth this flood,
Diana's wrath a virgin's blood
　Demands: 'tis ours t' obey."
Bound in necessity's iron chain
Reluctant Nature strives in vain:
Impure, unholy thoughts succeed,
　And darkening o'er his bosom roll;
While madness prompts the ruthless deed,
　Tyrant of the misguided soul:

Stern on the fleet he rolls his eyes,
And dooms the hateful sacrifice.

Antistrophe 3

Armed in a woman's cause, around
   Fierce for the war the princes rose;
No place affrighted pity found.
In vain the virgin's streaming tear,
Her cries in vain, her pleading prayer,
   Her agonizing woes.
Could the fond father hear unmoved?
The Fates decreed: the king approved:
Then to th' attendants gave command
   Decent her flowing robes to bind;
Prone on the altar with strong hand
   To place her, like a spotless hind;
And check her sweet voice, that no sound
Unhallowed might the rites confound.

Epode

Rent on the earth her maiden veil she throws,
     That emulates the rose;
   And on the sad attendants rolling
The trembling lustre of her dewy eyes,
   Their grief-impassioned souls controlling,
   That ennobled, modest grace,
   Which the mimic pencil tries
   In imaged form to trace,
     The breathing picture shows:
And as, amid his festal pleasures,
   Her father oft rejoiced to hear
Her voice in soft mellifluous measures
   Warble the sprightly-fancied air:
So now in act to speak the virgin stands:
   But when, the third libation paid,
     She heard her father's dread commands
Enjoining silence, she obeyed:

And for her country's good,
With patient, meek, submissive mind
To her hard fate resigned,
Poured out the rich stream of her blood.

What since hath past I know not, nor relate;
But never did the prophet speak in vain,
Th' afflicted, anxious for his future fate,
Looks forward, and with hope relieves his pain.

But since th' inevitable ill will come,
Much knowledge to much misery is allied;
Why strive we then t' anticipate the doom,
Which happiness and wisdom wish to hide?

Yet let this careful, age-enfeebled band
Breathe from our inmost soul one ardent vow,
Now the sole guardians of this Apian land,
" May fair success with glory bind her brow!"

CLYTEMNESTRA, CHORUS

Chorus. With reverence, Clytemnestra, I approach
Thy greatness; honour due to her that fills
The royal seat, yet vacant of its lord.
If aught of glad import hath reached thy ear.
Or to fair hope the victim bleeds, I wish,
But with submission to thy will, to hear.
Cly. The joy-importing Morn springs, as they say,
From Night, her mother. Thou shalt hear a joy
Beyond thy hopes to hear: the town of Priam
Is fallen beneath the conquering arms of Greece.
    Chor. What saidst thou? Passing credence fled thy
      word.
    Cly. In Troy Greece triumphs. Speak I clearly now?
    Chor. Joy steals upon me, and calls forth the tear.
    Cly. Thy glist'ning eye bespeaks an honest heart.
    Chor. Does aught of certain proof confirm these tid-
      ings?

Cly. It does.   Why not ? unless the gods deceive us.

Chor. Perchance the visions of persuasive dreams.

Cly. Sport of the slumbering soul; they move not me.

Chor. Hath then some wingèd rumour spread these transports ?

Cly. As a raw girl's, thou holdest my judgment cheap.

Chor. How long hath ruin crushed this haughty city?

Cly. This night, that gave this infant morning birth.

Chor. What speed could be the herald of this news?

Cly. The fire, that from the height of Ida sent
Its streaming light, as from th' announcing flame
Torch blazed to torch.   First Ida to the steep
Of Lemnos; Athos' sacred height received
The mighty splendour; from the surging back
Of the Hellespont the vigorous blaze held on
Its smiling way, and like the orient sun
Illumes with golden-gleaming rays the head
Of rocky Macetas; nor lingers there,
Nor winks unheedful, but its warning flames
Darts to the streams of Euripus, and gives
Its glittering signal to the guards that hold
Their high watch on Mesapius.   These enkindle
The joy-announcing fires, that spread the blaze
To where Erica hoar its shaggy brow
Waves rudely.   Unimpaired the active flame
Bounds o'er the level of Asopus, like
The jocund moon, and on Cithæron's steep
Wakes a successive flame ; the distant watch
Agnize its shine, and raise a brighter fire,
That o'er the lake Gorgopis streaming holds
Its rapid course, and on the mountainous heights
Of Ægiplanctus huge, swift-shooting spreads
The lengthened line of light.   Thence onward waves
Its fiery tresses, eager to ascend
The crags of Prone, frowning in their pride
O'er the Saronic gulf: it leaps, it mounts
The summit of Arachne, whose high head

Looks down on Argos: to this royal seat
Thence darts the light that from th' Idean fire
Derives its birth.   Rightly in order thus
Each to the next consigns the torch, and fills
The bright succession, while the first in speed
Vies with the last: the promised signal this
Given by my lord t' announce the fall of Troy.
 Chor. Anon my grateful praise shall rise to heaven:
Now, lady, would I willingly attend
Through each glad circumstance the wond'rous tale.
 Cly. This day the conquering Greeks are lords of Troy.
Methinks I hear the various clamours rise
Discordant through the city.   Pour thou oil
In the same vase and vinegar, in vain
Wouldst thou persuade th' unsocial streams to mix:
The captives' and the conqueror's voice distinct,
Marks of their different fortune, mayst thou hear:
Those rolling on the bodies of the slain,
Friends, husbands, brothers, fathers; the weak arms
Of children clasped around the bleeding limbs
Of hoary age, lament their fall, their necks
Bent to the yoke of slavery: eager these
From the fierce toils of war, who through the gloom
Of night ranged wide, fly on the spoils, as chance,
Not order, leads them; in the Trojan houses,
Won by their spears, they walk at large, relieved
From the cold dews dropped from th' unsheltered sky;
And at th' approach of eve, like those whose power
Commands security, the easy night
Shall sleep unguarded.   If with hallowed rites
They venerate the gods that o'er the city,
With those that o'er the vanquished country rule,
And reverence their shrines, the conquering troops
Shall not be conquered.   May no base desire,
No guilty wish urge them, enthralled to gain,
To break through sacred laws.   Behooves them now,
With safety in their train, backward to plough

The refluent wave.   Should they return exposed
To th' anger of the gods, vengeance would wake
To seize its prey, might they perchance escape
Life's incidental ills.   From me thou hearest
A woman's sentiment; and much I wish,
Their glories by no rude mischance depressed,
To cull from many blessings the most precious.

    Chor. With manly sentiment thy wisdom, lady,
Speaks well.   Confiding in thy suasive signs,
Prepare we to address the gods; our strains
Shall not without their meed of honour rise.

Prosode

Supreme of kings, Jove; and thou, friendly night,
    That wide o'er Heaven's star-spangled plain
      Holdest thy awful reign,
    Thou, that with resistless might
    O'er Troy's proud towers, and destined state,
    Hast thrown the secret net of fate,
In whose enormous sweep the young, the old,
      Without distinction rolled,
Are with unsparing fury dragged away
    To slavery and woe a prey;
Thee, hospitable Jove, whose vengeful power
    These terrors o'er the foe has spread,
    Thy bow long bent at Paris' head,
    Whose arrows know their time to fly,
    Not hurtling aimless in the sky,
      Our pious strains adore.

Strophe 1

The hand of Jove will they not own;
    And, as his marks they trace,
Confess he willed, and it was done?
    Who now of earth-born race
Shall dare contend that his high power
    Deigns not with eye severe to view

The wretch that tramples on his law?
　Hence with this impious lore:
Learn that the sons accursed shall rue
　The madly daring father's pride,
That furious drew th' unrighteous sword,
High in his house the rich spoils stored,
　And the avenging gods defied.
　　But be it mine to draw
From wisdom's fount, pure as it flows,
That calm of soul which virtue only knows.
For vain the shield that wealth shall spread,
　To guard the proud oppressor's head,
Who dares the rites of justice to confound,
And spurn her altars to the ground.

Antistrophe 1

But suasive is the voice of vice,
　That spreads th' insidious snare;
She, not concealed, through her disguise
　Emits a livid glare.
Her votary, like adult'rate brass
　Unfaithful to its use, unsound,
Proves the dark baseness of his soul;
　Fond as a boy to chase
The wingèd bird light-flitting round,
　And bent on his pernicious play
Draws desolation on his state.
His vows no god regards, when Fate
　In vengeance sweeps the wretch away.
　　With base intent and foul,
　　Each hospitable law defied,
From Sparta's king thus Paris stole his bride.
　To Greece she left the shield, the spear,
　The naval armament of war;
And, bold in ill, to Troy's devoted shore
　Destruction for her dowry bore.

Strophe 2

When through the gates her easy way
    She took, his pensive breast
Each prophet smote in deep dismay,
    And thus his grief expressed :
"What woes this royal mansion threat,
    This mansion, and its mighty lord?
Where now the chaste connubial bed?
    The traces of her feet,
By love to her blest consort led,
    Where now?   Ah! silent, see, she stands;
Each glowing tint, each radiant grace,
    That charm th' enraptured eye, we trace ;
    And still the blooming form commands,
        Still honoured, still adored,
    Though, careless of her former loves,
Far o'er the rolling sea the wanton roves ;
    The husband, with a bursting sigh,
    Turns from the pictured fair his eye ;
While love, by absence fed, without control
    Tumultuous rushes on his soul.

Antistrophe 2

"Oft as short slumbers close his eyes,
    His sad soul soothed to rest,
The dream-created visions rise,
    With all her charms impressed :
But vain th' ideal scene, that smiles
    With rapturous love and warm delight ;
Vain his fond hopes : his eager arms
    The fleeting form beguiles,
On sleep's quick pinions passing light."
    Such griefs, and more severe than these,
Their sad gloom o'er the palace spread ;
    Thence stretch their melancholy shade,
    And darken o'er the realms of Greece.
        Struck with no false alarms

Each house its home-felt sorrow knows,
Each bleeding heart is pierced with keenest woes;
When for the hero, sent to share
The glories of the crimson war,
Naught, save his arms stained with their master's gore,
And his cold ashes reach the shore.

Strophe 3

Thus in the dire exchange of war
   Does Mars the balance hold;
Helms are the scale, the beam a spear,
   And blood is weighed for gold.
Thus, for the warrior, to his friends
   His sad remains, a poor return,
Saved from the sullen fire that rose
   On Troy's cursed shore, he sends,
Placed decent in the mournful urn.
   With many a tear their dead they weep,
Their names with many a praise resound;
   One for his skill in arms renowned;
   One, that amid the slaughtered heap
      Of fierce-conflicting foes
Glorious in beauty's cause he fell:
Yet 'gainst th' avenging chiefs their murmurs swell
   In silence.   Some in youth's fresh bloom
   Beneath Troy's towers possess a tomb;
Their bodies buried on the distant strand,
   Seizing in death the hostile land.

Antistrophe 3

How dreadful, when the people raise
   Loud murmurs mixed with hate!
Yet this the tribute greatness pays
   For its exalted state.
E'en now some dark and horrid deed
   By my presaging soul is feared;
For never with unheedful eyes,

When slaughtered thousands bleed,
Did the just powers of Heaven regard
    The carnage of th' ensanguined plain.
The ruthless and oppressive power
May triumph for its little hour ;
    Full soon with all their vengeful train
    The sullen Furies rise,
Break his fell force, and whirl him down
Through life's dark paths, unpitied and unknown.
    And dangerous is the pride of fame,
    Like the red lightning's dazzling flame.
Nor envied wealth, nor conquest let me gain,
    Nor drag the conqueror's hateful chain.

Epode

But from these fires far streaming through the night
    Fame through the town her progress takes,
        And rapt'rous joy awakes ;
    If with truth's auspicious light
    They shine, who knows?   Her sacred reign
    Nor fraud, nor falsehood, dares profane.
But who, in wisdom's school so lightly taught,
        Suffers his ardent thought
From these informing flames to catch the fire,
    Full soon perchance in grief t' expire?
Yet when a woman holds the sovereign sway,
    Obsequious wisdom learns to bow,
    And hails the joy it does not know :
    Though, as the glitt'ring visions roll
    Before her easy, credulous soul,
        Their glories fade away.

Cly. Whether these fires, that with successive signals
Blaze through the night, be true, or like a dream
Play with a sweet delusion on the soul,
Soon shall we know.   A herald from the shore
I see ; branches of olive shade his brows.

That cloud of dust, raised by his speed, assures me .
That neither speechless, nor enkindling flames
Along the mountains, will he signify
His message; but his tongue shall greet our ears
With words of joy: far from my soul the thought
Of other, than confirm these fav'ring signals.
    Chor. May he, that to this state shall form a wish
Of other aim, on his own head receive it.

CLYTEMNESTRA, CHORUS, HERALD

    Herald. Hail, thou paternal soil of Argive earth!
In the fair light of the tenth year to thee
Returned, from the sad wreck of many hopes
This one I save; saved from despair e'en this;
For never thought I in this honoured earth
To share in death the portion of a tomb.
Hail then, loved earth; hail, thou bright sun; and thou,
Great guardian of my country, supreme Jove;
Thou, Pythian king, thy shafts no longer winged
For our destruction; on Scamander's banks
Enough we mourned thy wrath; propitious now
Come, King Apollo, our defence. And all
Ye gods, that o'er the works of war preside,
I now invoke; thee, Mercury, my avenger,
Revered by heralds, that from thee derive
Their high employ; you heroes, to the war
That sent us, friendly now receive our troops,
The relics of the spear. Imperial walls,
Mansion of kings, ye seats revered; ye gods,
That to the golden sun before these gates
Present your honoured forms; if e'er of old
Those eyes with favour have beheld the king,
Receive him now, after this length of time,
With glory; for he comes, and with him brings
To you, and all, a light that cheers this gloom:
Then greet him well; such honour is his meed.
The mighty king, that with the mace of Jove
5

Th' avenger, wherewith he subdues the earth,
Hath levelled with the dust the towers of Troy;
Their altars are o'erturned, their sacred shrines,
And all the race destroyed.   This iron yoke
Fixed on the neck of Troy, victorious comes
The great Atrides, of all mortal men
Worthy of highest honours.   Paris now,
And the perfidious state, shall boast no more
His proud deeds unrevenged; stripped of his spoils,
The debt of justice for his thefts, his rapines,
Paid amply, o'er his father's house he spreads
With twofold loss the wide-involving ruin.

 Cly. Joy to thee, herald of the Argive host.
 Her. For joy like this death were a cheap exchange.
 Cly. Strong thy affection to thy native soil.
 Her. So strong, the tear of joy starts from my eye.
 Cly. What, hath this sweet infection reached e'en you?
 Her. Beyond the power of language have I felt it.
 Cly. The fond desire of those, whose equal love——
 Her. This of the army sayst thou, whose warm love
Streams to this land?   Is this thy fond desire?
 Cly. Such that I oft have breathed the secret sigh.
 Her. Whence did the army cause this anxious sadness?
 Cly. Silence I long have held a healing balm.
 Her. The princes absent, hadst thou whom to fear?
 Cly. To use thy words, death were a wished exchange.
 Her. Well is the conflict ended.   In the tide
Of so long time, if 'midst the easy flow
Of wished events some tyrannous blast assail us,
What marvel?   Who, save the blest gods, can claim
Through life's whole course an unmixed happiness?
Should I relate our toils, our wretched plight
Wedged in our narrow ill-provided cabins,
Each irksome hour was loaded with fatigues.
Yet these were slight assays to those worse hardships
We suffered on the shore: our lodging near
The walls of the enemy, the dews of heaven

Fell on us from above, the damps beneath
From the moist marsh annoyed us, shrouded ill
In shaggy cov'rings.   Or should one relate
The winter's keen blasts, which from Ida's snows
Breathe frore, that, pierced through all their plumes, the
        birds
Shiver and die; or th' extreme heat that scalds,
When in his midday caves the sea reclines,
And not a breeze disturbs his calm repose.
But why lament these sufferings?   They are past;
Past to the dead indeed; they lie, no more
Anxious to rise.   What then avails to count
Those whom the wasteful war hath swept away,
And with their loss afflict the living?   Rather
Bid we farewell to misery : in our scale,
Who haply of the Grecian host remain,
The good preponderates, and in counterpoise
Our loss is light; and, after all our toils
By sea and land, before yon golden sun
It is our glorious privilege to boast,
" At length from vanquished Troy our warlike troops
Have to the gods of Greece brought home these spoils,
And in their temples, to record our conquests,
Fixed these proud trophies."   Those that hear this boast
It well becomes to gratulate the state,
And the brave chiefs; revering Jove's high power
That grace our conquering arms.   Thou hast my message.
    Chor. Thy words convince me; all my doubts are
        vanished :
But scrupulous inquiry grows with age.
On Clytemnestra and her house this charge,
Blessing e'en me with the rich joy, devolves.
    Cly. Long since my voice raised high each note of joy,
When through the night the streaming blaze first came,
And told us Troy was taken : not unblamed
That, as a woman lightly credulous,
I let a mountain fire transport my soul

With the fond hope that Ilion's haughty towers
Were humbled in the dust. At this rebuke,
Though somewhat shaken, yet I sacrificed ;
And, as weak woman wont, one voice of joy
Awoke another, till the city rang
Through all its streets ; and at the hallowed shrines
Each raised the pious strains of gratitude,
And fanned the altar's incense-breathing flame.
But it is needless to detain thee longer,
Soon from the king's own lips shall I learn all.
How best I may receive my honoured lord,
And grace his wished return, now claims my speed.
Can heaven's fair beam show a fond wife a sight
More grateful than her husband from his wars
Returned with glory, when she opes the gate,
And springs to welcome him ? Tell my lord this,
That he may hasten his desired return :
And tell him he will find his faithful wife,
Such as he left her, a domestic creature,
To him all fondness, to his enemies
Irreconcilable ; and tell him too
That ten long years have not effaced the seal
Of constancy ; that never knew I pleasure
In the blamed converse of another man,
More than the virgin metal in the mines
Knows an adulterate and debasing mixture.
    Her. This high boast, lady, sanctified by truth,
Is not unseemly in thy princely rank.

HERALD, CHORUS

    Chorus. This, for thy information, hath she spoken
With dignity and truth. Now tell me, herald,
Of Sparta's king wish I to question thee,
The pride of Greece : returns he safe with you ?
    Her. Never can I esteem a falsehood honest,
Though my friends long enjoy the sweet delusion.
    Chor. What then if thou relate an honest truth ?

From this distinction the conjecture's easy.

Her. Him from the Grecian fleet our eyes have lost,
The hero and his ship.   This is the truth.

Chor. Chanced this when in your sight he weighed
     from Troy;
Or in a storm that rent him from the fleet?

Her. Rightly is thy conjecture aimed, in brief
Touching the long recital of our loss.

Chor. How deemed the other mariners of this;
That the ship perished or rode out the storm?

Her. Who, save yon sun, the regent of the earth,
Can give a clear and certain information?

Chor. How saidst thou then a storm, not without loss,
Winged with Heaven's fury, tossed the shattered fleet?

Her. It is not meet, with inauspicious tongue
Spreading ill tidings, to profane a day
Sacred to festal joy : the gods require
Their pure rites undisturbed.   When with a brow
Witness of woe, the messenger relates
Unwelcome news, defeats, and slaughtered armies,
The wound with general grief affects the state;
And with particular and private sorrow
Full many a house, for many that have fall'n
Victims to Mars, who to his bloody car
Delights to yoke his terrors, sword and spear.
A pæan to the Furies would become
The bearer of such pond'rous heap of ills.
My tidings are of conquest and success,
Diffusing joy : with these glad sounds how mix
Distress, and speak of storm and angry gods?
The powers, before most hostile, now conspired,
Fire and the sea, in ruin reconciled :
And in a night of tempest wild from Thrace
In all their fury rushed the howling winds;
Tossed by the forceful blasts ship against ship
In hideous conflict dashed, or disappeared,
Driven at the boist'rous whirlwind's dreadful will;

But when the sun's fair light returned, we see
Bodies of Grecians, and the wreck of ships
Float on the chafed foam of th' Ægean Sea.
Us and our ship some god, the power of man
Were all too weak holding the helm preserved
Unhurt, or interceding for our safety;
And fortune, the deliverer, steered our course
To shun the waves, that near the harbour's mouth
Boil high, or break upon the rocky shore.
Escaped th' ingulfing sea, yet scarce secure
Of our escape, through the fair day we view
With sighs the recent sufferings of the host,
Cov'ring the sea with wrecks.   If any breathe
This vital air, they deem us lost, as we
Think the same ruin theirs.   Fair fall th' event!
But first and chief expect the Spartan king
T' arrive; if yet one ray of yon bright sun
Beholds him living, through the care of Jove,
Who wills not to destroy that royal race,
Well may we hope to joy in his return.
Having heard this, know thou hast heard the truth.

CHORUS.   *Strophe 1*

Is there to names a charm profound
Expressive of their fates assigned,
Mysterious potency of sound,
And truth in wondrous accord joined?
Why else this fatal name,
That Helen and destruction are the same?
Affianced in contention, led,
The spear her dowry, to the bridal bed:
With desolation in her train,
Fatal to martial hosts, to rampired towers,
From the rich fragrance of her gorgeous bowers,
Descending to the main,
She hastes to spread her flying sails,
And calls the earth-born zephyr's gales.

While heroes, breathing vengeance, snatch their shields,
 And trace her light oars o'er the pathless waves,
To the thick shades fresh waving o'er those fields,
 Which Simois with his silver windings laves.

Antistrophe 1

To Troy the shining mischief came;
 Before her, young-eyed pleasures play;
But in the rear with steadfast aim
 Grim-visaged Vengeance marks his prey,
 Waiting the dreadful hour
The terrors of offended Heaven to pour
 On those that dared, an impious train,
The rites of hospitable Jove profane;
 Nor revered that sacred song,
Whose melting strains the bride's approach declare,
As Hymen wakes the rapture-breathing air.
 Far other notes belong,
 The voice of mirth now heard no more,
 To Priam's state; its ruins o'er
Wailing instead, distress, and loud lament;
 Long sorrows sprung from that unholy bed,
And many a curse in heart-felt anguish sent
 On its woe-wedded Paris' hated head.

Strophe 2

The woodman, from his thirsty lair,
 Reft of his dam, a lion bore;
Fostered his future foe with care
 To mischiefs he must soon deplore:
 Gentle and tame, while young,
Harmless he frisked the fondling babes among;
 Oft in the father's bosom lay,
Oft licked his feeding hand in fawning play;
 Till, conscious of his firmer age,
His lion-race the lordly savage shows;
No more his youth-protecting cottage knows,

But with insatiate rage
Flies on the flocks, a baleful guest,
And riots in th' unbidden feast:
While through his mangled folds the hapless swain
    With horror sees th' unbounded carnage spread ;
And learns too late that from th' infernal reign
    A priest of Até in his house was bred.

Antistrophe 2

To Ilion's towers in wanton state
    With speed she wings her easy way ;
Soft gales obedient round her wait,
    And pant on the delighted sea.
        Attendant on her side
The richest ornaments of splendid pride :
    The darts, whose golden points inspire,
Shot from her eyes the flames of soft desire ;
    The youthful bloom of rosy love,
That fills with ecstasy the willing soul :
With duteous zeal obey her sweet control.
        But, such the doom of Jove,
    Vindictive round her nuptial bed,
    With threat'ning mien and footstep dread,
Rushes to Priam and his state severe,
    To rend the bleeding heart his stern delight,
And from the bridal eye to force the tear,
    Erinnys, rising from the realms of night.

Epode

From ev'ry mouth we oft have heard
This saying, for its age revered :
" With joy we see our offspring rise,
And happy, who not childless dies :
But Fortune, when her flow'rets blow,
Oft bears the bitter fruit of woe."
Though these saws are as truths allowed,
Thus I dare differ from the crowd :

" One base deed, with prolific power,
Like its cursed stock engenders more :
But to the just, with blooming grace
Still flourishes, a beauteous race."

The old Injustice joys to breed
Her young, instinct with villanous deed ;
The young her destined hour will find
To rush in mischief on mankind :
She too in Até's murky cell,
Brings forth the hideous child of hell,
A burden to th' offended sky,
The power of bold impiety.

But Justice bids her ray divine
E'en on the low-roofed cottage shine ;
And beams her glories on the life,
That knows not fraud, nor ruffian strife.
The gorgeous glare of gold, obtained
By foul polluted hands, disdained
She leaves, and with averted eyes
To humbler, holier mansions flies ;
And looking through the times to come
Assigns each deed its righteous doom.

CHORUS, AGAMEMNON

Chorus. My royal lord, by whose victorious hand
The towers of Troy are fall'n, illustrious son
Of Atreus, with what words, what reverence
Shall I address thee, not t' o'erleap the bounds
Of modest duty, nor to sink beneath
An honourable welcome? Some there are,
That form themselves to seem, more than to be,
Transgressing honesty : to him that feels
Misfortune's rugged hand, full many a tongue
Shall drop condolence, though th' unfeeling heart
Knows not the touch of sorrow ; these again

In fortune's summer gale, with the like art,
Shall dress in forced smiles th' unwilling face:
But him the penetrating eye soon marks,
That in the seemly garb of honest zeal
Attempts to clothe his meagre blandishments.
When first in Helen's cause my royal lord
Levied his host, let me not hide the truth,
Notes, other than music, echoed wide
In loud complaints from such as deemed him rash,
And void of reason, by constraint to plant
In breast averse the martial soul, that glows
Despising death.   But now their eager zeal
Streams friendly to those chiefs, whose prosp'rous valour
Is crowned with conquest.   Soon then shalt thou learn,
As each supports the state, or strives to rend it
With faction, who reveres thy dignity.

    Aga. To Argos first, and to my country's gods,
I bow with reverence, by whose holy guidance
On Troy's proud towers I poured their righteous venge-
    ance,
And now revisit safe my native soil.
No loud-tongued pleader heard, they judged the cause,
And in the bloody urn, without one vote
Dissentient, cast the lots that fixed the fate
Of Ilion and its sons: the other vase
Left empty, save of widowed hope.   The smoke,
Rolling in dusky wreaths, shows that the town
Is fall'n; the fiery storm yet lives, and high
The dying ashes toss rich clouds of wealth
Consumed.   For this behooves us to the gods
Render our grateful thanks, and that they spread
The net of fate sweeping with angry ruin.
In beauty's cause the Argive monster reared
Its bulk enormous, to th' affrighted town
Portending devastation; in its womb
Hiding embattled hosts, rushed furious forth,
About the setting of the Pleiades,

And, as a lion rav'ning for its prey,
Ramped o'er their walls, and lapped the blood of kings.
This to the gods addressed, I turn me now
Attentive to thy caution: I approve
Thy just remark, and with my voice confirm it.
Few have the fortitude of soul to honour
A friend's success, without a touch of envy;
For that malignant passion to the heart
Cleaves close, and with a double burden loads
The man infected with it; first he feels
In all their weight his own calamities,
Then sighs to see the happiness of others.
This of my own experience have I learned;
And this I know, that many, who in public
Have borne the semblance of my firmest friends,
Are but the flatt'ring image of a shadow
Reflected from a mirror; save Ulysses
Alone, who, though averse to join our arms,
Yoked in his martial harness from my side
Swerved not; living or dead be this his praise.
But what concerns our kingdom and the gods,
Holding a general council of the state,
We will consult; that what is well may keep
Its goodness permanent, and what requires
Our healing hand, with mild severity
May be corrected. But my royal roof
Now will I visit, and before its hearths
Offer libations to the gods, who sent me
To this far-distant war, and led me back.
Firm stands the victory that attends our arms.

CLYTEMNESTRA, AGAMEMNON, CHORUS

Clytemnestra. Friends, fellow-citizens, whose counsels
    guide
The state of Argos, in your reverend presence
A wife's fond love I blush not to disclose:
Thus habit softens dread. From my full heart

Will I recount my melancholy life
Through the long stay of my loved lord at Troy:
For a weak woman, in her husband's absence,
Pensive to sit and lonely in her house,
'Tis dismal, list'ning to each frightful tale:
First one alarms her, then another comes
Charged with worse tidings. Had my poor lord here
Suffered as many wounds as common fame
Reported, like a net he had been pierced;
Had he been slain oft as the loud-tongued rumour
Was noised abroad, this triple-formed Geryon,
A second of the name, while yet alive,
For of the dead I speak not, well might boast
To have received his triple mail, to die
In each form singly. Such reports oppressed me,
Till life became distasteful, and my hands
Were prompted oft to deeds of desperation.
Nor is thy son Orestes, the dear tie
That binds us each to th' other, present here
To aid me, as he ought: nay, marvel not,
The friendly Strophius with a right strong arm
Protects him in Phocæa; while his care
Saw danger threat me in a double form,
The loss of thee at Troy, the anarchy
That might ensue, should madness drive the people
To deeds of violence, as men are prompt
Insultingly to trample on the fall'n:
Such care dwells not with fraud. At thy return
The gushing fountains of my tears are dried,
Save that my eyes are weak with midnight watchings,
Straining, through tears, if haply they might see
Thy signal fires, that claimed my fixed attention.
If they were closed in sleep, a silly fly
Would, with its slightest murm'rings, make me start,
And wake me to more fears. For thy dear sake
All this I suffered: but my jocund heart
Forgets it all, while I behold my lord,

My guardian, the strong anchor of my hope,
The stately column that supports my house,
Dear as an only child to a fond parent;
Welcome as land, which the tossed mariner
Beyond his hope descries; welcome as day
After a night of storms with fairer beams
Returning; welcome as the liquid lapse
Of fountain to the thirsty traveller:
So pleasant is it to escape the chain
Of hard constraint. Such greeting I esteem
Due to thy honour: let it not offend,
For I have suffered much. But, my loved lord,
Leave now that car; nor on the bare ground set
That royal foot, beneath whose mighty tread
Troy trembled.—Haste, ye virgins, to whose care
This pleasing office is intrusted, spread
The streets with tapestry; let the ground be covered
With richest purple, leading to the palace;
That honour with just state may grace his entry,
Though unexpected. My attentive care
Shall, if the gods permit, dispose the rest
To welcome his high glories, as I ought.
 Aga. Daughter of Leda, guardian of my house,
Thy words are correspondent to my absence,
Of no small length. With better grace my praise
Would come from others: soothe me not with strains
Of adulation, as a girl; nor raise,
As to some proud barbaric king, that loves
Loud acclamations echoed from the mouths
Of prostrate worshippers, a clamorous welcome:
Nor spread the streets with tapestry; 'tis invidious;
These are the honours we should pay the gods.
For mortal man to tread on ornaments
Of rich embroidery—— No: I dare not do it:
Respect me as a man, not as a god.
Why should my foot pollute these vests, that glow
With various tinctured radiance? My full fame

Swells high without it; and the temperate rule
Of cool discretion is the choicest gift
Of favouring Heaven. Happy the man, whose life
Is spent in friendship's calm security.
These sober joys be mine, I ask no more.

Cly. Do not thou thwart the purpose of my mind.

Aga. My mind, be well assured, shall not be tainted.

Cly. Hast thou in fear made to the gods this vow?

Aga. Free, from my soul in prudence have I said it.

Cly. Had Priam's arms prevailed, how had he acted?

Aga. On rich embroidery he had proudly trod.

Cly. Then dread not thou th' invidious tongues of men.

Aga. Yet has the popular voice much potency.

Cly. But the unenvied is not of the happy.

Aga. Ill suits it thy soft sex to love contention.

Cly. To yield sometimes adds honour to the mighty.

Aga. Art thou so earnest to obtain thy wish?

Cly. Let me prevail: indulge me with this conquest.

Aga. If such thy will, haste some one, from my feet
Unloose these high-bound buskins, lest some god
Look down indignant, if with them I press
These vests sea-tinctured: shame it were to spoil
With unclean tread their rich and costly texture.
Of these enough.—This stranger, let her find
A gentle treatment: from high heaven the god
Looks with an eye of favour on the victor
That bears his high state meekly; for none wears
Of his free choice the yoke of slavery.
And she, of many treasures the prime flower
Selected by the troops, has followed me.
Well, since I yield me vanquished by thy voice,
I go, treading on purple, to my house.

Cly. Does not the sea, and who shall drain it, yield
Unfailing stores of these rich tints, that glow
With purple radiance? These this lordly house
Commands, blest with abundance, but to want
A stranger. I had vowed his foot should tread

On many a vestment, when the victims bled,
The hallowed pledge which this fond breast devised
For his return. For while the vig'rous root
Maintains its grasp, the stately head shall rise,
And with its waving foliage screen the house
From the fierce dog-star's fiery pestilence.
And on thy presence at thy household hearth,
Ev'n the cold winter feels a genial warmth.
But when the hot sun in the unripe grape
Matures the wine, the husband's perfect virtues
Spread a refreshing coolness. Thou, O Jove,
Source of perfection, perfect all my vows,
And with thy influence favour my intents!

CHORUS. *Strophe I*

What may this mean? Along the skies
    Why do these dreadful portents roll?
Visions of terror, spare my aching eyes,
    Nor shake my sad presaging soul!
In accents dread, not tuned in vain,
    Why bursts the free, unbidden strain?
    These are no phantoms of the night,
    That vanish at the faithful light
Of steadfast confidence. Thou sober power,
    Whither, ah, whither art thou gone?
    For since the long-passed hour,
When first for Troy the naval band
Unmoored their vessels from the strand,
Thou hast not in my bosom fixed thy throne.

Antistrophe I

At length they come: these faithful eyes,
    See them returned to Greece again:
Yet, while the sullen lyre in silence lies,
    Erinnys wakes the mournful strain:
    Her dreadful powers possess my soul,
    And bid the untaught measures roll;

Swell in rude notes the dismal lay,
And fright enchanting hope away ;
While, ominous of ill, grim-visaged care
Incessant whirls my tortured heart.
Vain be each anxious fear !
Return, fair hope, thy seat resume,
Dispel this melancholy gloom,
And to my soul thy gladsome light impart !

Strophe 2

Ah me, what hope ! This mortal state
Nothing but cruel change can know.
Should cheerful health our vig'rous steps await,
Enkindling all her roseate glow ;
Disease creeps on with silent pace,
And withers ev'ry blooming grace.
Proud sails the bark ; the fresh gales breathe,
And dash her on the rocks beneath.
In the rich house her treasures plenty pours ;
Comes sloth, and from her well-poised sling
Scatters the piled-up stores.
Yet disease makes not all her prey :
Nor sinks the bark beneath the sea :
And famine sees the heaven-sent harvest spring.

Antistrophe 2

But when forth-welling from the wound
The purple-streaming blood shall fall,
And the warm tide disdain the reeking ground,
Who shall the vanished life recall ?
Nor verse, nor music's magic power,
Nor the famed leech's boasted lore ;
Not that his art restored the dead,
Jove's thunder burst upon his head.
But that the Fates forbid, and chain my tongue,
My heart, at inspiration's call,
Would the rapt strain prolong :

Now all is dark; it raves in vain,
And, as it pants with trembling pain,
Desponding feels its fiery transports fall.

CLYTEMNESTRA, CASSANDRA, CHORUS

Clytemnestra. Thou too, Cassandra, enter; since high
    Jove,
Gracious to thee, hath placed thee in this house,
With many slaves to share the common rites,
And deck the altar of the fav'ring god.
Come from that chariot, and let temperance rule
Thy lofty spirit: ev'n Alcmena's son,
Sold as a slave, submitted to the yoke
Perforce; and if necessity's hard hand
Hath sunk thee to this fortune, our high rank,
With greatness long acquainted, knows to use
Its power with gentleness: the low-born wretch,
That from his mean degree rises at once
To unexpected riches, treats his slaves
With barbarous and unbounded insolence.
From us thou wilt receive a juster treatment.
Chor. These are plain truths: since in the toils of fate
Thou art inclosed, submit, if thou canst brook
Submission; haply I advise in vain.
Cly. If that her language, like the twittering swallow's,
Be not all barbarous and unknown, my words
Within shall with persuasion move her mind.
Chor. She speaks what best beseems thy present state;
Follow, submit, and leave that lofty car.
Cly. I have not leisure here before the gates
T' attend on her; for at the inmost altar,
Blazing with sacred fires, the victims stand
Devoted to the gods for his return
So much beyond our hopes. If to comply
Thou form thy mind, delay not: if thy tongue
Knows not to sound our language, let thy signs
Supply the place of words, speak with thy hand.
6

Chor. Of foreign birth she understands us not:
But as new-taken struggles in the net.

Cly. 'Tis frenzy this, the impulse of a mind
Disordered; from a city lately taken
She comes, and knows not how to bear the curb,
Till she has spent her rage in bloody foam.
But I no more waste words to be disdained.

Chor. My words, for much I pity her, shall bear
No mark of anger. Go, unhappy fair one,
Forsake thy chariot, unreluctant learn
To bear this new yoke of necessity.

Cas. Woe, woe! O Earth! Apollo, O Apollo!

Chor. Why with that voice of woe invoke Apollo?
Ill do these notes of grief accord with him.

Cas. Woe, woe! O Earth! Apollo, O Apollo!

Chor. Again her inauspicious voice invokes
The god, whose ears are not attuned to woe.

Cas. Apollo, O Apollo, fatal leader,
Yet once more, god, thou leadest me to ruin!

Chor. She seems prophetic of her own misfortunes,
Retaining, though a slave, the divine spirit.

Cas. Apollo, O Apollo, fatal leader,
Ah, whither hast thou led me? to what house?

Chor. Is that unknown? Let me declare it then;
This is the royal mansion of th' Atridæ.

Cas. It is a mansion hated by the gods,
Conscious to many a foul and horrid deed;
A slaughter-house, that reeks with human gore.

Chor. This stranger seems, like the nice-scented hound,
Quick in the trace of blood, which she will find.

Cas. These are convincing proofs. Look there, look
 there,
While pity drops a tear, the children butchered,
The father feasting on their roasted flesh!

Chor. Thy fame, prophetic virgin, we have heard;
We know thy skill; but wish no prophets now.

Cas. Ye powers of Heaven, what does she now design?

What new and dreadful deed of woe is this?
What dreadful ill designs she in the house,
Intolerable, irreparable mischief,
While far she sends the succouring power away?

Chor. These prophecies surpass my apprehension;
The first I knew, they echo through the city.

Cas. Ah! daring wretch, dost thou achieve this deed,
Thus in the bath the partner of thy bed
Refreshing? How shall I relate th' event?
Yet speedy shall it be. Ev'n now advanced
Hand above hand extended threatens high.

Chor. I comprehend her not; her words are dark,
Perplexing me like abstruse oracles.

Cas. Ah! What is this, that I see here before me?
Is it the net of hell? Or rather hers,
Who shares the bed and plans the murderous deed.
Let discord, whose insatiable rage
Pursues this race, howl through the royal rooms
Against the victim destined to destruction.

Chor. What fury dost thou call within this house
To hold her orgies? The dread invocation
Appals me; to my heart the purple drops
Flow back; a deathlike mist covers my eyes,
With expectation of some sudden ruin.

Cas. See, see there: from the heifer keep the bull!
O'er his black brows she throws th' entangling vest,
And smites him with her huge two-handed engine.
He falls, amid the cleansing laver falls:
I tell thee of the bath, the treach'rous bath.

Chor. T' unfold the obscure oracles of Heaven
Is not my boast; beneath the shadowing veil
Misfortune lies; when did th' inquirer learn
From the dark sentence an event of joy?
From time's first records the diviner's voice
Gives the sad heart a sense of misery.

Cas. Ah me, unhappy! Wretched, wretched fate!
For my own sufferings joined call forth these wailings.

Why hast thou brought me hither? Wretched me!
Is it for this, that I may die with him?

Chor. This is the frenzy of a mind possessed
With wildest ravings. Thy own woes thou wailest
In mournful melody; like the sweet bird,
That darkling pours her never-ceasing plaint;
And for her Itys, her lost Itys, wastes
In sweetest woe her melancholy life.

Cas. Ah me! the fortune of the nightingale
Is to be envied: on her light-poised plumes
She wings at will her easy way, nor knows
The anguish of a tear, while o'er my head
Th' impending sword threatens the fatal wound.

Chor. Whence is this violent, this wild presage
Of ill? Thy fears are vain; yet with a voice
That terrifies, though sweet, aloud thou speakest
Thy sorrows. Whence hast thou derived these omens,
Thus deeply marked with characters of death?

Cas. Alas! the bed, the bridal bed of Paris,
Destructive to his friends! Paternal stream,
Scamander, on thy banks with careless steps
My childhood strayed: but now methinks I go,
Alas, how soon! to prophesy around
Cocytus, and the banks of Acheron!

Chor. Perspicuous this, and clear! the new-born babe
Might comprehend it; but thy piercing griefs,
Bewailing thus the miseries of thy fate,
Strike deep; they wound me to my very soul.

Cas. Ah, my poor country, my poor bleeding country,
Fall'n, fall'n forever! And you, sacred altars,
That blazed before my father's towered palace,
Not all your victims could avert your doom!
And on the earth soon shall my warm blood flow.

Chor. This is consistent with thy former ravings.
Or does some god indeed incumbent press
Thy soul, and modulate thy voice to utter
These lamentable notes of woe and death?

What th' event shall be, exceeds my knowledge.

 Cas. The oracle no more shall shroud its visage
Beneath a veil, as a new bride that blushes
To meet the gazing eye; but like the sun,
When with his orient ray he gilds the east,
Shall burst upon you in a flood of light,
Disclosing deeds of deeper dread. Away,
Ye mystic coverings! And you, reverend men,
Bear witness to me, that with steady step
I trace foul deeds that smell above the earth.
For never shall that band, whose yelling notes
In dismal accord pierce th' affrighted ear,
Forsake this house. The genius of the feast,
Drunk with the blood of men, and fired from thence
To bolder daring, ranges through the rooms
Linked with his kindred Furies: these possess
The mansion, and in horrid measures chant
The first base deed; recording with abhorrence
Th' adulterous lust, that stained a brother's bed.
What, like a skilful archer, have I lodged
My arrow in the mark? No trifling this,
T' alarm you with false sounds. But swear to me,
In solemn attestation, that I know,
And speak the old offences of this house.

 Chor. In such a rooted ill what healing power
Resides there in an oath? But much I marvel
That thou, the native of a foreign realm,
Of foreign tongue, canst speak our language freely,
As Greece had been thy constant residence.

 Cas. Apollo graced me with this skill. At first
The curb of modesty was on my tongue.

 Chor. Did the god feel the force of young desire?
In each gay breast ease fans the wanton flame.

 Cas. With all the fervour of impatient love
He strove to gratify my utmost wish.

 Chor. And didst thou listen to his tempting lures?

 Cas. First I assented, then deceived the god.

Chor. Wast thou then fraught with these prophetic arts?
Cas. Even then I told my country all its woes.
Chor. The anger of the god fell heavy on thee?
Cas. My voice, for this offence, lost all persuasion.
Chor. To us it seems a voice of truth divine.
Cas. Woe, woe is me! Again the furious power
Swells in my lab'ring breast; again commands
My bursting voice; and what I speak is fate.
Look, look, behold those children. There they sit;
Such are the forms, that in the troubled night
Distract our sleep. By a friend's hands they died:
Are these the ties of blood? See, in their hands
Their mangled limbs, horrid repast, they bear:
Th' invited father shares th' accursed feast.
For this the sluggard savage, that at ease
Rolls on his bed, nor rouses from his lair,
'Gainst my returning lord, for I must wear
The yoke of slavery, plans the dark design
Of death. Ah me! the chieftain of the fleet,
The vanquisher of Troy, but little knows
What the smooth tongue of mischief, filed to words
Of glozing courtesy, with fate her friend,
Like Até ranging in the dark can do
Calmly: such deeds a woman dares: she dares
Murder a man. What shall I call this mischief?
An Amphisbæna? or a Scylla rather,
That in the vexed rocks holds her residence,
And meditates the mariner's destruction?
Mother of hell, 'midst friends enkindling discord
And hate implacable! With dreadful daring
How did she shout, as if the battle swerved?
Yet with feigned joy she welcomes his return.
These words may want persuasion. What of that?
What must come, will come: and ere long with grief
Thou shalt confess my prophecies are true.
Chor. Thyestes' bloody feast oft have I heard of,
Always with horror; and I tremble now

Hearing th' unaggravated truth. What else
She utters, leads my wand'ring thoughts astray
In wild uncertainty.

    Cas.   Then mark me well,
Thou shalt behold the death of Agamemnon.

    Chor. To better omens tune that voice unblessed,
Or in eternal silence be it sunk.

    Cas. This is an ill no medicine can heal.

    Chor. Not if it happens : but avert it, Heaven !

    Cas. To pray be thine ; the murd'rous deed is theirs.

    Chor. What man dares perpetrate this dreadful act ?

    Cas. How widely dost thou wander from my words !

    Chor. I heard not whose bold hand should do the deed.

    Cas. Yet speak I well the language of your Greece.

    Chor. The gift of Phœbus this ; no trivial grace.

    Cas. Ah, what a sudden flame comes rushing on me !
I burn, I burn. Apollo, O Apollo !
This lioness, that in a sensual sty
Rolled with the wolf, the generous lion absent,
Will kill me. And the sorc'ress, as she brews
Her philtred cup, will drug it with my blood,
She glories, as against her husband's life
She whets the axe, her vengeance falls on him
For that he came accompanied by me.
Why do I longer wear these useless honours,
This laurel wand, and these prophetic wreaths ?
Away ! before I die I cast you from me ;
Lie there and perish ; I am rid of you ;
Or deck the splendid ruin of some other.
Apollo rends from me these sacred vestments,
Who saw me in his rich habiliments
Mocked 'midst my friends, doubtless without a cause.
When in opprobrious terms they jeered my skill,
And treated me as a poor vagrant wretch,
That told events from door to door for bread,
I bore it all : but now the prophet god,
That with his own arts graced me, sinks me down

To this low ruin.   As my father fell
Butchered ev'n at the altar, like the victim's
My warm blood at the altar shall be shed :
Nor shall we die unhonoured by the gods.
He comes, dreadful in punishment, the son
Of this bad mother, by her death t' avenge
His murdered father : distant though he roams
An outcast and an exile, by his friends
Fenced from these deeds of violence, he comes
In solemn vengeance for his father laid
Thus low.   But why for foreign miseries
Does the tear darken in my eye, that saw
The fall of Ilium, and its haughty conquerors
In righteous judgment thus received their meed?
But forward now ; I go to close the scene,
Nor shrink from death. I have a vow in heaven :
And further, I adjure these gates of hell,
Well may the blow be aimed, that while my blood
Flows in a copious stream, I may not feel
The fierce, convulsive agonies of death ;
But gently sink, and close my eyes in peace.
   Chor. Unhappy, in thy knowledge most unhappy,
Long have thy sorrows flowed.   But if indeed
Thou dost foresee thy death, why, like the heifer
Led by a heavenly impulse, do thy steps
Advance thus boldly to the cruel altar?
   Cas. I could not by delay escape my fate.
   Chor. Yet is there some advantage in delay.
   Cas. The day is come : by flight I should gain little.
   Chor. Thy boldness adds to thy unhappiness.
   Cas. None of the happy shuns his destined end.
   Chor. True ; but to die with glory crowns our praise.
   Cas. So died my father, so his noble sons.
   Chor. What may this mean?   Why backward dost
      thou start?
Do thy own thoughts with horror strike thy soul?
   Cas. The scent of blood and death breathes from this
      house.

Chor. The victims now are bleeding at the altar.
Cas. 'Tis such a smell as issues from the tomb.
Chor. This is no Syrian odour in the house.
Cas. Such though it be, I enter to bewail
My fate, and Agamemnon's. To have lived,
Let it suffice. And think not, gen'rous strangers,
Like the poor bird that flutters o'er the bough,
Through fear I linger. But my dying words
You will remember, when her blood shall flow
For mine, woman's for woman's: and the man's,
For his that falls by his accursèd wife.
    Chor. Thy fate, poor sufferer, fills my eyes with tears.
    Cas. Yet once more let me raise my mournful voice.
Thou sun, whose rising beams shall bless no more
These closing eyes! You, whose vindictive rage
Hangs o'er my hated murderers, oh avenge me,
Though, a poor slave, I fall an easy prey!
This is the state of man: in prosperous fortune
A shadow, passing light, throws to the ground
Joy's baseless fabric: in adversity
Comes Malice with a sponge moistened in gall,
And wipes each beauteous character away;
More than the first this melts my soul to pity.
    Chor. By nature man is formed with boundless wishes
For prosperous fortune; and the great man's door
Stands ever open to that envied person,
On whom she smiles; but enter not with words,
Like this poor sufferer, of such dreadful import.
His arms the powers of Heaven have graced with con-
       quest;
Troy's proud walls lie in dust; and he returns
Crowned by the gods with glory: but if now
His blood must for the blood there shed atone,
If he must die for those that died, too dearly
He buys his triumph. Who of mortal men
Hears this, and dares to think his state secure?
    Aga. [*within*] Oh! I am wounded with a deadly blow.

Semichor. List, list! What cry is this of wounds and
    death?
Aga. Wounded again, oh, basely, basely murdered!

SEMICHORUS

'Tis the king's cry; the dreadful deed is doing.
What shall we do? What measures shall we form?

What if we spread th' alarm, and with our outcries
Call at the palace gates the citizens?

Nay, rather rush we in, and prove the deed,
While the fresh blood is reeking on the sword.

I readily concur; determine then;
For something must be done, and instantly.

That's evident. This bloody prelude threatens
More deeds of violence and tyranny.

We linger: those that tread the paths of honour,
Late though she meets them, sleep not in their task.

Perplexity and doubt distract my thoughts:
Deeds of high import ask maturest counsel.

Such are my thoughts, since fruitless were th' attempt
By all our pleas to raise the dead to life.

To save our wretched lives then shall we bow
To these imperious lords, these stains of honour?

That were a shame indeed! No; let us die:
Death is more welcome than such tyranny.

Shall we then take these outcries, which we heard,
For proofs, and thence conclude the king is slain?

We should be well assured ere we pronounce:
To know, and to conjecture, differ widely.

There's reason in thy words. Best enter then,
And see what fate attends the son of Atreus.

CLYTEMNESTRA, CHORUS

Clytemnestra. To many a fair speech suited to the times,
If my words now be found at variance,
I shall not blush. For when the heart conceives
Thoughts of deep vengeance on a foe, what means
T' achieve the deed more certain, than to wear
The form of friendship, and with circling wiles
Inclose him in th' insuperable net?
This was no hasty, rash-conceived design;
But formed with deep, premeditated thought,
Incensed with wrongs; and often have I stood,
T' assay the execution, where he fell;
And planned it so, for I with pride avow it,
He had no power t' escape, or to resist,
Entangled in the gorgeous robe, that shone
Fatally rich. I struck him twice, and twice
He groaned, then died. A third time as he lay
I gored him with a wound, a grateful present
To the stern god, that in the realms below
Reigns o'er the dead: there let him take his seat.
He lay; and spouting from his wounds a stream
Of blood, bedewed me with these crimson drops.
I glory in them, like the genial earth,
When the warm showers of heaven descend, and wake
The flow'rets to unfold their vermeil leaves.
Come then, ye reverend senators of Argos,
Joy with me, if your hearts be tuned to joy;
And such I wish them. Were it decent now
To pour libations o'er the dead, with justice
It might be done; for his injurious pride
Filled for this house the cup of desolation,
Fated himself to drain it to the dregs.
    Chor. We are astonished at thy daring words,
Thus vaunting o'er the ruins of thy husband.
    Cly. Me, like a witless woman, wouldst thou fright?
I tell thee, my firm soul disdains to fear.
Be thou disposed t' applaud, or censure me,

I reck it not: there Agamemnon lies,
My husband, slaughtered by this hand: I dare
Avow his death, and justify the deed.

   Chor. What poison hath the baleful teeming earth,
Or the chafed billows of the foamy sea,
Given thee for food, or mingled in thy cup,
To work thee to this frenzy? Thy cursed hand
Hath struck, hath slain. For this thy country's wrath
Shall in just vengeance burst upon thy head,
And with abhorrence drive thee from the city.

   Cly. And dost thou now denounce upon my head
Vengeance, and hate, and exile? 'Gainst this man
Urging no charge? Yet he without remorse,
As if a lamb that wantoned in his pastures
Were doomed to bleed, could sacrifice his daughter,
For whose dear sake I felt a mother's pains,
T' appease the winds of Thrace. Should not thy voice
Adjudge this man to exile, in just vengeance
For such unholy deeds? Scarce hast thou heard
What I have done, but sentence is pronounced,
And that with rigour too. But mark me well,
I boldly tell thee that I bear a soul
Prepared for either fortune; if thy hand
Be stronger, use thy power: but if the gods
Prosper my cause, be thou assured, old man,
Thou shalt be taught a lesson of discretion.

   Chor. Aspiring are thy thoughts, and thy proud vaunts
Swell with disdain; ev'n yet thy madding mind
Is drunk with slaughter; with a savage grace
The thick blood stains thine eye. But soon thy friends
Faithless shall shrink from thy unsheltered side,
And leave thee to just vengeance, blow for blow.

   Cly. Hear then this solemn oath: By that revenge,
Which for my daughter I have greatly taken;
By the dread powers of Até and Erinnys,
To whom my hand devoted him a victim,
Without a thought of fear I range these rooms,

While present to my aid Ægisthus stands,
As he hath stood, guarding my social hearth:
He is my shield, my strength, my confidence.
Here lies my base betrayer, who at Troy
Could revel in the arms of each Chryseis;
He, and his captive minion; she that marked
Portents and prodigies, and with ominous tongue
Presaged the Fates; a wanton harlotry,
True to the rower's benches; their just meed
Have they received. See where he lies; and she,
That like the swan warbled her dying notes,
His paranymph lies with him, to my bed
Leaving the darling object of my wishes.

Chor. No slow-consuming pains, to torture us
Fixed to the groaning couch, await us now;
But Fate comes rushing on, and brings the sleep
That wakes no more. There lies the king, whose vir-
    tues
Were truly royal. In a woman's cause
He suffered much; and by a woman perished.
Ah, fatal Helen! in the fields of Troy
How many has thy guilt, thy guilt alone,
Stretched in the dust? But now by murd'rous hands
Hast thou sluiced out this rich and noble blood,
Whose foul stains never can be purged. This ruin
Hath discord, raging in the house, effected.

Cly. Wish not for death; nor bow beneath thy griefs;
Nor turn thy rage on Helen, as if she
Had drenched the fields with blood, as she alone
Fatal to Greece had caused these dreadful ills.

Chor. Tremendous fiend, that breathest through this
    house
Thy baleful spirit, and with equal daring
Hast steeled these royal sisters to fierce deeds
That rend my soul, now, like the baleful raven,
Incumbent o'er the body dost thou joy
T' affright us with thy harsh and dissonant notes!

Cly. There's sense in this: now hast thou touched
   the key,
Rousing the fury that from sire to son
Hath bade the stream of blood, first poured by her,
Descend: one sanguine tide scarce rolled away,
Another flows in terrible succession.

   Chor. And dost thou glory in these deeds of death,
This vengeance of the fury? Thus to pride thee
In ruin, and the havoc of thy house,
Becomes thee ill. Ah! 'tis a higher power,
That thus ordains: we see the hand of Jove,
Whose will directs the fate of mortal man.
My king, my royal lord, what words can show
My grief, my reverence for thy princely virtues!
Art thou thus fall'n, caught in a cobweb snare,
By impious murder breathing out thy life?
Art thou thus fall'n, ah the disloyal bed!
Secretly slaughtered by a treach'rous hand?

   Cly. Thou say'st, and say'st aloud, I did this deed:
Say not that I, that Agamemnon's wife,
Did it: the fury, fatal to this house,
In vengeance for Thyestes' horrid feast,
Assumed this form, and with her ancient rage
Hath for the children sacrificed the man.

   Chor. That thou art guiltless of this blood, what proof,
What witness? From the father, in his cause,
Rise an avenger! Stained with the dark streams
Of kindred blood fierce waves the bick'ring sword,
And points the ruthless boy to deeds of horror.
My king, my royal lord, what words can show
My grief, my reverence for thy princely virtues!
Art thou thus fall'n, caught in a cobweb snare,
By impious murder breathing out thy life?
Art thou thus fall'n, ah the disloyal bed!
Secretly slaughtered by a treach'rous hand?

   Cly. No: of his death far otherwise I deem,
Nothing disloyal. Nor with secret guile

Wrought he his murd'rous mischiefs on this house.
For my sweet flow'ret, opening from his stem,
My Iphigenia, my lamented child,
Whom he unjustly slew, he justly died.
Nor let him glory in the shades below;
For as he taught his sword to thirst for blood,
So by the thirsty sword his blood was shed.

Chor. Perplexed and troubled in my anxious thought,
Amid the ruins of this house, despair
Hangs heavy on me.   Drop by drop no more
Descends the shower of blood; but the wild storm
In one red torrent shakes the solid walls;
While vengeance, ranging through the dreadful scene,
For further mischief whets her fatal sword.

Semichor. O Earth, that I had rested in thy bosom,
Ere I had seen him lodged with thee, and shrunk
To the brief compass of a silver urn!
Who shall attend the rites of sepulture?
Who shall lament him?   Thou, whose hand has shed
Thy husband's blood, wilt thou dare raise the voice
Of mourning o'er him?   Thy unhallowed hand
Renders these honours, should they come from thee,
Unwelcome to his shade.   What faithful tongue,
Fond to recount his great and godlike acts,
Shall steep in tears his funeral eulogy?

Cly. This care concerns not thee: by us he fell,
By us he died: and we will bury him
With no domestic grief.   But Iphigenia,
His daughter, as is meet, jocund and blithe
Shall meet him on the banks of that sad stream,
The flood of sorrow, and with filial duty
Hang fondling on her father's neck, and kiss him.

Chor. Thus insult treads on insult.   Of these things
Hard is it to decide.   Th' infected stain
Communicates th' infection; murder calls
For blood; and outrage on th' injurious head,
At Jove's appointed time, draws outrage down.

Thus, by the laws of Nature, son succeeds
To sire; and who shall drive him from the house?
   Cly. These are the oracles of truth. But hear me;
It likes me to the genius of the race
Of Plisthenes to swear that what is past,
Though poor the satisfaction, bounds my wishes.
Hither he comes no more: no, let him stain
Some other house with gore. For me, some poor,
Some scanty pittance of the goods contents me,
Well satisfied that from this house I've driven
These frantic Furies red with kindred blood.

ÆGISTHUS, CLYTEMNESTRA, CHORUS

   Ægisthus. Hail to this joyful day, whose welcome light
Brings vengeance! Now I know that the just gods
Look from their skies, and punish impious mortals,
Seeing this man rolled in the blood-wove woof,
The tissue of the Furies, grateful sight,
And suffering for his father's fraudful crimes.
Atreus, his father, sovereign of this land,
Brooking no rival in his power, drove out
My father and his brother, poor Thyestes,
A wretched exile: from his country far
He wandered; but at length returned, and stood
A suppliant before the household gods,
Secure in their protection that his blood
Should not distain the pavement. This man's father,
The sacrilegious Atreus, with more show
Of courtesy than friendship, spread the feast;
Devoting, such the fair pretence, the day
To hospitality and genial mirth:
Then to my father in that feast served up
The flesh of his own sons: their hands and feet
Hacked off before, their undistinguished parts
He ate, without suspicion ate, a food
Destructive to the race. But when he knew
Th' unhallowed deed, he raised a mournful cry,

And starting up with horror spurned to the ground
The barb'rous banquet, utt'ring many a curse
Of deepest vengeance on the house of Pelops.
Thus perish all the race of Plisthenes!
And for this cause thou seest him fall'n! His death
With justice I devised; for me he chased,
The thirteenth son, an infant in my cradle,
With my unhappy father. Nursed abroad,
Vengeance led back my steps, and taught my hand
From far to reach him. All this plan of ruin
Was mine, reckless of what ensues; ev'n death
Were glorious, now he lies caught in my vengeance.

    Chor. T' embitter ills with insult, this, Ægisthus,
I praise not. Thou, of thine own free accord,
Hast slain this man; such is thy boast; this plan
Of ruin, which we mourn, is thine alone.
But be thou well assured thou shalt not 'scape,
When, roused to justice, the avenging people
Shall hurl their stones with curses on thy head.

    Ægis. From thee, who labourest at the lowest oar,
This language, and to him that holds the helm!
Thou shalt be taught, old man, what at thy age
Is a hard lesson, prudence. Chains and hunger,
Besides the load of age, have sovereign virtue
To physic the proud heart. Behold this sight;
Does it not ope thine eyes? Rest quiet then;
Contend not with the strong; there's danger in it.

    Chor. And could thy softer sex, while the rough
      war
Demands its chieftain, violate his bed,
And on his first return contrive his death?

    Ægis. No more: this sounds th' alarm to rude com-
      plaints.
The voice of Orpheus with its soothing notes
Attracted ev'n the savage; while thy yells
To rage inflame the gentle: but take heed;
Dungeons and chains may teach thee moderation.

    7

Chor. Shalt thou reign king in Argos? Thou, whose
    soul
Plotted this murder; while thy coward hand
Shrunk back, nor dared to execute the deed?
    Ægis. Wiles and deceit are female qualities:
The memory of my ancient enmity
Had waked suspicion. Master of his treasures,
Be it my next attempt to gain the people:
Whome'er I find unwilling to submit,
Him, like a high-fed and unruly horse
Reluctant to the harness, rigour soon
Shall tame: confinement, and her meagre comrade,
Keen hunger, will abate his fiery mettle.
    Chor. Did not the baseness of thy coward soul
Unman thee to this murder, that a woman,
Shame to her country and her country's gods,
Must dare the horrid deed? But when Orestes,
Where'er he breathes the vital air, returns,
Good fortune be his guide, shall not his hand
Take a bold vengeance in the death of both?
    Ægis. Since such thy thoughts and words, soon shalt
    thou feel——
    Chor. Help, ho! soldiers and friends; the danger's
    near;
Help, ho! advance in haste with your drawn swords!
    Ægis. My sword is drawn: Ægisthus dares to die.
    Chor. Prophetic be thy words! We hail the omen.
    Cly. Dearest of men, do not heap ills on ills:
I wish not to exasperate, but to heal,
Misfortune's past: enough is given to vengeance;
Let no more blood be spilt. Go then, old men,
Each to your homes; go, while ye may, in peace.
What hath been done the rigour of the times
Compelled, and hard necessity; the weight
Of these afflictions, grievous as they are,
By too severe a doom falls on our heads.
Disdain not to be taught, though by a woman.

Ægis. Ay; but to hear this vain, tongue-doughty bab-
    bler,
Lavish of speech that tempts to desperate deeds,
It moves me from the firmness of my temper.
    Chor. An Argive scorns to fawn on guilty greatness.
    Ægis. My vengeance shall o'ertake thee at the last.
    Chor. Not if just Heaven shall guide Orestes hither.
    Ægis. An exile, I well know, feeds on vain hopes.
    Chor. Go on then, gorge with blood; thou hast the
    means.
    Ægis. This folly, be assured, shall cost thee dear.
    Chor. The craven, in her presence, rears his crest.
    Cly. Slight men, regard them not; but let us enter,
Assume our state, and order all things well.

THE
ANTIGONE OF SOPHOCLES

TRANSLATED BY

RICHARD CLAVERHOUSE JEBB

SOPHOCLES was born in 496 B. C. and lived to the age of ninety-one. His father, Sophillus, was a wealthy citizen of Colonos, a fashionable suburb of Athens, and the young dramatist received the best education that Greece could afford. In music, which he studied under Lamprocles, he was particularly apt, and at the age of sixteen he was chosen to lead a chorus of youths in the celebration of the victory of Salamis (480 B. C.). He was frequently employed as ambassador, and in other high offices in the republic, and in the Samian War was given the generalship in joint command with Pericles. This appointment is said to have been influenced by the great popular success of "Antigone." At twenty-eight he competed with Æschylus, and was awarded the prize by Cimon and his fellow-generals, who had just returned from Scyros and were the judges for that year (468 B. C.). From that time until the death of Æschylus he divided honours about equally with his great predecessor, never taking less than a third prize, and continually growing in popularity. Seven of the eighty or more plays that he is supposed to have written remain for our study and enjoyment, together with many fragments of those less fortunate in the wreck of time. The probable order of their production is as follows: "Ajax," "Antigone," "Electra," "Œdipus Tyrannus," "Trachiniæ," "Œdipus Coloneus," and "Philoctetes." Cicero voices a popular tradition where he says, in his essay "On Old Age": "Sophocles continued in extreme old age to write tragedies. As he seemed to neglect his family affairs while he was wholly intent on his dramatic compositions, his sons instituted a suit against him in a court of judicature, suggesting that his understanding was impaired, and praying that he might be removed from the management of his estate. It is said that when the old bard appeared in court on this occasion he desired that he might be permitted to read a play which he had lately finished, and which he then held in his hand; it was his 'Œdipus Coloneus.' His request being granted, after he had finished the recital he appealed to the judges whether they could discover in his performance any symptoms of an insane mind, and the result was that the court unanimously dismissed the complainants' petition." The poet died in 405. "Philoctetes" was produced in 409, and "Œdipus Coloneus" is said not to have been acted until after the poet's death.

DRAMATIS PERSONÆ

Antigone.
Ismene.
Eurydice.
Creon.
Hæmon,
Teiresias.
Guard.
Messenger.
Second Messenger.
Chorus of Theban Elders.

Scene: An open space before the Royal Palace (once that of Œdipus) at Thebes. The back-scene represents the front of the palace, with three doors, of which the central is the largest, being the principal entrance to the court of the house.

ANTIGONE

———— ❖ ————

At daybreak, on the morning after the fall of the two brothers and the flight of the Argives. ANTIGONE calls ISMENE forth from the house, in order to speak with her apart.

ANTIGONE. Ismene, my sister, mine own dear sister, knowest thou what ill there is, of all bequeathed by Œdipus, that Zeus fulfils not for us twain while we live? Nothing painful is there, nothing fraught with ruin, no shame, no dishonour, that I have not seen in thy woes and mine.

And now what new edict is this of which they tell, that our Captain hath just published to all Thebes? Knowest thou aught? Hast thou heard? Or is it hidden from thee that our friends are threatened with the doom of our foes?

Ismene. No word of friends, Antigone, gladsome or painful, hath come to me, since we two sisters were bereft of brothers twain, killed in one day by a twofold blow; and since in this last night the Argive host has fled, I know no more, whether my fortune be brighter, or more grievous.

An. I knew it well, and therefore sought to bring thee beyond the gates of the court, that thou mightest hear alone.

Is. What is it? 'Tis plain that thou art brooding on some dark tidings.

An. What! hath not Creon destined our brothers, the one to honoured burial, the other to unburied shame? Eteocles, they say, with due observance of right and custom, he hath laid in the earth, for his honour among the dead below. But the hapless corpse of Polyneices—as rumour saith, it hath been published to the town that none shall entomb him or mourn, but leave unwept, unsepulchred, a welcome store for the birds, as they espy him, to feast on at will.

Such, 'tis said, is the edict that the good Creon hath set forth for thee and for me—yes, for *me*—and is coming hither to proclaim it clearly to those who know it not; nor counts the matter light, but, whoso disobeys in aught, his doom is death by stoning before all the folk. Thou knowest it now; and thou wilt soon show whether thou art nobly bred, or the base daughter of a nobler line.

Is. Poor sister—and if things stand thus, what could I help to do or undo?

An. Consider if thou wilt share the toil and the deed.

Is. In what venture? What can be thy meaning?

An. Wilt thou aid this hand to lift the dead?

Is. Thou wouldst bury him—when 'tis forbidden to Thebes?

An. I will do my part—and thine, if thou wilt not—to a brother. False to him will I never be found.

Is. Ah, over-bold! when Creon hath forbidden?

An. Nay, he hath no right to keep me from mine own.

Is. Ah me! think, sister, how our father perished, amid hate and scorn, when sins bared by his own search had moved him to strike both eyes with self-blinding hand; then the mother wife, two names in one, with twisted noose did despite unto her life; and last, our two brothers in one day—each shedding, hapless one, a kinsman's blood—wrought out with mutual hands their common doom. And now *we* in turn—we two left all alone—think how we shall perish, more miserably than all the rest, if, in defiance of the law, we brave a king's decree or his powers. Nay, we must remember, first, that we were born women, as who should not strive with men; next, that we are ruled of the stronger, so that we must obey in these things, and in things yet sorer. I, therefore, asking the spirits infernal to pardon, seeing that force is put on me herein, will hearken to our rulers; for 'tis witless to be over-busy.

An. I will not urge thee—no, nor, if thou yet shouldst have the mind, wouldst thou be welcome as a worker with *me.* Nay, be what thou wilt; but I will bury him: well for me to die in doing that. I shall rest, a loved one with him whom I have loved, sinless in my crime; for I owe a longer allegiance to the dead than to the living: in that world I shall abide forever. But if *thou* wilt, be guilty of dishonouring laws which the gods have established in honour.

Is. I do them no dishonour; but to defy the state—I have no strength for that.

An. Such be thy plea: I, then, will go to heap the earth above the brother whom I love.

Is. Alas, unhappy one! How I fear for thee!

An. Fear not for me: guide thine own fate aright.

Is. At least, then, disclose this plan to none, but hide it closely—and so, too, will I.

An. Oh, denounce it! Thou wilt be far more hateful for thy silence, if thou proclaim not these things to all.

Is. Thou hast a hot heart for chilling deeds.

An. I know that I please where I am most bound to please.

Is. Ay, if thou canst; but thou wouldst what thou canst not.

An. Why, then, when my strength fails, I shall have done.

Is. A hopeless quest should not be made at all.

An. If thus thou speakest, thou wilt have hatred from me, and wilt justly be subject to the lasting hatred of the dead. But leave me, and the folly that is mine alone, to suffer this dread thing; for I shall not suffer aught so dreadful as an ignoble death.

Is. Go, then, if thou must; and of this be sure—that, though thine errand is foolish, to thy dear ones thou art truly dear.

[*Exit* ANTIGONE *on the spectators' left.* ISMENE *retires into the palace by one of the two side-doors.*

Chorus. Beam of the sun, fairest light that ever dawned on Thebè of the seven gates, thou hast shone forth at last, eye of golden day, arisen above Dircè's streams! The warrior of the white shield, who came from Argos in his panoply, hath been stirred by thee to headlong flight, in swifter career; who set forth against our land by reason of the vexed claims of Polyneices; and, like shrill-screaming eagle, he flew over into our land, in snow-white pinion sheathed, with an armèd throng, and with plumage of helms.

He paused above our dwellings; he ravened around our sevenfold portals with spears athirst for blood; but he went hence, or ever his jaws were glutted with our gore, or the Fire-god's pine-fed flame had seized our crown of towers. So fierce was the noise of battle raised behind him, a thing too hard for him to conquer, as he wrestled with his dragon foe.

For Zeus utterly abhors the boasts of a proud tongue; and when he beheld them coming on in a great stream, in the haughty pride of clanging gold, he smote with brandished fire one who was now hasting to shout victory at his goal upon our ramparts.

Swung down, he fell on the earth with a crash, torch in hand, he who so lately, in the frenzy of the mad onset, was raging against us with the blasts of his tempestuous hate. But those threats fared not as he hoped; and to other foes the mighty War-god dispensed their several dooms, dealing havoc around, a mighty helper at our need.

For seven captains at seven gates, matched against

seven, left the tribute of their panoplies to Zeus who turns the battle; save those two of cruel fate, who, born of one sire and one mother, set against each other their twain conquering spears, and are sharers in a common death.

But since Victory of glorious name hath come to us, with joy responsive to the joy of Thebè whose chariots are many, let us enjoy forgetfulness after the late wars, and visit all the temples of the gods with night-long dance and song; and may Bacchus be our leader, whose dancing shakes the land of Thebè.

But lo, the king of the land comes yonder, Creon, son of Menœceus, our new ruler by the new fortunes that the gods have given; what counsel is he pondering, that he hath proposed this special conference of elders, summoned by his general mandate?

Enter CREON, *from the central doors of the palace, in the garb of king; with two attendants*

Creon. Sirs, the vessel of our state, after being tossed on wild waves, hath once more been safely steadied by the gods: and ye, out of all the folk, have been called apart by my summons, because I knew, first of all, how true and constant was your reverence for the royal power of Laius; how, again, when Œdipus was ruler of our land, and when he had perished, your steadfast loyalty still upheld their children. Since, then, his sons have fallen in one day by a twofold doom—each smitten by the other, each stained with a brother's blood—I now possess the throne and all its powers, by nearness of kinship to the dead.

No man can be fully known, in soul and spirit and mind, until he hath been seen versed in rule and law-giving. For if any, being supreme guide of the state, cleaves not to the best counsels, but, through some fear, keeps his lips locked, I hold, and have ever held, him most base; and if any makes a friend of more account than his fatherland, that man hath no place in my regard. For I—be Zeus my witness, who sees all things always—

would not be silent if I saw ruin, instead of safety, coming to the citizens; nor would I ever deem the country's foe a friend to myself; remembering this, that our country is the ship that bears us safe, and that only while she prospers in our voyage can we make true friends.

Such are the rules by which I guard this city's greatness. And in accord with them is the edict which I have now published to the folk touching the sons of Œdipus; that Eteocles, who hath fallen fighting for our city, in all renown of arms, shall be entombed, and crowned with every rite that follows the noblest dead to their rest. But for his brother, Polyneices—who came back from exile, and sought to consume utterly with fire the city of his fathers and the shrines of his fathers' gods—sought to taste of kindred blood, and to lead the remnant into slavery—touching this man, it hath been proclaimed to our people that none shall grace him with sepulture or lament, but leave him unburied, a corpse for birds and dogs to eat, a ghastly sight of shame.

Such the spirit of my dealing; and never, by deed of mine, shall the wicked stand in honour before the just; but whoso hath good-will to Thebes, he shall be honoured of me, in his life and in his death.

Ch. Such is thy pleasure, Creon, son of Menœceus, touching this city's foe, and its friend; and thou hast power, I ween, to take what order thou wilt, both for the dead and for all of us who live.

Cr. See, then, that ye be guardians of the mandate.

Ch. Lay the burden of this task on some younger man.

Cr. Nay, watchers of the corpse have been found.

Ch. What, then, is this further charge that thou wouldst give?

Cr. That ye side not with the breakers of these commands.

Ch. No man is so foolish that he is enamoured of death.

Cr. In sooth, that is the meed; yet lucre hath oft ruined men through their hopes.

Enter GUARD

Guard. My liege, I will not say that I come breathless from speed, or that I have plied a nimble foot; for often did my thoughts make me pause, and wheel round in my path, to return. My mind was holding large discourse with me: "Fool, why goest thou to thy certain doom?" "Wretch, tarrying again? And if Creon hears this from another, must not thou smart for it?" So debating, I went on my way with lagging steps, and thus a short road was made long. At last, however, it carried the day that I should come hither—to thee; and, though my tale be naught, yet will I tell it; for I come with a good grip on one hope—that I can suffer nothing but what is my fate.

Cr. And what is it that disquiets thee thus?

Gu. I wish to tell thee first about myself—I did not do the deed—I did not see the doer—it were not right that I should come to any harm.

Cr. Thou hast a shrewd eye for thy mark; well dost thou fence thyself round against the blame—clearly thou hast some strange thing to tell.

Gu. Ay, truly; dread news makes one pause long.

Cr. Then tell it, wilt thou, and so get thee gone?

Gu. Well, this is it.—The corpse—some one hath just given it burial, and gone away—after sprinkling thirsty dust on the flesh with such other rites as piety enjoins.

Cr. What sayest thou? What living man hath dared this deed?

Gu. I know not; no stroke of pickaxe was seen there, no earth thrown up by mattock; the ground was hard and dry, unbroken, without track of wheels; the doer was one who had left no trace. And when the first day-watchman showed it to us, sore wonder fell on all. The dead man was veiled from us; not shut within a tomb, but lightly strewn with dust, as by the hand of one who shunned a curse. And no sign met the eye as though any beast of prey or any dog had come nigh to him, or torn him.

Then evil words flew fast and loud among us, guard accusing guard ; and it would e'en have come to blows at last, nor was there any to hinder. Every man was the culprit, and no one was convicted, but all disclaimed knowledge of the deed. And we were ready to take red-hot iron in our hands—to walk through fire—to make oath by the gods that we had not done the deed—that we were not privy to the planning or the doing.

At last, when all our searching was fruitless, one spake, who made us all bend our faces on the earth in fear; for we saw not how we could gainsay him, or escape mischance if we obeyed. His counsel was that this deed must be reported to thee, and not hidden. And this seemed best; and the lot doomed my hapless self to win this prize. So here I stand—as unwelcome as unwilling, well I wot; for no man delights in the bearer of bad news.

Ch. O King, my thoughts have long been whispering, can this deed, perchance, be e'en the work of gods?

Cr. Cease, ere thy words fill me utterly with wrath, lest thou be found at once an old man and foolish. For thou sayest what is not to be borne, in saying that the gods have care for this corpse. Was it for high reward of trusty service that they sought to hide his nakedness, who came to burn their pillared shrines and sacred treasures, to burn their land, and scatter its laws to the winds? Or dost thou behold the gods honouring the wicked? It can not be. No! From the first there were certain in the town that muttered against me, chafing at this edict, wagging their heads in secret; and kept not their necks duly under the yoke, like men contented with my sway.

'Tis by them, well I know, that these have been beguiled and bribed to do this deed. Nothing so evil as money ever grew to be current among men. This lays cities low, this drives men from their homes, this trains and warps honest souls till they set themselves to works of shame; this still teaches folk to practise villanies, and to know every godless deed.

But all the men who wrought this thing for hire have made it sure that, soon or late, they shall pay the price. Now, as Zeus still hath my reverence, know this—I tell it thee on my oath: If ye find not the very author of this burial, and produce him before mine eyes, death alone shall not be enough for you, till first hung up alive, ye have revealed this outrage—that henceforth ye may thieve with better knowledge whence lucre should be won, and learn that it is not well to love gain from every source. For thou wilt find that ill-gotten pelf brings more men to ruin than to weal.

Gu. May I speak? Or shall I just turn and go?

Cr. Knowest thou not that even now thy voice offends?

Gu. Is thy smart in the ears, or in the soul?

Cr. And why wouldst thou define the seat of my pain?

Gu. The doer vexes thy mind, but I, thine ears.

Cr. Ah, thou art a born babbler, 'tis well seen.

Gu. May be, but never the doer of this deed.

Cr. Yea, and more—the seller of thy life for silver.

Gu. Alas! 'Tis sad, truly, that he who judges should misjudge.

Cr. Let thy fancy play with "judgment" as it will: but, if ye show me not the doers of these things, ye shall avow that dastardly gains work sorrows.   [*Exit.*

Gu. Well, may he be found! so 'twere best. But, be he caught or be he not—fortune must settle that—truly thou wilt not see me here again. Saved, even now, beyond hope and thought, I owe the gods great thanks.

[*Exit.*

Chorus. Wonders are many, and none is more wonderful than man; the power that crosses the white sea, driven by the stormy south wind, making a path under surges that threaten to ingulf him; and Earth, the eldest of the gods, the immortal, the unwearied, doth he wear, turning the soil with the offspring of horses, as the ploughs go to and fro from year to year.

8

And the light-hearted race of birds, and the tribes of savage beasts, and the sea-brood of the deep, he snares in the meshes of his woven toils, he leads captive—man excellent in wit! And he masters by his arts the beast whose lair is in the wilds, who roams the hills; he tames the horse of shaggy mane, he puts the yoke upon its neck, he tames the tireless mountain bull.

And speech, and wind-swift thought, and all the moods that mould a state, hath he taught himself; and how to flee the arrows of the frost, when 'tis hard lodging under the clear sky, and the arrows of the rushing rain; yea, he hath resource for all; without resource he meets nothing that must come: only against Death shall he call for aid in vain; but from baffling maladies he hath devised escapes.

Cunning beyond fancy's dream is the fertile skill which brings him, now to evil, now to good. When he honours the laws of the land, and that justice which he hath sworn by the gods to uphold, proudly stands his city: no city hath he who, for his rashness, dwells with sin. Never may he share my hearth, never think my thoughts, who doth these things!

Enter the GUARD, *on the spectators' left, leading*
ANTIGONE

What portent from the gods is this?—my soul is amazed. I know her—how can I deny that yon maiden is Antigone?

O hapless, and child of hapless sire—of Œdipus! What means this? Thou brought a prisoner?—thou, disloyal to the king's laws, and taken in folly?

Gu. Here she is, the doer of the deed: we caught this girl burying him—but where is Creon?

Ch. Lo, he comes forth again from the house, at our need.

Cr. What is it? What hath chanced, that makes my coming timely?

Gu. O King, against nothing should men pledge their word ; for the after-thought belies the first intent. I could have vowed that I should not soon be here again— scared by thy threats, with which I had just been lashed : but—since the joy that surprises and transcends our hopes is like in fulness to no other pleasure—I have come, though 'tis in breach of my sworn oath, bringing this maid ; who was taken showing grace to the dead. This time there was no casting of lots ; no, this luck hath fallen to me, and to none else. And now, Sire, take her thyself, question her, examine her, as thou wilt ; but I have a right to free and final quittance of this trouble.

Cr. And thy prisoner here—how and whence hast thou taken her ?

Gu. She was burying the man ; thou knowest all.

Cr. Dost thou mean what thou sayest ? Dost thou speak aright ?

Gu. I saw her burying the corpse that thou hadst forbidden to bury. Is that plain and clear ?

Cr. And how was she seen ? how taken in the act ?

Gu. It befell on this wise : When we had come to the place—with those dread menaces of thine upon us—we swept away all the dust that covered the corpse, and bared the dank body well ; and then sat us down on the brow of the hill, to windward, heedful that the smell from him should not strike us ; every man was wide awake, and kept his neighbour alert with torrents of threats, if any one should be careless of this task.

So went it, until the sun's bright orb stood in mid heaven, and the heat began to burn : and then suddenly a whirlwind lifted from the earth a storm of dust, a trouble in the sky, and filled the plain, marring all the leafage of its woods ; and the wide air was choked therewith : we closed our eyes, and bore the plague from the gods.

And when, after a long while, this storm had passed, the maid was seen ; and she cried aloud with the sharp cry of a bird in its bitterness—even as when, within the empty nest, it sees the bed stripped of its nestlings. So she also, when she saw the corpse bare, lifted up a voice of wailing, and called down curses on the doers of that deed. And straightway she brought thirsty dust in her hands; and from a shapely ewer of bronze, held high, with thrice-poured drink-offering she crowned the dead.

We rushed forward when we saw it, and at once closed upon our quarry, who was in no wise dismayed. Then we taxed her with her past and present doings; and she stood not on denial of aught—at once to my joy and to my pain. To have escaped from ills one's self is a great joy; but 'tis painful to bring friends to ill. Howbeit, all such things are of less account to me than mine own safety.

Cr. Thou—thou whose face is bent to earth—dost thou avow, or disavow, this deed?

An. I avow it; I make no denial.

Cr. (*To* GUARD.) Thou canst betake thee whither thou wilt, free and clear of a grave charge. [*Exit* GUARD.

(*To* ANTIGONE.) Now, tell me thou—not in many words, but briefly—knewest thou that an edict had forbidden this?

An. I knew it: could I help it? It was public.

Cr. And thou didst indeed dare to transgress that law?

An. Yes; for it was not Zeus that had published me that edict; not such are the laws set among men by the Justice who dwells with the gods below; nor deemed I that thy decrees were of such force, that a mortal could override the unwritten and unfailing statutes of Heaven. For their life is not of to-day or yesterday, but from all time, and no man knows when they were first put forth.

Not through dread of any human pride could I answer to the gods for breaking *these*. Die I must—I knew that well (how should I not?)—even without thy edicts. But if I am to die before my time, I count that a gain: for when any one lives, as I do, compassed about with evils, can such a one find aught but gain in death?

So for me to meet this doom is trifling grief; but if I

had suffered my mother's son to lie in death an unburied corpse, that would have grieved me; for this, I am not grieved. And if my present deeds are foolish in thy sight, it may be that a foolish judge arraigns my folly.

Ch. The maid shows herself passionate child of passionate sire, and knows not how to bend before troubles.

Cr. Yet I would have thee know that o'er-stubborn spirits are most often humbled; 'tis the stiffest iron, baked to hardness in the fire, that thou shalt oftenest see snapped and shivered; and I have seen horses that show temper brought to order by a little curb; there is no room for pride, when thou art thy neighbour's slave. This girl was already versed in insolence when she transgressed the laws that had been set forth; and, that done, lo! a second insult—to vaunt of this, and exult in her deed.

Now verily I am no man, she is the man, if this victory shall rest with her, and bring no penalty. No! be she sister's child, or nearer to me in blood than any that worships Zeus at the altar of our house—she and her kinsfolk shall not avoid a doom most dire; for indeed I charge that other with a like share in the plotting of this burial.

And summon her—for I saw her e'en now within— raving, and not mistress of her wits. So oft, before the deed, the mind stands self-convicted in its treason, when folks are plotting mischief in the dark. But verily this, too, is hateful—when one who hath been caught in wickedness then seeks to make the crime a glory.

An. Wouldst thou do more than take and slay me?

Cr. No more, indeed; having that, I have all.

An. Why then dost thou delay? In thy discourse there is naught that pleases me—never may there be!— and so my words must needs be unpleasing to thee. And yet, for glory—whence could I have won a nobler, than by giving burial to mine own brother? All here would own that they thought it well, were not their lips sealed by fear. But royalty, blest in so much besides, hath the power to do and say what it will.

Cr. Thou differest from all these Thebans in that view.

An. These also share it; but they curb their tongues for thee.

Cr. And art thou not ashamed to act apart from them?

An. No; there is nothing shameful in piety to a brother.

Cr. Was it not a brother, too, that died in the opposite cause?

An. Brother by the same mother and the same sire.

Cr. Why, then, dost thou render a grace that is impious in his sight?

An. The dead man will not say that he so deems it.

Cr. Yea, if thou makest him but equal in honour with the wicked.

An. It was his brother, not his slave, that perished.

Cr. Wasting this land; while *he* fell as its champion.

An. Nevertheless, Hades desires these rites.

Cr. But the good desires not a like portion with the evil.

An. Who knows but this seems blameless in the world below?

Cr. A foe is never a friend—not even in death.

An. 'Tis not my nature to join in hating, but in loving.

Cr. Pass, then, to the world of the dead, and, if thou must needs love, love them. While I live, no woman shall rule me.

Enter ISMENE *from the house, led in by two attendants*

Ch. Lo, yonder Ismene comes forth, shedding such tears as fond sisters weep; a cloud upon her brow casts its shadow over her darkly flushing face, and breaks in on her fair cheek.

Cr. And thou, who, lurking like a viper in my house, wast secretly draining my life-blood, while I knew not that I was nurturing two pests, to rise against my throne—

come, tell me now, wilt thou also confess thy part in this burial, or wilt thou forswear all knowledge of it?

Is. I have done the deed—if she allows my claim—and share the burden of the charge.

An. Nay, justice will not suffer thee to do that: thou didst not consent to the deed, nor did I give thee part in it.

Is. But, now that ills beset thee, I am not ashamed to sail the sea of trouble at thy side.

An. Whose was the deed, Hades and the dead are witnesses: a friend in words is not the friend that I love.

Is. Nay, sister, reject me not, but let me die with thee, and duly honour the dead.

An. Share not thou my death, nor claim deeds to which thou hast not put thy hand: my death will suffice.

Is. And what life is dear to me, bereft of thee?

An. Ask Creon; all thy care is for him.

Is. Why vex me thus, when it avails thee naught?

An. Indeed, if I mock, 'tis with pain that I mock thee.

Is. Tell me—how can I serve thee, even now?

An. Save thyself: I grudge not thy escape.

Is. Ah, woe is me! And shall I have no share in thy fate?

An. Thy choice was to live; mine, to die.

Is. At least thy choice was not made without my protest.

An. One world approved thy wisdom; another mine.

Is. Howbeit, the offence is the same for both of us.

An. Be of good cheer; thou livest; but my life hath long been given to death, that so I might serve the dead.

Cr. Lo, one of these maidens hath newly shown herself foolish, as the other hath been since her life began.

Is. Yea, O King, such reason as Nature may have given abides not with the unfortunate, but goes astray.

Cr. Thine did, when thou chosest vile deeds with the vile.

Is. What life could I endure, without her presence?

Cr. Nay, speak not of her "presence"; she lives no more.

Is. But wilt thou slay the betrothed of thine own son?

Cr. Nay, there are other fields for him to plough.

Is. But there can never be such love as bound him to her.

Cr. I like not an evil wife for my son.

An. Hæmon, beloved! How thy father wrongs thee!

Cr. Enough, enough of thee and of thy marriage!

Ch. Wilt thou indeed rob thy son of this maiden?

Cr. 'Tis Death that shall stay these bridals for me.

Ch. 'Tis determined, it seems, that she shall die.

Cr. Determined, yes, for thee and for me.—(*To the two attendants.*) No more delay—servants, take them within! Henceforth they must be women, and not range at large; for verily even the bold seek to fly, when they see Death now closing on their life.

[*Exeunt attendants, guarding* ANTIGONE *and* ISMENE.— CREON *remains*

Ch. Blest are they whose days have not tasted of evil. For when a house hath once been shaken from heaven, there the curse fails nevermore, passing from life to life of the race; even as, when the surge is driven over the darkness of the deep by the fierce breath of Thracian sea-winds, it rolls up the black sand from the depths, and there is a sullen roar from wind-vexed headlands that front the blows of the storm.

I see that from olden time the sorrows in the house of the Labdacidæ are heaped upon the sorrows of the dead; and generation is not freed by generation, but some god strikes them down, and the race hath no deliverance.

For now that hope of which the light had been spread above the last root of the house of Œdipus—that hope, in turn, is brought low—by the blood-stained dust due to the gods infernal, and by folly in speech, and frenzy at the heart.

Thy power, O Zeus, what human trespass can limit? That power which neither Sleep, the all-ensnaring, nor the untiring months of the gods can master; but thou, a ruler to whom time brings not old age, dwellest in the dazzling splendour of Olympus.

And through the future, near and far, as through the past, shall this law hold good: Nothing that is vast enters into the life of mortals without a curse.

For that hope whose wanderings are so wide is to many men a comfort, but to many a false lure of giddy desires; and the disappointment comes on one who knoweth naught till he burn his foot against the hot fire.

For with wisdom hath some one given forth the famous saying, that evil seems good, soon or late, to him whose mind the god draws to mischief; and but for the briefest space doth he fare free of woe.

But lo, Hæmon, the last of thy sons—comes he grieving for the doom of his promised bride, Antigone, and bitter for the baffled hope of his marriage?

Enter HÆMON

Cr. We shall know soon, better than seers could tell us.—My son, hearing the fixed doom of thy betrothed, art thou come in rage against thy father? Or have I thy good-will, act how I may?

Hæ. Father, I am thine; and thou, in thy wisdom, tracest for me rules which I shall follow. No marriage shall be deemed by me a greater gain than thy good guidance.

Cr. Yea, this, my son, should be thy heart's fixed law —in all things to obey thy father's will. 'Tis for this that men pray to see dutiful children grow up around them in their homes—that such may requite their father's foe with evil, and honour, as their father doth, his friend. But he who begets unprofitable children—what shall we say that he hath sown, but troubles for himself, and much triumph for his foes? Then do not thou, my son, at pleasure's beck, dethrone thy reason for a woman's sake; knowing that this is a joy that soon grows cold in clasping arms— an evil woman to share thy bed and thy home. For what wound could strike deeper than a false friend? Nay, with loathing, and as if she were thine enemy, let this girl go to find a husband in the house of Hades. For since I have taken her, alone of all the city, in open disobedi- ence, I will not make myself a liar to my people—I will slay her.

So let her appeal as she will to the majesty of kindred blood. If I am to nurture mine own kindred in naughti- ness, needs must I bear with it in aliens. He who does his duty in his own household will be found righteous in the state also. But if any one transgresses, and does vio- lence to the laws, or thinks to dictate to his rulers, such a one can win no praise from me. No, whomsoever the city may appoint, that man must be obeyed, in little things and great, in just things and unjust; and I should feel sure that one who thus obeys would be a good ruler no less than a good subject, and in the storm of spears would stand his ground where he was set, loyal and dauntless at his comrade's side.

But disobedience is the worst of evils. This it is that ruins cities; this makes homes desolate; by this, the ranks of allies are broken into headlong rout: but, of the lives whose course is fair, the greater part owes safety to obe- dience. Therefore we must support the cause of order, and in no wise suffer a woman to worst us. Better to fall from power, if we must, by a man's hand; then we should not be called weaker than a woman.

Ch. To us, unless our years have stolen our wit thou seemest to say wisely what thou sayest.

Hæ. Father, the gods implant reason in men, the highest of all things that we call our own. Not mine the skill—far from me be the quest!—to say wherein thou speakest not aright; and yet another man, too, might have some useful thought. At least, it is my natural office to watch, on thy behalf, all that men say, or do, or find to blame. For the dread of thy frown forbids the citizen to speak such words as would offend thine ear; but I can hear these murmurs in the dark, these moanings of the city for this maiden; "No woman," they say, "ever merited her doom less—none ever was to die so shamefully for deeds so glorious as hers; who, when her own brother had fallen in bloody strife, would not leave him unburied, to be devoured by carrion dogs, or by any bird:—deserves not *she* the meed of golden honour?"

Such is the darkling rumour that spreads in secret. For me, my father, no treasure is so precious as thy welfare. What, indeed, is a nobler ornament for children than a prospering sire's fair fame, or for sire than son's? Wear not, then, one mood only in thyself; think not that thy word, and thine alone, must be right. For if any man thinks that he alone is wise—that in speech, or in mind, he hath no peer—such a soul, when laid open, is ever found empty.

No, though a man be wise, 'tis no shame for him to learn many things, and to bend in season. Seest thou, beside the wintry torrent's course, how the trees that yield to it save every twig, while the stiff-necked perish root and branch? And even thus he who keeps the sheet of his sail taut, and never slackens it, upsets his boat, and finishes his voyage with keel uppermost.

Nay, forego thy wrath; permit thyself to change. For if I, a younger man, may offer my thought, it were far best, I ween, that men should be all-wise by nature; but, otherwise—and oft the scale inclines not so—'tis good also to learn from those who speak aright.

Ch. Sire, 'tis meet that thou shouldst profit by his words, if he speaks aught in season, and thou, Hæmon, by thy father's; for on both parts there hath been wise speech.

Cr. Men of my age—are we indeed to be schooled, then, by men of his?

Hæ. In nothing that is not right; but if I am young, thou shouldst look to my merits, not to my years.

Cr. Is it a merit to honour the unruly?

Hæ. I could wish no one to show respect for evil-doers.

Cr. Then is not she tainted with that malady?

Hæ. Our Theban folk, with one voice, denies it.

Cr. Shall Thebes prescribe to me how I must rule?

Hæ. See, there thou hast spoken like a youth indeed.

Cr. Am I to rule this land by other judgment than mine own?

Hæ. That is no city, which belongs to one man.

Cr. Is not the city held to be the ruler's?

Hæ. Thou wouldst make a good monarch of a desert.

Cr. This boy, it seems, is the woman's champion.

Hæ. If thou art a woman; indeed, my care is for thee.

Cr. Shameless, at open feud with thy father!

Hæ. Nay, I see thee offending against justice.

Cr. Do I offend, when I respect mine own prerogatives?

Hæ. Thou dost not respect them, when thou tramplest on the gods' honours.

Cr. O dastard nature, yielding place to a woman!

Hæ. Thou wilt never find me yield to baseness.

Cr. All thy words, at least, plead for that girl.

Hæ. And for thee, and for me, and for the gods below.

Cr. Thou canst never marry her, on this side the grave.

Hæ. Then she must die, and in death destroy another.

Cr. How! doth thy boldness run to open threats?

Hæ. What threat is it, to combat vain resolves?

Cr. Thou shalt rue thy witless teaching of wisdom.

Hæ. Wert thou not my father, I would have called thee unwise.

Cr. Thou woman's slave, use not wheedling speech with me.

Hæ. Thou wouldst speak, and then hear no reply?

Cr. Sayest thou so? Now, by the heaven above us— be sure of it—thou shalt smart for taunting me in this opprobrious strain.—Bring forth that hated thing, that she may die forthwith in his presence—before his eyes— at her bridegroom's side!

Hæ. No, not at my side—never think it—shall she perish; nor shalt thou ever set eyes more upon my face:— rave, then, with such friends as can endure thee.

[*Exit* HÆMON.

Ch. The man is gone, O King, in angry haste; a youthful mind, when stung, is fierce.

Cr. Let him do, or dream, more than man—good speed to him!—But he shall not save these two girls from their doom.

Ch. Dost thou indeed purpose to slay both?

Cr. Not her whose hands are pure: thou sayest well.

Ch. And by what doom mean'st thou to slay the other?

Cr. I will take her where the path is loneliest, and hide her, living, in a rocky vault, with so much food set forth as piety prescribes, that the city may avoid a public stain. And there, praying to Hades, the only god whom she worships, perchance she will obtain release from death; or else will learn, at last, though late, that it is lost labour to revere the dead. [*Exit* CREON.

Ch. Love, unconquered in the fight, Love, who makest havoc of wealth, who keepest thy vigil on the soft cheek of a maiden; thou roamest over the sea, and among the homes of dwellers in the wilds; no immortal can escape thee, nor any among men whose life is for a day; and he to whom thou hast come is mad. [ANTIGONE *is led in.*

The just themselves have their minds warped by thee to wrong, for their ruin: 'tis thou that hast stirred up this present strife of kinsmen; victorious is the love-kindling light from the eyes of the fair bride; it is a power enthroned in sway beside the eternal laws; for there the goddess Aphrodite is working her unconquerable will.

But now I also am carried beyond the bounds of loyalty, and can no more keep back the streaming tears, when I see Antigone thus passing to the bridal chamber where all are laid to rest.

An. See me, citizens of my fatherland, setting forth on my last way, looking my last on the sunlight that is for me no more; no, Hades, who gives sleep to all, leads me living to Acheron's shore; who have had no portion in the chant that brings the bride, nor hath any song been mine for the crowning of bridals; whom the lord of the Dark Lake shall wed.

Ch. Glorious, therefore, and with praise, thou departest to that deep place of the dead: wasting sickness hath not smitten thee; thou hast not found the wages of the sword; no, mistress of thine own fate, and still alive, thou shalt pass to Hades, as no other of mortal kind hath passed.

An. I have heard in other days how dread a doom befell our Phrygian guest, the daughter of Tantalus, on the Sipylian heights; how, like clinging ivy, the growth of stone subdued her; and the rains fail not, as men tell, from her wasting form, nor fails the snow, while beneath her weeping lids the tears bedew her bosom; and most like to hers is the fate that brings me to my rest.

Ch. Yet she was a goddess, thou knowest, and born of gods; we are mortals, and of mortal race. But, 'tis great renown for a woman who hath perished that she should have shared the doom of the godlike, in her life, and afterward in death.

An. Ah, I am mocked! In the name of our fathers' gods, can ye not wait till I am gone—must ye taunt me to my face, O my city, and ye, her wealthy sons? Ah, fount of Dircè, and thou holy ground of Thebè whose chariots are many; ye, at least, will bear me witness, in what sort, unwept of friends, and by what laws I pass to the rock-closed prison of my strange tomb, ah me, unhappy! who have no home on the earth or in the shades, no home with the living or with the dead.

Ch. Thou hast rushed forward to the utmost verge of

daring; and against that throne where Justice sits on high thou hast fallen, my daughter, with a grievous fall. But in this ordeal thou art paying, haply, for thy father's sin.

An. Thou hast touched on my bitterest thought— awaking the ever-new lament for my sire and for all the doom given to us, the famed house of Labdacus. Alas for the horrors of the mother's bed! alas for the wretched mother's slumber at the side of her own son—and my sire! From what manner of parents did I take my miserable being! And to them I go thus, accursed, unwed, to share their home. Alas, my brother, ill-starred in thy marriage, in thy death thou hast undone my life!

Ch. Reverent action claims a certain praise for reverence; but an offence against power can not be brooked by him who hath power in his keeping. Thy self-willed temper hath wrought thy ruin.

An. Unwept, unfriended, without marriage-song, I am led forth in my sorrow on this journey that can be delayed no more. No longer, hapless one, may I behold yon day-star's sacred eye; but for my fate no tear is shed, no friend makes moan.

Enter CREON

Cr. Know ye not that songs and wailings before death would never cease, if it profited to utter them? Away with her—away! And when ye have inclosed her, according to my word, in her vaulted grave, leave her alone, forlorn—whether she wishes to die, or to live a buried life in such a home. Our hands are clean as touching this maiden. But this is certain—she shall be deprived of her sojourn in the light.

An. Tomb, bridal chamber, eternal prison in the caverned rock, whither I go to find mine own, those many who have perished, and whom Persephone hath received among the dead! Last of all shall I pass thither, and far most miserably of all, before the term of my life is spent. But I cherish good hope that my coming will be welcome

to my father, and pleasant to thee, my mother, and welcome, brother, to thee; for, when you died, with mine
own hands I washed and dressed you, and poured drink-
offerings at your graves; and now, Polyneices, 'tis for
tending thy corpse that I win such recompense as this.

[And yet I honoured thee, as the wise will deem,
rightly. Never had I been a mother of children, or if a
husband had been mouldering in death, would I have
taken this task upon me in the city's despite. What law,
ye ask, is my warrant for that word? The husband lost,
another might have been found, and child from another,
to replace the first-born; but, father and mother hidden
with Hades, no brother's life could ever bloom for me
again. Such was the law whereby I held thee first in
honour; but Creon deemed me guilty of error therein,
and of outrage, ah brother mine! And now he leads me
thus, a captive in his hands; no bridal bed, no bridal song
hath been mine, no joy of marriage, no portion in the
nurture of children; but thus, forlorn of friends, unhappy
one, I go living to the vaults of death.]

And what law of Heaven have I transgressed? Why,
hapless one, should I look to the gods any more—what
ally should I invoke—when by piety I have earned the
name of impious? Nay, then, if these things are pleasing
to the gods, when I have suffered my doom, I shall come
to know my sin; but if the sin is with my judges, I could
wish them no fuller measure of evil than they, on their
part, mete wrongfully to me.

Ch. Still the same tempest of the soul vexes this maiden
with the same fierce gusts.

Cr. Then for this shall her guards have cause to rue
their slowness.

An. Ah me! that word hath come very near to death.

Cr. I can cheer thee with no hope that this doom is
not thus to be fulfilled.

An. O city of my fathers in the land of Thebè! O ye
gods, eldest of our race!—they lead me hence—now, now

—they tarry not! Behold me, princes of Thebes, the last daughter of the house of your kings—see what I suffer, and from whom, because I feared to cast away the fear of Heaven! [ANTIGONE *is led away by the guards.*

Ch. Even thus endured Danaë in her beauty to change the light of day for brass-bound walls; and in that chamber, secret as the grave, she was held close prisoner; yet was she of a proud lineage, O my daughter, and charged with the keeping of the seed of Zeus, that fell in the golden rain.

But dreadful is the mysterious power of fate; there is no deliverance from it by wealth or by war, by fenced city, or dark, sea-beaten ships.

And bonds tamed the son of Dryas, swift to wrath, that king of the Edonians; so paid he for his frenzied taunts, when, by the will of Dionysus, he was pent in a rocky prison. There the fierce exuberance of his madness slowly passed away. That man learned to know the god, whom in his frenzy he had provoked with mockeries; for he had sought to quell the god-possessed women, and the Bacchanalian fire; and he angered the Muses that love the flute.

And by the waters of the Dark Rocks, the waters of the twofold sea, are the shores of Bosporus, and Thracian Salmydessus; where Ares, neighbour to the city, saw the accursed, blinding wound dealt to the two sons of Phineus by his fierce wife—the wound that brought darkness to those vengeance-craving orbs, smitten with her bloody hands, smitten with her shuttle for a dagger.

Pining in their misery, they bewailed their cruel doom, those sons of a mother hapless in her marriage; but she traced her descent from the ancient line of the Erechtheidæ; and in far-distant caves she was nursed amid her father's storms, that child of Boreas, swift as a steed over the steep hills, a daughter of gods; yet upon her also the gray Fates bore hard, my daughter.

9

Enter TEIRESIAS, *led by a boy, on the spectators' right*

Te. Princes of Thebes, we have come with linked steps, both served by the eyes of one; for thus, by a guide's help, the blind must walk.

Cr. And what, aged Teiresias, are thy tidings?

Te. I will tell thee; and do thou hearken to the seer.

Cr. Indeed, it has not been my wont to slight thy counsel.

Te. Therefore didst thou steer our city's course aright.

Cr. I have felt, and can attest, thy benefits.

Te. Mark that now, once more, thou standest on fate's fine edge.

Cr. What means this? How I shudder at thy message!

Te. Thou wilt learn, when thou hearest the warnings of mine art. As I took my place on mine old seat of augury, where all birds have been wont to gather within my ken, I heard a strange voice among them; they were screaming with dire, feverish rage, that drowned their language in a jargon; and I knew that they were rending each other with their talons, murderously; the whirr of wings told no doubtful tale.

Forthwith, in fear, I essayed burnt-sacrifice on a duly kindled altar: but from my offerings the Fire-god showed no flame; a dank moisture, oozing from the thigh-flesh, trickled forth upon the embers, and smoked, and sputtered; the gall was scattered to the air; and the streaming thighs lay bared of the fat that had been wrapped round them.

Such was the failure of the rites by which I vainly asked a sign, as from this boy I learned; for he is my guide, as I am guide to others. And 'tis thy counsel that hath brought this sickness on our state. For the altars of our city and of our hearths have been tainted, one and all, by birds and dogs, with carrion from the hapless corpse, the son of Œdipus: and therefore the gods no more accept prayer and sacrifice at our hands, or the flame of meat-offering; nor doth any bird give a clear sign by its shrill cry, for they have tasted the fatness of a slain man's blood.

Think, then, on these things, my son. All men are liable to err; but when an error hath been made, that man is no longer witless or unblest who heals the ill into which he hath fallen, and remains not stubborn. Self-will, we know, incurs the charge of folly. Nay, allow the claim of the dead; stab not the fallen; what prowess is it to slay the slain anew? I have sought thy good, and for thy good I speak: and never is it sweeter to learn from a good counsellor than when he counsels for thine own gain.

Cr. Old man, ye all shoot your shafts at me, as archers at the butts; ye must needs practise on me with seer-craft also; ay, the seer-tribe hath long trafficked in me, and made me their merchandise. Gain your gains, drive your trade, if ye list, in the silver-gold of Sardis and the gold of India; but ye shall not hide that man in the grave—no, though the eagles of Zeus should bear the carrion morsels to their Master's throne—no, not for dread of that defilement will I suffer his burial: for well I know that no mortal can defile the gods. But, aged Teiresias, the wisest fall with a shameful fall, when they clothe shameful thoughts in fair words, for lucre's sake.

Te. Alas! Doth any man know, doth any consider. . .

Cr. Whereof? What general truth dost thou announce?

Te. How precious, above all wealth, is good counsel.

Cr. As folly, I think, is the worst mischief.

Te. Yet thou art tainted with that distemper.

Cr. I would not answer the seer with a taunt.

Te. But thou dost, in saying that I prophesy falsely.

Cr. Well, the prophet-tribe was ever fond of money.

Te. And the race bred of tyrants loves base gain.

Cr. Knowest thou that thy speech is spoken of thy king?

Te. I know it; for through me thou hast saved Thebes.

Cr. Thou art a wise seer; but thou lovest evil deeds.

Te. Thou wilt rouse me to utter the dread secret in my soul.

Cr. Out with it!—Only speak it not for gain.

Te. Indeed, methinks, I shall not—as touching thee.

Cr. Know that thou shalt not trade on my resolve.

Te. Then know thou—ay, know it well—that thou shalt not live through many more courses of the sun's swift chariot, ere one begotten of thine own loins shall have been given by thee, a corpse for corpses; because thou hast thrust children of the sunlight to the shades, and ruthlessly lodged a living soul in the grave; but keepest in this world one who belongs to the gods infernal, a corpse unburied, unhonoured, all unhallowed. In such thou hast no part, nor have the gods above, but this is a violence done to them by thee. Therefore the avenging destroyers lie in wait for thee, the Furies of Hades and of the gods, that thou mayest be taken in these same ills.

And mark well if I speak these things as a hireling. A time not long to be delayed shall awaken the wailing of men and of women in thy house. And a tumult of hatred against thee stirs all the cities whose mangled sons had the burial-rite from dogs, or from wild beasts, or from some winged bird that bore a polluting breath to each city that contains the hearths of the dead.

Such arrows for thy heart—since thou provokest me— have I launched at thee, archer-like, in my anger—sure arrows, of which thou shalt not escape the smart.—Boy, lead me home, that he may spend his rage on younger men, and learn to keep a tongue more temperate, and to bear within his breast a better mind than now he bears.

[*Exit* TEIRESIAS.

Ch. The man hath gone, O King, with dread prophecies. And, since the hair on this head, once dark, hath been white, I know that he hath never been a false prophet to our city.

Cr. I, too, know it well, and am troubled in soul. 'Tis dire to yield; but, by resistance, to smite my pride with ruin—this, too, is a dire choice.

Ch. Son of Menœceus, it behooves thee to take wise counsel.

Cr. What should I do, then? Speak, and I will obey.

Ch. Go thou, and free the maiden from her rocky chamber, and make a tomb for the unburied dead.

Cr. And this is thy counsel? Thou wouldst have me yield?

Ch. Yea, King, and with all speed; for swift harms from the gods cut short the folly of men.

Cr. Ah me, 'tis hard, but I resign my cherished resolve —I obey. We must not wage a vain war with destiny.

Ch. Go, thou, and do these things; leave them not to others.

Cr. Even as I am I'll go.—On, on, my servants, each and all of you—take axes in your hands, and hasten to the ground that ye see yonder! Since our judgment hath taken this turn, I will be present to unloose her, as I myself bound her. My heart misgives me, 'tis best to keep the established laws, even to life's end.

Ch. O thou of many names, glory of the Cadmeian bride, offspring of loud-thundering Zeus! thou who watchest over famed Italia, and reignest, where all guests are welcomed, in the sheltered plain of Eleusinian Deô! O Bacchus, dweller in Thebè, mother-city of Bacchants, by the softly-gliding stream of Ismenus, on the soil where the fierce dragon's teeth were sown!

Thou hast been seen where torch-flames glare through smoke, above the crests of the twin peaks, where move the Corycian nymphs, thy votaries, hard by Castalia's stream.

Thou comest from the ivy-mantled slopes of Nysa's hills, and from the shore green with many-clustered vines, while thy name is lifted up on strains of more than mortal power, as thou visitest the ways of Thebè:

Thebè, of all cities, thou holdest first in honour, thou, and thy mother whom the lightning smote; and now, when all our people is captive to a violent plague, come thou with healing feet over the Parnassian height, or over the moaning strait!

O thou with whom the stars rejoice as they move, the stars whose breath is fire; O master of the voices of the night; son begotten of Zeus; appear, O king, with thine attendant Thyiads, who in night-long frenzy dance before thee, the giver of good gifts, Iacchus!

Enter MESSENGER, *on the spectators' left*

Me. Dwellers by the house of Cadmus and of Amphion, there is no estate of mortal life that I would ever praise or blame as settled. Fortune raises and Fortune humbles the lucky or unlucky from day to day, and no one can prophesy to men concerning those things which are established. For Creon was blest once, as I count bliss; he had saved this land of Cadmus from its foes; he was clothed with sole dominion in the land; he reigned, the glorious sire of princely children. And now all hath been lost. For when a man hath forfeited his pleasures, I count him not as living—I hold him but a breathing corpse. Heap up riches in thy house, if thou wilt; live in kingly state; yet, if there be no gladness therewith, I would not give the shadow of a vapour for all the rest, compared with joy.

Ch. And what is this new grief that thou hast to tell for our princes?

Me. Death; and the living are guilty for the dead.

Ch. And who is the slayer? Who the stricken? Speak.

Me. Hæmon hath perished; his blood hath been shed by no stranger.

Ch. By his father's hand, or by his own?

Me. By his own, in wrath with his sire for the murder.

Ch. O prophet, how true, then, hast thou proved thy word!

Me. These things stand thus; ye must consider of the rest.

Ch. Lo, I see the hapless Eurydicè, Creon's wife, approaching; she comes from the house by chance, haply— or because she knows the tidings of her son.

Enter EURYDICÈ

Eu. People of Thebes, I heard your words as I was going forth, to salute the goddess Pallas with my prayers. Even as I was loosing the fastenings of the gate, to open it, the message of a household woe smote on mine ear: I sank back, terror-stricken, into the arms of my handmaids, and my senses fled. But say again what the tidings were; I shall hear them as one who is no stranger to sorrow.

Me. Dear lady, I will witness of what I saw, and will leave no word of the truth untold. Why, indeed, should I soothe thee with words in which I must presently be found false? Truth is ever best.—I attended thy lord as his guide to the farthest part of the plain, where the body of Polyneices, torn by dogs, still lay unpitied. We prayed the goddess of the roads, and Pluto, in mercy to restrain their wrath; we washed the dead with holy washing; and with freshly-plucked boughs we solemnly burned such relics as there were. We raised a high mound of his native earth; and then we turned away to enter the maiden's nuptial chamber with rocky couch, the caverned mansion of the bride of Death. And, from afar off, one of us heard a voice of loud wailing at that bride's unhallowed bower; and came to tell our master Creon.

And as the king drew nearer, doubtful sounds of a bitter cry floated around him; he groaned, and said in accents of anguish: "Wretched that I am, can my foreboding be true? Am I going on the wofullest way that ever I went? My son's voice greets me.—Go, my servants—haste ye nearer, and when ye have reached the tomb, pass through the gap, where the stones have been wrenched away, to the cell's very mouth—and look, and see if 'tis Hæmon's voice that I know, or if mine ear is cheated by the gods."

This search, at our despairing master's word, we went to make; and in the farthest part of the tomb we descried *her* hanging by the neck, slung by a thread-wrought halter of fine linen; while *he* was embracing her with arms thrown around her waist—bewailing the loss of his bride who is with the dead, and his father's deeds, and his own ill-starred love.

But his father, when he saw him, cried aloud with a dread cry, and went in, and called to him with a voice of wailing: "Unhappy, what a deed hast thou done! What thought hath come to thee? What manner of mischance hath marred thy reason? Come forth, my child! I pray thee—I implore!" But the boy glared at him with fierce eyes, spat in his face, and, without a word of answer, drew his cross-hilted sword: as his father rushed forth in flight, he missed his aim; then, hapless one, wroth with himself, he straightway leaned with all his weight against his sword, and drove it, half its length, into his side; and while sense lingered, he clasped the maiden to his faint embrace, and, as he gasped, sent forth on her pale cheek the swift stream of the oozing blood.

Corpse enfolding corpse he lies; he has won his nuptial rites, poor youth, not here, yet in the halls of Death; and he hath witnessed to mankind that, of all curses which leave to man, ill counsel is the sovereign curse.

[EURYDICÈ *retires into the house.*

Ch. What wouldst thou augur from this? The lady hath turned back, and is gone, without a word, good or evil.

Me. I, too, am startled; yet I nourish the hope that, at these sore tidings of her son, she can not deign to give her sorrow public vent, but in the privacy of the house will set her handmaids to mourn the household grief. For she is not untaught of discretion, that she should err.

Ch. I know not ; but to me, at least, a strained silence seems to portend peril, no less than vain abundance of lament.

Me. Well, I will enter the house, and learn whether indeed she is not hiding some repressed purpose in the depths of a passionate heart. Yea, thou sayest well : excess of silence, too, may have a perilous meaning.

[*Exit* MESSENGER.

Enter CREON, *on the spectators' left, with attendants, carrying the shrouded body of* HÆMON *on a bier*

Ch. Lo, yonder the king himself draws near, bearing that which tells too clear a tale—the work of no stranger's madness—if we may say it—but of his own misdeeds.

Cr. Woe for the sins of a darkened soul, stubborn sins, fraught with death ! Ah, ye behold us, the sire who hath slain, the son who hath perished ! Woe is me, for the wretched blindness of my counsels !—Alas, my son, thou hast died in thy youth, by a timeless doom, woe is me !—thy spirit hath fled—not by thy folly, but by mine own !

Ch. Ah me, how all too late thou seemest to see the right !

Cr. Ah me, I have learned the bitter lesson ! But then, methinks, oh then, some god smote me from above with crushing weight, and hurled me into ways of cruelty, woe is me—overthrowing and trampling on my joy ! Woe, woe for the troublous toils of men !

Enter SECOND MESSENGER *from the house*

Sec. Me. Sire, thou hast come, methinks, as one whose hands are not empty, but who hath store laid up besides ; thou bearest yonder burden with thee ; and thou art soon to look upon the woes within thy house.

Cr. And what worse ill is yet to follow upon ills ?

Sec. Me. Thy queen hath died, true mother of yon corpse—ah, hapless lady !—by blows newly dealt.

Cr. O Hades, all-receiving, whom no sacrifice can

appease! Hast thou, then, no mercy for me? O thou
herald of evil, bitter tidings, what word dost thou utter?
Alas! I was already as dead, and thou hast smitten me
anew! What sayest thou, my son? What is this new
message that thou bringest—woe, woe is me!—of a wife's
doom—of slaughter heaped on slaughter?

Ch. Thou canst behold: 'tis no longer hidden within.

> [*The doors of the palace are opened, and the
> corpse of* EURYDICÈ *is disclosed.*

Cr. Ah me—yonder I behold a new, a second woe!
What destiny, ah what, can yet await me? I have but
now raised my son in my arms—and there, again, I see a
corpse before me! Alas, alas, unhappy mother! Alas,
my child!

Sec. Me. There, at the altar, self-stabbed with a keen
knife, she suffered her darkening eyes to close, when she
had wailed for the noble fate of Megareus who died before, and then for his fate who lies there—and when, with
her last breath, she had invoked evil fortunes upon thee,
the slayer of thy sons.

Cr. Woe, woe! I thrill with dread. Is there none to
strike me to the heart with two-edged sword? Oh, miserable that I am, and steeped in miserable anguish!

Sec. Me. Yea, both this son's doom, and that other's,
were laid to thy charge by her whose corpse thou seest.

Cr. And what was the manner of the violent deed by
which she passed away?

Sec. Me. Her own hand struck her to the heart, when
she had learned her son's sorely lamented fate.

Cr. Ah me, this guilt can never be fixed on any other
of mortal kind, for my acquittal! I, even I, was thy slayer,
wretched that I am—I own the truth.—Lead me away, O
my servants, lead me hence with all speed, whose life is
but as death!

Ch. Thy counsels are good, if there can be good with
ills; briefest is best, when trouble is in our path.

Cr. Oh, let it come, let it appear, that fairest of fates

for me, that brings my last day—ay, best fate of all! Oh, let it come, that I may never look upon to-morrow's light!

Ch. These things are in the future; present tasks claim our care: the ordering of the future rests where it should rest.

Cr. All my desires, at least, were summed in that prayer.

Ch. Pray thou no more; for mortals have no escape from destined woe.

Cr. Lead me away, I pray you; a rash, foolish man; who have slain thee, ah my son, unwittingly, and thee, too, my wife—unhappy that I am! I know not which way I should bend my gaze, or where I should seek support; for all is amiss with that which is in my hands—and yonder, again, a crushing fate hath leapt upon my head.

[*As* CREON *is being conducted into the house, the Coryphæus speaks the closing verses.*

Ch. Wisdom is the supreme part of happiness; and reverence toward the gods must be inviolate. Great words of prideful men are ever punished with great blows, and, in old age, teach the chastened to be wise.

THE ŒDIPUS TYRANNUS
OF SOPHOCLES

TRANSLATED BY

THOMAS FRANCKLIN

DRAMATIS PERSONÆ

ŒDIPUS, King of Thebes.
JOCASTA, Wife of Œdipus.
CREON, Brother of Jocasta.
TIRESIAS, a Blind Prophet of Thebes.
A SHEPHERD, from Corinth.
A MESSENGER.
AN OLD SHEPHERD, formerly belonging to Laius.
HIGH PRIEST OF JUPITER.
CHORUS, composed of the Priests and Ancient
    Men of Thebes, Theban Youths, Children of
    Œdipus, Attendants, etc.

SCENE: THEBES, before the PALACE OF ŒDIPUS.

ŒDIPUS TYRANNUS

—▸◆◂—

ŒDIPUS, HIGH PRIEST OF JUPITER

OEDIPUS. O my loved sons! the youthful
progeny
Of ancient Cadmus, wherefore sit you here,
And suppliant thus, with sacred boughs adorned,
Crowd to our altars? Frequent sacrifice
And prayers and sighs and sorrows fill the land.
I could have sent to learn the fatal cause;
But see, your anxious sovereign comes himself
To know it all from you; behold your king,
Renowned Œdipus; do thou, old man,
For best that office suits thy years, inform me,
Why are you come; is it the present ill
That calls you here, or dread of future woe?
Hard were indeed the heart that did not feel
For grief like yours, and pity such distress:
If there be aught that Œdipus can do
To serve his people, know me for your friend.
  Priest. O king! thou seest what numbers throng thy
altars;
Here, bending sad beneath the weight of years,
The hoary priests, here crowd the chosen youth
Of Thebes, with these a weak and suppliant train
Of helpless infants, last in me behold
The minister of Jove: far off thou seest

Assembled multitudes, with laurel crowned,
To where Minerva's hallowed temples rise
Frequent repair, or where Ismenus laves
Apollo's sacred shrine: too well thou knowst
Thy wretched Thebes, with dreadful storms oppressed,
Scarce lifts her head above the whelming flood;
The teeming earth her blasted harvest mourns,
And on the barren plain the flocks and herds
Unnumbered perish; dire abortion thwarts
The mother's hopes, and painful she brings forth
The half-formed infant; baleful pestilence
Hath laid our city waste, the fiery god
Stalks o'er deserted Thebes; while with our groans
Enriched, the gloomy god of Erebus
Triumphant smiles. O Œdipus! to thee
We bend; behold these youths, with me they kneel,
And suppliant at thy altars sue for aid,
To thee the first of men, and only less
Than them whose favour thou alone canst gain,
The gods above; thy wisdom yet may heal
The deep-felt wounds, and make the powers divine
Propitious to us. Thebes long since to thee
Her safety owed, when from the Sphinx delivered
Thy grateful people saw thee, not by man
But by the gods instructed, save the land:
Now then, thou best of kings, assist us now.
Oh! by some mortal or immortal aid
Now succour the distress! On wisdom oft,
And prudent counsels in the hour of ill,
Success awaits. O dearest prince! support,
Relieve thy Thebes; on thee, its saviour once,
Again it calls. Now, if thou wouldst not see
The mem'ry perish of thy former deeds,
Let it not call in vain, but rise and save!
With happiest omens once and fair success
We saw thee crowned: oh, be thyself again,
And may thy will and fortune be the same!

If thou art yet to reign, O king! remember
A sovereign's riches is a peopled realm;
For what will ships or lofty towers avail
Unarmed with men to guard and to defend them?

Œdi. O my unhappy sons! too well I know
Your sad estate. I know the woes of Thebes;
And yet among you lives not such a wretch
As Œdipus; for oh! on me, my children,
Your sorrows press. Alas! I feel for you
My people, for myself, for Thebes, for all!
Think not I slept regardless of your ills;
Oh no! with many a tear I wept your fate,
And oft in meditation deep revolved
How best your peace and safety to restore:
The only medicine that my thoughts could find
I have administered: Menœceus' son,
The noble Creon, went by my command
To Delphos from Apollo's shrine, to know
What must be done to save this wretched land:
'Tis time he were returned: I wonder much
At his delay. If, when he comes, your king
Perform not all the god enjoins, then say
He is the worst of men.

Priest. O king! thy words
Are gracious, and if right these youths inform me,
Creon is here.

Œdi. O Phœbus! grant he come
With tidings cheerful as the smile he wears!

Priest. He is the messenger of good; for see,
His brows are crowned with laurel.

Œdi. We shall soon
Be satisfied: he comes.

CREON, ŒDIPUS, PRIEST, CHORUS

Œdi. My dearest Creon,
Oh! say, what answer bear'st thou from the god:
Or good, or ill?

Creon.   Good, very good ; for know,
The worst of ills, if rightly used, may prove
The means of happiness.

Œdi.   What says my friend ?
This answer gives me naught to hope or fear.

Creon. Shall we retire, or would you that I speak
In public here ?

Œdi.   Before them all declare it ;
Their woes sit heavier on me than my own.

Creon. Then mark what I have heard : the god com-
    mands
That instant we drive forth the fatal cause
Of this dire pestilence, nor nourish here
The accursèd monster.

Œdi.   Who ? What monster ? How
Remove it ?

Creon.   Or by banishment, or death,
Life must be given for life ; for yet his blood
Rests on the city.

Œdi.   Whose ? What means the god ?

Creon. O king ! before thee Laius ruled o'er Thebes.

Œdi. I know he did, though I did ne'er behold him.

Creon. Laius was slain, and on his murderers,
So Phœbus says, we must have vengeance.

Œdi.   Where,
Where are the murderers ? Who shall trace the guilt
Buried so long in silence ?

Creon.   Here, he said,
E'en in this land, what's sought for may be found,
But truth unsearched for seldom comes to light.

Œdi. How did he fall, and where ?—at home, abroad ?
Died he at Thebes, or in a foreign land ?

Creon. He left his palace, fame reports, to seek
Some oracle ; since that, we ne'er beheld him.

Œdi. But did no messenger return ? Not one
Of all his train, of whom we might inquire
Touching this murder ?

Creon.   One, and one alone,
Came back, who, flying, 'scaped the general slaughter.
But nothing save one little circumstance
Or knew, or e'er related.
          Œdi.   What was that?
Much may be learned from that.   A little dawn
Of light appearing may discover all.
          Creon. Laius, attacked by robbers, and oppressed
By numbers, fell.   Such is his tale.
          Œdi.   Would they—
Would robbers do so desperate a deed,
Unbribed and unassisted?
          Creon.   So, indeed,
Suspicion whispered then.   But—Laius dead—
No friend was found to vindicate the wrong.
          Œdi. But what strange cause could stop inquiry thus
Into the murder of a king?
          Creon.   The Sphinx.
Her dire enigma kept our thoughts intent
On present ills, nor gave us time to search
The past mysterious deed.
          Œdi.   Myself will try
Soon to unveil it.   Thou, Apollo, well,
And well hast thou, my Creon, lent thy aid.
Your Œdipus shall now perform his part.
Yes, I will fight for Phœbus and my country.
And so I ought.   For not to friends alone,
Or kindred, owe I this, but to myself.
Who murdered him, perchance would murder me!
His cause is mine.   Wherefore, my children, rise;
Take hence your suppliant boughs, and summon here
The race of Cadmus—my assembled people.
Naught shall be left untried.   Apollo leads,
And we shall rise to joy, or sink forever.
          Priest. Haste, then, my sons, for this we hither came:
About it quick, and may the god who sent
This oracle, protect, defend, and save us!   [*Exeunt.*

Chorus
Strophe 1

O thou great oracle divine!
Who didst to happy Thebes remove
　From Delphi's golden shrine,
And in sweet sounds declare the will of Jove.
　Daughter of hope, oh! soothe my soul to rest,
　And calm the rising tumult in my breast.
Look down, O Phœbus! on thy loved abode.
　Speak, for thou knowst the dark decrees of fate,
　Our present and our future state.
O Delian! be thou still our healing god?

Antistrophe 1

Minerva, first on thee I call,
Daughter of Jove, immortal maid,
　Low beneath thy feet we fall:
Oh! bring thy sister Dian to our aid.
　Goddess of Thebes, from thy imperial throne
　Look with an eye of gentle pity down;
And thou, far-shooting Phœbus, once the friend
　Of this unhappy, this devoted land,
　Oh! now, if ever, let thy hand
Once more be stretched to save and to defend!

Strophe 2

Great Thebes, my sons, is now no more;
She falls and ne'er again shall rise,
　Naught can her health or strength restore,
The mighty nation sinks, she droops, she dies.
　Stripped of her fruits, behold the barren earth—
　The half-formed infant struggles for a birth.
The mother sinks unequal to her pain:
　While quick as birds in airy circles fly,
　Or lightnings from an angry sky,
Crowds press on crowds to Pluto's dark domain.

Antistrophe 2

Behold what heaps of wretches slain,
Unburied, unlamented lie,
  Nor parents now nor friends remain
To grace their deaths with pious obsequy.
  The aged matron and the blooming wife,
  Cling to the altars—sue for added life.
With sighs and groans united pæans rise;
  Re-echoed, still doth great Apollo's name
  Their sorrows and their wants proclaim.
Frequent to him ascends the sacrifice.

Strophe 3

Haste then, Minerva, beauteous maid,
Descend in this afflictive hour,
  Haste to thy dying people's aid,
Drive hence this baneful, this destructive power!
  Who comes not armed with hostile sword or shield,
  Yet strews with many a corse th' ensanguined field;
To Amphitrite's wide-extending bed
  Oh! drive him, goddess, from thy favourite land,
  Or let him, by thy dread command,
Bury in Thracian waves his ignominious head.

Antistrophe 3

Father of all, immortal Jove!
Oh! now thy fiery terrors send;
  From thy dreadful stores above
Let lightnings blast him and let thunders rend!
  And thou, O Lydian king! thy aid impart;
  Send from thy golden bow th' unerring dart;
Smile, chaste Diana, on this loved abode,
  While Theban Bacchus joins the maddening throng,
  O god of wine and mirth and song!
Now with thy torch destroy the base, inglorious god.

                              [Exeunt.

ŒDIPUS, CHORUS. *The People assembled*

Œdi. Your prayers are heard: and if you will obey
Your king, and hearken to his words, you soon
Shall find relief; myself will heal your woes.
I was a stranger to the dreadful deed,
A stranger e'en to the report till now;
And yet without some traces of the crime
I should not urge this matter; therefore hear me.
I speak to all the citizens of Thebes,
Myself a citizen—observe me well:
If any know the murderer of Laius,
Let him reveal it; I command you all.
But if restrained by dread of punishment
He hide the secret, let him fear no more;
For naught but exile shall attend the crime
Whene'er confessed; if by a foreign hand
The horrid deed was done, who points him out
Commands our thanks, and meets a sure reward;
But if there be who knows the murderer,
And yet conceals him from us, mark his fate,
Which here I do pronounce: Let none receive
Throughout my kingdom, none hold converse with him,
Nor offer prayer, nor sprinkle o'er his head
The sacred cup; let him be driven from all,
By all abandoned, and by all accursed,
For so the Delphic oracle declared;
And therefore to the gods I pay this duty
And to the dead. Oh! may the guilty wretch,
Whether alone, or by his impious friends
Assisted, he performed the horrid deed,
Denied the common benefits of Nature,
Wear out a painful life! And oh! if here,
Within my palace, I conceal the traitor,
On me and mine alight the vengeful curse!
To you, my people, I commit the care
Of this important business; 'tis my cause,
The cause of Heaven, and your expiring country.

E'en if the god had naught declared, to leave
This crime unexpiated were most ungrateful.
He was the best of kings, the best of men;
That sceptre now is mine which Laius bore;
His wife is mine; so would his children be
Did any live; and therefore am I bound,
E'en as he were my father, to revenge him.
Yes, I will try to find this murderer,
I owe it to the son of Labdacus,
To Polydorus, Cadmus, and the race
Of great Agenor. Oh! if yet there are,
Who will not join me in the pious deed,
From such may earth withhold her annual store,
And barren be their bed, their life most wretched,
And their death cruel as the pestilence
That wastes our city! But on you, my Thebans,
Who wish us fair success, may justice smile
Propitious, and the gods forever bless!

 Chor. O king! thy imprecations unappalled
I hear, and join thee, guiltless of the crime,
Nor knowing who committed it. The god
Alone, who gave the oracle, must clear
Its doubtful sense, and point out the offender.

 Œdi. 'Tis true. But who shall force the powers divine
To speak their hidden purpose?

 Chor.   One thing more,
If I might speak.

 Œdi.   Say on, whate'er thy mind
Shall dictate to thee.

 Chor.   As among the gods
All-knowing Phœbus, so to mortal men
Doth sage Tiresias in foreknowledge sure
Shine forth pre-eminent. Perchance his aid
Might much avail us.

 Œdi.   Creon did suggest
The same expedient, and by his advice
Twice have I sent for this Tiresias; much

I wonder that he comes not.

Chor.   'Tis most fitting
We do consult him ; for the idle tales
Which rumour spreads are not to be regarded.

Œdi. What are those tales? for naught should we
    despise.

Chor. 'Tis said some travellers did attack the king.

Œdi. It is ; but still no proof appears.

Chor.   And yet,
If it be so, thy dreadful execration
Will force the guilty to confess.

Œdi.   Oh no!
Who fears not to commit the crime will ne'er
Be frightened at the curse that follows it.

Chor. Behold he comes, who will discover all,
The holy prophet. See! they lead him hither;
He knows the truth and will reveal it to us.

TIRESIAS, ŒDIPUS, CHORUS

Œdi. O sage Tiresias, thou who knowest all
That can be known, the things of heaven above
And earth below, whose mental eye beholds,
Blind as thou art, the state of dying Thebes,
And weeps her fate, to thee we look for aid,
On thee alone for safety we depend.
This answer, which perchance thou hast not heard,
Apollo gave: the plague, he said, should cease
When those who murdered Laius were discovered
And paid the forfeit of their crime by death
Or banishment. Oh! do not then conceal
Aught that thy art prophetic from the flight
Of birds or other omens may disclose.
Oh! save thyself, save this afflicted city,
Save Œdipus, avenge the guiltless dead
From this pollution! Thou art all our hope;
Remember, 'tis the privilege of man,
His noblest function, to assist the wretched.

Tir. Alas! what misery it is to know
When knowledge is thus fatal! O Tiresias!
Thou art undone! Would I had never come!

Œdi. What sayst thou? Whence this strange dejec-
tion? Speak.

Tir. Let me be gone; 'twere better for us both
That I retire in silence: be advised.

Œdi. It is ingratitude to Thebes, who bore
And cherished thee—it is unjust to all,
To hide the will of Heaven.

Tir.   'Tis rash in thee
To ask, and rash I fear will prove my answer.

Chor. Oh! do not, by the gods, conceal it from us,
Suppliant we all request, we all conjure thee.

Tir. You know not what you ask; I'll not unveil
Your miseries to you.

Œdi.   Knowst thou then our fate,
And wilt not tell it? Meanst thou to betray
Thy country and thy king?

Tir.   I would not make
Myself and thee unhappy; why thus blame
My tender care, nor listen to my caution?

Œdi. Wretch as thou art, thou wouldst provoke a
stone—
Inflexible and cruel—still implored
And still refusing.

Tir.   Thou condemn'st my warmth,
Forgetful of thy own.

Œdi.   Who would not rage
To see an injured people treated thus
With vile contempt?

Tir.   What is decreed by Heaven
Must come to pass, though I reveal it not,

Œdi. Still, 'tis thy duty to inform us of it.

Tir. I'll speak no more, not though thine anger swell
E'en to its utmost.

Œdi.   Nor will I be silent.

I tell thee once for all thou wert thyself
Accomplice in this deed. Nay, more, I think,
But for thy blindness, wouldst with thy own hand
Have done it too.

Tir.   'Tis well. Now hear Tiresias.
The sentence, which thou didst thyself proclaim,
Falls on thyself. Henceforth shall never man
Hold converse with thee, for thou art accursed—
The guilty cause of all this city's woes.

Œdi. Audacious traitor ! thinkst thou to escape
The hand of vengeance?

Tir.   Yes, I fear thee not ;
For truth is stronger than a tyrant's arm.

Œdi. Whence didst thou learn this? Was it from
     thy art?

Tir. I learned it from thyself. Thou didst compel me
To speak, unwilling as I was.

Œdi.   Once more
Repeat it then, that I may know my fate
More plainly still.

Tir.   Is it not plain already ?
Or meanst thou but to tempt me ?

Œdi.   No, but say,
Speak it again.

Tir.   Again then I declare
Thou art thyself the murderer whom thou seekst.

Œdi. A second time thou shalt not pass unpunished.

Tir. What wouldst thou say, if I should tell thee all ?

Œdi. Say what thou wilt. For all is false.

Tir.   Know then,
That Œdipus, in shameful bonds united
With those he loves, unconscious of his guilt,
Is yet most guilty.

Œdi.   Dar'st thou utter more,
And hope for pardon ?

Tir.   Yes, if there be strength
In sacred truth.

Œdi.　　　　But truth dwells not in thee :
Thy body and thy mind are dark alike,
For both are blind.　Thy ev'ry sense is lost.
　Tir. Thou dost upbraid me with the loss of that
For which thyself ere long shall meet reproach
From every tongue.
　Œdi.　　　　Thou blind and impious traitor !
Thy darkness is thy safeguard, or this hour
Had been thy last.
　Tir.　　　　It is not in my fate
To fall by thee.　Apollo guards his priest.
　Œdi. Was this the tale of Creon, or thy own ?
　Tir. Creon is guiltless, and the crime is thine.
　Œdi. O riches, power, dominion ! and thou far
Above them all, the best of human blessings,
Excelling wisdom, how doth envy love
To follow and oppress you !　This fair kingdom,
Which by the nation's choice, and not my own,
I here possess, Creon, my faithful friend,
For such I thought him once, would now wrest from me,
And hath suborned this vile impostor here,
This wandering hypocrite, of sharpest sight
When interest prompts, but ignorant and blind
When fools consult him.　Tell me, prophet, where
Was all thy art when the abhorred Sphinx
Alarmed our city ?　Wherefore did not then
Thy wisdom save us ?　Then the man divine
Was wanting.　But thy birds refused their omens,
Thy god was silent.　Then came Œdipus,
This poor, unlearned, uninstructed sage ;
Who not from birds uncertain omens drew,
But by his own sagacious mind explored
The hidden mystery.　And now thou com'st
To cast me from the throne my wisdom gained,
And share with Creon my divided empire.
But you should both lament your ill-got power,
You and your bold compeer.　For thee, this moment,

But that I bear respect unto thy age,
I'd make thee rue thy execrable purpose.

Chor. You both are angry, therefore both to blame;
Much rather should you join, with friendly zeal
And mutual ardour, to explore the will
Of all-deciding Heaven.

Tir.   What though thou rul'st
O'er Thebes despotic, we are equal here:
I am Apollo's subject, and not thine,
Nor want I Creon to protect me.   No;
I tell thee, king, this blind Tiresias tells thee,
Seeing thou seest not, knowst not where thou art,
What, or with whom.   Canst thou inform me who
Thy parents are, and what thy horrid crimes
'Gainst thy own race, the living and the dead?
A father's and a mother's curse attend thee;
Soon shall their furies drive thee from the land,
And leave thee dark like me.   What mountain then,
Or conscious shore, shall not return the groans
Of Œdipus, and echo to his woes?
When thou shalt look on the detested bed,
And in that haven where thou hop'st to rest,
Shalt meet with storm and tempest, then what ills
Shall fall on thee and thine!   Now vent thy rage
On old Tiresias and the guiltless Creon;
We shall be soon avenged, for ne'er did Heaven
Cut off a wretch so base, so vile as thou art.

Œdi. Must I bear this from thee?   Away, begone!
Home, villain, home!

Tir.   I did not come to thee
Unsent for.

Œdi. Had I thought thou wouldst have thus
Insulted me, I had not called thee hither.

Tir. Perhaps thou holdst Tiresias as a fool
And madman; but thy parents thought me wise.

Œdi. My parents, saidst thou?   Speak, who were my
   parents?

Tir. This day, that gives thee life, shall give thee death.

Œdi. Still dark, and still perplexing are the words thou utter'st.

Tir. 'Tis thy business to unriddle,
And therefore thou canst best interpret them.

Œdi. Thou dost reproach me for my virtues.

Tir.   They,
And thy good fortune, have undone thee.

Œdi.   Since
I saved the city, I'm content.

Tir.   Farewell.—
Boy, lead me hence.

Œdi. Away with him, for here
His presence but disturbs us ; being gone,
We shall be happier.

Tir.   Œdipus, I go,
But first inform me, for I fear thee not,
Wherefore I came.   Know, then, I came to tell thee,
The man thou seekst, the man on whom thou pouredst
Thy execrations, e'en the murderer
Of Laius, now is here—a seeming stranger
And yet a Theban.   He shall suffer soon
For all his crimes : from light and affluence driven
To penury and darkness, poor and blind,
Propped on his staff, and from his native land
Expelled, I see him in a foreign clime
A helpless wanderer ; to his sons at once
A father and a brother ; child and husband
Of her from whom he sprang.   Adulterous,
Incestuous parricide, now fare thee well !
Go, learn the truth, and if it be not so,
Say I have ne'er deserved the name of prophet.

Chorus

Strophe 1

When will the guilty wretch appear,
  Whom Delphi's sacred oracle demands;
  Author of crimes too black for mortal ear,
  Dipping in royal blood his sacrilegious hands?
Swift as the storm by rapid whirlwinds driven;
Quick let him fly th' impending wrath of Heaven;
    For lo! the angry son of Jove,
    Armed with red lightnings from above,
Pursues the murderer with immortal hate,
And round him spreads the snares of unrelenting fate.

Antistrophe 1

From steep Parnassus' rocky cave,
  Covered with snow, came forth the dread command;
  Apollo thence his sacred mandate gave,
  To search the man of blood through every land:
Silent and sad, the weary wanderer roves
O'er pathless rocks and solitary groves,
    Hoping to 'scape the wrath divine,
    Denounced from great Apollo's shrine;
Vain hopes to 'scape the fate by Heaven decreed,
For vengeance hovers still o'er his devoted head.

Strophe 2

Tiresias, famed for wisdom's lore,
  Hath dreadful ills to Œdipus divined;
  And as his words mysterious I explore,
  Unnumbered doubts perplex my anxious mind.
Now raised by hope, and now with fears oppressed,
Sorrow and joy alternate fill my breast:
    How should these hapless kings be foes,
    When never strife between them rose?
Or why should Laius, slain by hands unknown,
Bring foul disgrace on Polybus' unhappy son?

Antistrophe 2

From Phœbus and all-seeing Jove
Naught can be hid of actions here below;
 But earthly prophets may deceitful prove,
 And little more than other mortals know:
Though much in wisdom man doth man excel,
In all that's human error still must dwell:
  Could he commit the bloody deed,
  Who from the Sphinx our city freed?
Oh, no! he never shed the guiltless blood;
The Sphinx declares him wise, and innocent, and good.

          [*Exeunt.*

CREON, CHORUS

Creon. O citizens! with grief I hear your king
Hath blasted the fair fame of guiltless Creon!
And most unjustly brands me with a crime
My soul abhors: while desolation spreads
On every side, and universal ruin
Hangs o'er the land, if I in word or deed
Could join to swell the woes of hapless Thebes,
I were unworthy—nay, I would not wish—
To live another day: alas! my friends,
Thus to be deemed a traitor to my country,
To you my fellow-citizens, to all
That hear me, 'tis infamy and shame;
I can not, will not bear it.
 Chor.   'Twas th' effect
Of sudden anger only—what he said
But could not think.
 Creon.   Who told him I suborned
The prophet to speak falsely? What could raise
This vile suspicion?
 Chor.   Such he had, but whence
I know not.
 Creon.   Talked he thus with firm composure
And confidence of mind?

II

Chor.   I can not say;
'Tis not for me to know the thoughts of kings,
Or judge their actions! But behold! he comes.

ŒDIPUS, CREON, CHORUS

Œdi. Ha! Creon here? And dar'st thou thus approach
My palace, thou who wouldst have murdered me,
And ta'en my kingdom? By the gods I ask thee;
Answer me, traitor, didst thou think me fool,
Or coward, that I could not see thy arts,
Or had not strength to vanquish them? What madness,
What strange infatuation led thee on,
Without or force or friends, to grasp at empire
Which only their united force can give?
What wert thou doing?

Creon.   Hear what I shall answer,
Then judge impartial.

Œdi.   Thou canst talk it well,
But I shall ne'er attend to thee; thy guilt
Is plain; thou art my deadliest foe.

Creon.   But hear
What I shall urge.

Œdi.   Say not thou art innocent.

Creon. If self-opinion void of reason seem
Conviction to thee, know, thou err'st most grossly.

Œdi. And thou more grossly, if thou thinkst to pass
Unpunished for this injury to thy friend.

Creon. I should not, were I guilty; but what crime
Have I committed? Tell me.

Œdi.   Wert not thou
The man who urged me to require the aid
Of your all-knowing prophet?

Creon.   True, I was;
I did persuade you; so I would again.

Œdi. How long is it since Laius——

Creon.   Laius! What?

Œdi. Since Laius fell by hands unknown?

Creon.   A long,
Long tract of years.

Œdi.   Was this Tiresias then
A prophet?

Creon.   Ay; in wisdom and in fame
As now excelling.

Œdi.   Did he then say aught
Concerning me?

Creon.   I never heard he did.

Œdi. Touching this murder, did you ne'er inquire
Who were the authors?

Creon.   Doubtless; but in vain.

Œdi. Why did not this same prophet then inform you?

Creon. I know not that, and when I'm ignorant
I'm always silent.

Œdi.   What concerns thyself
At least thou knowst, and therefore shouldst declare it.

Creon. What is it? Speak; and if 'tis in my power,
I'll answer thee.

Œdi.   Thou knowst, if this Tiresias
Had not combined with thee, he would not thus
Accuse me as the murderer of Laius.

Creon. What he declares, thou best canst tell: of me,
What thou requirest, myself am yet to learn.

Œdi. Go, learn it then; but ne'er shalt thou discover
That Œdipus is guilty.

Creon.   Art not thou
My sister's husband?

Œdi.   Granted.

Creon.   Joined with her,
Thou rul'st o'er Thebes.

Œdi.   'Tis true, and all she asks
Most freely do I give her.

Creon.   Is not Creon
In honour next to you?

Œdi.   Thou art; and therefore

The more ungrateful.

    Creon.   Hear what I shall plead,
And thou wilt never think so. Tell me, prince,
Is there a man who would prefer a throne,
With all its dangers, to an equal rank
In peace and safety? I am not of those
Who choose the name of king before the power;
Fools only make such wishes: I have all
From thee, and fearless I enjoy it all:
Had I the sceptre, often must I act
Against my will. Know then, I am not yet
So void of sense and reason as to quit
A real 'vantage for a seeming good.
Am I not happy, am I not revered,
Embraced, and loved by all? To me they come
Who want thy favour, and by me acquire it:
What then should Creon wish for; shall he leave
All this for empire? Bad desires corrupt
The fairest mind. I never entertained
A thought so vile, nor would I lend my aid
To forward such base purposes. But go
To Delphi, ask the sacred oracle
If I have spoke the truth; if there you find
That with the prophet I conspired, destroy
The guilty Creon; not thy voice alone
Shall then condemn me, for myself will join
In the just sentence. But accuse me not
On weak suspicion's most uncertain test.
Justice would never call the wicked good,
Or brand fair virtue with the name of vice,
Unmerited: to cast away a friend,
Faithful and just, is to deprive ourselves
Of life and being, which we hold most dear:
But time and time alone revealeth all;
That only shows the good man's excellence:
A day sufficeth to unmask the wicked.

    Chor. O king! his caution merits your regard;

Who judge in haste do seldom judge aright.

Œdi. When they are quick who plot against my life,
'Tis fit I should be quick in my defence;
If I am tame and silent, all they wish
Will soon be done, and Œdipus must fall.

Creon. What wouldst thou have? my banishment?

Œdi. Thy death.

Creon. But first inform me wherefore I should die.

Œdi. Dost thou rebel then? Wilt thou not submit?

Creon. Not when I see thee thus deceived.

Œdi. 'Tis fit
I should defend my own.

Creon. And so should I.

Œdi. Thou art a traitor.

Creon. What if it should prove
I am not so?

Œdi. A king must be obeyed.

Creon. Not if his orders are unjust.

Œdi. O Thebes!
O citizens!

Creon. I too can call on Thebes;
She is my country.

Chor. Oh! no more, my lords;
For see, Jocasta comes in happiest hour
To end your contest.

JOCASTA, CREON, ŒDIPUS, CHORUS

Joc. Whence this sudden tumult?
O princes! Is this well, at such a time
With idle broils to multiply the woes
Of wretched Thebes? Home, home, for shame! nor thus
With private quarrels swell the public ruin.

Creon. Sister, thy husband hath most basely used me;
He threatens me with banishment or death.

Œdi. I do confess it; for he did conspire
With vile and wicked arts against my life.

Creon. Oh! may I never prosper, but accursed,

Unpitied, perish if I ever did.

Joc. Believe him, Œdipus; revere the gods
Whom he contests, if thou dost love Jocasta;
Thy subjects beg it of thee.

Chor.   Hear, O king!
Consider, we entreat thee.

Œdi.   What wouldst have?
Think you I'll e'er submit to him?

Chor.   Revere
His character, his oath, both pleading for him.

Œdi. But know you what you ask?

Chor.   We do.

Œdi.   What is it?

Chor. We ask thee to believe a guiltless friend,
Nor cast him forth dishonoured thus, on slight
Suspicion's weak surmise.

Œdi.   Requesting this,
You do request my banishment, or death.

Chor. No; by yon leader of the heavenly host,
Th' immortal sun, I had not such a thought;
I only felt for Thebes' distressful state,
And would not have it by domestic strife
Embittered thus.

Œdi.   Why, let him then depart:
If Œdipus must die, or leave his country
For shameful exile, be it so; I yield
To thy request, not his; for hateful still
Shall Creon ever be.

Creon.   Thy stubborn soul
Bends with reluctance, and when anger fires it
Is terrible; but natures formed like thine
Are their own punishment.

Œdi.   Wilt thou not hence?
Wilt not begone?

Creon.   I go; thou knowest me not;
But these will do me justice.   [*Exit* CREON.

JOCASTA, ŒDIPUS, CHORUS

Chor.   Princess, now
Persuade him to retire.
Joc.   First, let me know
The cause of this dissension.
Chor.   From reports
Uncertain, and suspicions most injurious,
The quarrel rose.
Joc.   Was th' accusation mutual?
Chor. It was.
Joc.   What followed then?
Chor.   Ask me no more;
Enough's already known; we'll not repeat
The woes of hapless Thebes.
Œdi.   You are all blind,
Insensible, unjust; you love me not,
Yet boast your piety.
Chor.   I said before,
Again I say, that not to love my king
E'en as myself, would mark me for the worst
Of men.   For thou didst save expiring Thebes.
Oh! rise once more, protect, preserve thy country!
Joc. O king! inform me, whence this strange dissen-
    sion?
Œdi. I'll tell thee, my Jocasta, for thou knowst
The love I bear thee, what this wicked Creon
Did artfully devise against me.
Joc.   Speak it,
If he indeed be guilty.
Œdi.   Creon says
That I did murder Laius.
Joc.   Spake he this
As knowing it himself, or from another?
Œdi. He had suborned that evil-working priest,
And sharpens every tongue against his king.
Joc. Let not a fear perplex thee, Œdipus;
Mortals know nothing of futurity,

And these prophetic seers are all impostors;
I'll prove it to thee.   Know then, Laius once,
Not from Apollo, but his priests, received
An oracle, which said it was decreed
He should be slain by his own son, the offspring
Of Laius and Jocasta.   Yet he fell
By strangers, murdered, for so fame reports,
By robbers, in the place where three ways meet.
A son was born, but ere three days had passed
The infant's feet were bored.   A servant took
And left him on the pathless mountain's top,
To perish there.   Thus Phœbus ne'er decreed
That he should kill his father, or that Laius,
Which much he feared, should by his son be slain.
Such is the truth of oracles.   Henceforth
Regard them not.   What Heaven would have us know,
It can with ease unfold, and will reveal it.

 Œdi. What thou hast said, Jocasta, much disturbs me;
I tremble at it.

 Joc.   Wherefore shouldst thou fear?

 Œdi. Methought I heard thee say, Laius was slain
Where three ways meet.

 Joc.   'Twas so reported then,
And is so still.

 Œdi.   Where happened the misfortune?

 Joc. In Phocis, where the roads unite that lead
To Delphi and to Daulia.

 Œdi.   How long since?

 Joc. A little time ere you began to reign
O'er Thebes, we heard it.

 Œdi.   O almighty Jove!
What wilt thou do with me?

 Joc.   Why talkst thou thus?

 Œdi. Ask me no more; but tell me of this Laius:
What was his age and stature?

 Joc.   He was tall;
His hairs just turning to the silver hue;

His form not much unlike thy own.

Œdi.   Oh me!
Sure I have called down curses on myself
Unknowing.

    Joc.   Ha! what sayst thou, Œdipus?
I tremble while I look on thee.

Œdi.   Oh! much
I fear the prophet saw too well; but say,
One thing will make it clear.

    Joc.   I dread to hear it;
Yet speak, and I will tell thee.

Œdi.   Went he forth
With few attendants, or a numerous train,
In kingly pomp?

    Joc.   They were but five in all,
The herald with them; but one chariot there,
Which carried Laius.

Œdi.   Oh! 'tis but too plain.
Who brought the news?

    Joc.   A servant, who alone
Escaped with life.

Œdi.   That servant, is he here?

    Joc. Oh, no! His master slain, when he returned
And saw thee on the throne of Thebes, with prayer
Most earnest he beseeched me to dismiss him,
That he might leave this city, where he wished
No longer to be seen, but to retire,
And feed my flocks; I granted his request;
For that and more his honest services
Had merited.

Œdi.   I beg he may be sent for
Immediately.

    Joc.   He shall; but wherefore is it?

    Œdi. I fear thou'st said too much, and therefore wish
To see him.

    Joc.   He shall come; but, O my lord!
Am I not worthy to be told the cause

Of this distress?

    Œdi.   Thou art, and I will tell thee;
Thou art my hope—to whom should I impart
My sorrows, but to thee? Know then, Jocasta,
I am the son of Polybus, who reigns
At Corinth, and the Dorian Merope
His queen; there long I held the foremost rank,
Honoured and happy, when a strange event
(For strange it was, though little meriting
The deep concern I felt) alarmed me much:
A drunken reveller at a feast proclaimed
That I was only the supposed son
Of Corinth's king. Scarce could I bear that day
The vile reproach. The next, I sought my parents
And asked of them the truth; they too, enraged,
Resented much the base indignity.
I liked their tender warmth, but still I felt
A secret anguish, and, unknown to them,
Sought out the Pythian oracle. In vain.
Touching my parents nothing could I learn;
But dreadful were the miseries it denounced
Against me. 'Twas my fate, Apollo said,
To wed my mother, to produce a race
Accursed and abhorred; and last, to slay
My father who begat me. Sad decree!
Lest I should e'er fulfil the dire prediction,
Instant I fled from Corinth, by the stars
Guiding my hapless journey to the place
Where thou report'st this wretched king was slain.
But I will tell thee the whole truth. At length
I came to where the three ways meet, when, lo!
A herald, with another man like him
Whom thou describ'st, and in a chariot, met me.
Both strove with violence to drive me back;
Enraged, I struck the charioteer, when straight,
As I advanced, the old man saw, and twice
Smote me o' th' head, but dearly soon repaid

The insult on me; from his chariot rolled
Prone on the earth, beneath my staff he fell,
And instantly expired! Th' attendant train
All shared his fate. If this unhappy stranger
And Laius be the same, lives there a wretch
So cursed, so hateful to the gods as I am?
Nor citizen nor alien must receive,
Or converse, or communion hold with me,
But drive me forth with infamy and shame.
The dreadful curse pronounced with my own lips
Shall soon o'ertake me. I have stained the bed
Of him whom I had murdered; am I then
Aught but pollution? If I fly from hence,
The bed of incest meets me, and I go
To slay my father Polybus, the best,
The tenderest parent. This must be the work
Of some malignant power. Ye righteous gods!
Let me not see that day, but rest in death,
Rather than suffer such calamity.

   Chor. O king! we pity thy distress; but wait
With patience his arrival, and despair not.

   Œdi. That shepherd is my only hope: Jocasta,
Would he were here!

   Joc.   Suppose he were; what then?
What wouldst thou do?

   Œdi.   I'll tell thee: if he says
The same as thou dost, I am safe and guiltless.

   Joc. What said I then?

   Œdi.   Thou saidst he did report
Laius was slain by robbers; if 'tis true
He fell by numbers, I am innocent,
For I was unattended; if but one
Attacked and slew him, doubtless I am he.

   Joc. Be satisfied it must be as he first
Reported it; he can not change the tale:
Not I alone, but the whole city heard it.
Or grant he should, the oracle was ne'er

Fulfilled: for Phœbus said, Jocasta's son
Should slay his father. That could never be;
For, oh! Jocasta's son long since is dead.
He could not murder Laius; therefore never
Will I attend to prophecies again.

Œdi. Right, my Jocasta; but, I beg thee, send
And fetch this shepherd; do not fail.

Joc.   I will
This moment; come, my lord, let us go in:
I will do nothing but what pleases thee.   [*Exeunt.*

CHORUS. *Strophe 1*

Grant me henceforth, ye powers divine,
    In virtue's purest paths to tread!
    In every word, in every deed,
May sanctity of manners ever shine!
    Obedient to the laws of Jove,
    The laws descended from above,
Which, not like those by feeble mortals given,
    Buried in dark oblivion lie,
    Or worn by time decay, and die,
But bloom eternal like their native heaven!

Antistrophe 1

Pride first gave birth to tyranny:
    That hateful vice, insulting pride,
    When, every human power defied,
She lifts to glory's height her votary;
    Soon stumbling, from her tottering throne
    She throws the wretched victim down.
But may the god indulgent hear my prayer,
    That god whom humbly I adore;
    Oh! may he smile on Thebes once more,
And take its wretched monarch to his care!

Strophe 2

Perish the impious and profane,
    Who, void of reverential fear,

Nor justice nor the laws revere,
Who leave their god for pleasure or for gain!
Who swell by fraud their ill-got store,
Who rob the wretched and the poor!
If vice unpunished virtue's meed obtain,
Who shall refrain the impetuous soul,
The rebel passions who control,
Or wherefore do I lead this choral train?

Antistrophe 2

No more to Delphi's sacred shrine
Need we with incense now repair,
No more shall Phocis hear our prayer;
Nor fair Olympia see her rites divine;
If oracles no longer prove,
The power of Phœbus and of Jove.
Great lord of all, from thy eternal throne
Behold, how impious men defame
Thy loved Apollo's honoured name;
Oh! guard his rights, and vindicate thy own.

[*Exeunt.*

JOCASTA, CHORUS

Jocasta. Sages and rulers of the land, I come
To seek the altars of the gods, and there
With incense and oblations to appease
Offended Heaven. My Œdipus, alas!
No longer wise and prudent, as you all
Remember once he was, with present things
Compares the past, nor judges like himself;
Unnumbered cares perplex his anxious mind,
And every tale awakes new terrors in him;
Vain is my counsel, for he hears me not.
First, then, to thee, O Phœbus! for thou still
Art near to help the wretched, we appeal,
And suppliant beg thee now to grant thy aid
Propitious; deep is our distress; for, oh!

We see our pilot sinking at the helm,
And much already fear the vessel lost.

SHEPHERD FROM CORINTH, JOCASTA, CHORUS

Shep. Can you instruct me, strangers, which way lies
The palace of King Œdipus? himself
I would most gladly see. Can you inform me?

Chor. This is the palace; he is now within;
Thou seest his queen before thee.

Shep. Ever blest
And happy with the happy mayst thou live!

Joc. Stranger, the same good wish to thee, for well
Thy words deserve it; but say, wherefore com'st thou,
And what's thy news?

Shep. To thee, and to thy husband,
Pleasure and joy.

Joc. What pleasure? And whence art thou?

Shep. From Corinth. To be brief, I bring thee tidings
Of good and evil.

Joc. Ha! what mean thy words
Ambiguous?

Shep. Know then, if report say true,
The Isthmian people will choose Œdipus
Their sovereign.

Joc. Is not Polybus their king?

Shep. No; Polybus is dead.

Joc. What sayst thou? Dead?

Shep. If I speak falsely, may death seize on me!

Joc. [*to one of her* ATTENDANTS]. Why fliest thou not
to tell thy master? Hence!
What are you now, you oracles divine?
Where is your truth? The fearful Œdipus
From Corinth fled, lest he should slay the king,
This Polybus, who perished, not by him,
But by the hand of Heaven.

ŒDIPUS, JOCASTA, SHEPHERD, CHORUS

Œdi.   My dear Jocasta,
Why hast thou called me hither?
    Joc.   Hear this man,
And when thou hear'st him, mark what faith is due
To your revered oracles.
    Œdi.   Who is he?
And what doth he report?
    Joc.   He comes from Corinth,
And says thy father Polybus is dead.
    Œdi. What sayst thou, stranger? Speak to me—oh!
    speak!
    Shep. If touching this thou first desir'st my answer;
Know, he is dead.
    Œdi.   How died he? Say, by treason,
Or some disease?
    Shep.   Alas! a little force
Will lay to rest the weary limbs of age.
    Œdi. Distemper then did kill him?
    Shep.   That in part,
And part a length of years that wore him down,
    Œdi. Now, my Jocasta, who shall henceforth trust
To prophecies, and seers, and clamorous birds
With their vain omens—they who had decreed
That I should kill my father? He thou seest
Beneath the earth lies buried, while I live
In safety here and guiltless of his blood:
Unless perhaps sorrow for loss of me
Shortened his days, thus only could I kill
My father. But he's gone, and to the shades
Hath carried with him those vain oracles
Of fancied ills, no longer worth my care.
    Joc. Did I not say it would be thus?
    Œdi.   Thou didst;
But I was full of fears.
    Joc.   Henceforth, no more
Indulge them.

Œdi. But my mother's bed—that still
Must be avoided. I must fly from that.

Joc. Why should man fear, whom chance, and chance
alone,
Doth ever rule? Foreknowledge, all is vain,
And can determine nothing. Therefore best
It is to live as fancy leads, at large,
Uncurbed, and only subject to our will.
Fear not thy mother's bed. Ofttimes in dreams
Have men committed incest. But his life
Will ever be most happy who contemns
Such idle phantoms.

Œdi. Thou wert right, Jocasta,
Did not my mother live. But as it is,
Spite of thy words, I must be anxious still.

Joc. Think on thy father's death ; it is a light
To guide thee here.

Œdi. It is so. Yet I fear
While she survives him.

Shep. Who is it you mean?
What woman fear you?

Œdi. Merope, the wife
Of Polybus.

Shep. And wherefore fear you her?

Œdi. Know, stranger, a most dreadful oracle
Concerning her affrights me.

Shep. May I know it,
Or must it be revealed to none but thee?

Œdi. Oh, no! I'll tell thee. Phœbus hath declared
That Œdipus should stain his mother's bed,
And dip his hands in his own father's blood ;
Wherefore I fled from Corinth, and lived here,
In happiness indeed. But still thou knowst
It is a blessing to behold our parents,
And that I had not.

Shep. Was it for this cause
Thou wert an exile then?

Œdi.   It was.   I feared
That I might one day prove my father's murderer.
  Shep. What if I come, O king! to banish hence
Thy terrors, and restore thy peace?
  Œdi.   Oh, stranger!
Couldst thou do this, I would reward thee nobly.
  Shep. Know then, for this I came.   I came to serve,
And make thee happy.
   Œdi.   But I will not go
Back to my parents.
  Shep.   Son, I see thou knowst not
What thou art doing.
   Œdi.   Wherefore thinkst thou so?
By Heaven I beg thee then do thou instruct me.
  Shep. If thou didst fly from Corinth for this cause——
  Œdi. Apollo's dire predictions still affright me.
  Shep. Fearst thou pollution from thy parents?
  Œdi.   That,
And that alone I dread.
  Shep.   Thy fears are vain.
  Œdi. Not if they are my parents.
  Shep.   Polybus
Was not akin to thee.
   Œdi.   What sayst thou?   Speak,
Say, was not Polybus my father?
  Shep.   No;
No more than he is mine.
   Œdi.   Why call me then
His son?
  Shep.   Because long since I gave thee to him—
He did receive thee from these hands.
  Œdi.   Indeed!
And could he love another's child so well?
  Shep. He had no children; that persuaded him
To take and keep thee.
  Œdi.   Didst thou buy me, then,
Or am I thine, and must I call thee father?

12

Shep. I found thee in Cithæron's woody vale.

Œdi. What brought thee there?

Shep.   I came to feed my flocks
On the green mountain's side.

Œdi.   It seems thou wert
A wandering shepherd.

Shep.   Thy deliverer;
I saved thee from destruction.

Œdi.   How? What then
Had happened to me?

Shep.   Thy own feet will best
Inform thee of that circumstance.

Œdi.   Alas!
Why callst thou to remembrance a misfortune
Of so long date?

Shep.   'Twas I who loosed the tendons
Of thy bored feet.

Œdi.   It seems in infancy
I suffered much, then.

Shep.   To this incident
Thou ow'st thy name.

Œdi.   My father, or my mother,
Who did it? Knowst thou?

Shep.   He who gave thee to me
Must tell thee that.

Œdi.   Then from another's hand
Thou didst receive me.

Shep.   Ay, another shepherd.

Œdi. Who was he? Canst thou recollect?

Shep.   'Twas one,
At least so called, of Laius' family.

Œdi. Laius, who ruled at Thebes?

Shep.   The same; this man
Was shepherd to King Laius.

Œdi.   Lives he still?
And could I see him?

Shep. [*pointing to the* CHORUS]. Some of these perhaps,

His countrymen, may give you information.

Œdi. [*to the* CHORUS]. Oh! speak, my friends, if any
   of you know
This shepherd; whether still he lives at Thebes,
Or in some neighbouring country. Tell me quick,
For it concerns us near.

Chor.   It must be he
Whom thou didst lately send for; but the queen
Can best inform thee.

Œdi.   Knowst thou, my Jocasta,
Whether the man whom thou didst order hither,
And whom the shepherd speaks of, be the same?

Joc. Whom meant he? for I know not. Œdipus,
Think not so deeply of this thing.

Œdi.   Good heaven!
Forbid, Jocasta, I should now neglect
To clear my birth, when thus the path is marked
And open to me.

Joc.   Do not, by the gods
I beg thee, do not, if thy life be dear,
Make further search, for I have felt enough
Already from it.

Œdi.   Rest thou satisfied;
Were I descended from a race of slaves,
'Twould not dishonour thee.

Joc.   Yet hear me; do not,
Once more I beg thee, do not search this matter.

Œdi. I will not be persuaded. I must search
And find it too.

Joc.   I know it best, and best
Advise thee.

Œdi.   That advice perplexes more.

Joc. Oh! would to Heaven that thou mayst never know
Or who or whence thou art!

Œdi. [*to the* ATTENDANTS]. Let some one fetch
That shepherd quick, and leave this woman here
To glory in her high descent.

Joc.   Alas!
Unhappy Œdipus! that word alone
I now can speak: remember 'tis my last.

                        [*Exit* JOCASTA.

ŒDIPUS, CHORUS

Chor. Why fled the queen in such disorder hence?
Sorely distressed she seemed, and much I fear
Her silence bodes some sad event.
    Œdi.   Whate'er
May come of that, I am resolved to know
The secret of my birth, how mean soever
It chance to prove. Perhaps her sex's pride
May make her blush to find I was not born
Of noble parents; but I call myself
The son of fortune, my indulgent mother,
Whom I shall never be ashamed to own,
The kindred months that are like me, her children,
The years that roll obedient to her will,
Have raised me from the lowest state to power
And splendour. Wherefore, being what I am,
I need not fear the knowledge of my birth.

CHORUS. *Strophe*

If my prophetic soul doth well divine,
Ere on thy brow to-morrow's sun shall shine,
   Cithæron, thou the mystery shalt unfold;
The doubtful Œdipus, no longer blind,
Shall soon his country and his father find,
   And all the story of his birth be told.
       Then shall we in grateful lays
       Celebrate our monarch's praise,
And in the sprightly dance our songs triumphant raise.

Antistrophe

What heavenly power gave birth to thee, O king!
From Pan, the god of mountains, didst thou spring,

With some fair daughter of Apollo joined;
Art thou from him who o'er Cyllene reigns,
Swift Hermes, sporting in Arcadia's plains?
Some nymph of Helicon did Bacchus find—
    Bacchus, who delights to rove
    Through the forest, hill, and grove—
And art thou, prince, the offspring of their love?

ŒDIPUS, CHORUS, SHEPHERD FROM CORINTH

Œdi. If I may judge of one whom yet I ne'er
Had converse with, yon old man, whom I see
This way advancing, must be that same shepherd
We lately sent for, by his age and mien,
E'en as this stranger did describe him to us;
My servants too are with him. But you best
Can say, for you must know him well.
    Chor.   'Tis he,
My lord; the faithful shepherd of King Laius.
    Œdi. [*to the* SHEPHERD *from Corinth*]. What sayst
        thou, stranger?—is it he?
    Shep.   It is.

OLD SHEPHERD, ŒDIPUS, SHEPHERD FROM CORINTH,
CHORUS

Œdi. Now answer me, old man; look this way—speak;
Didst thou belong to Laius?
    Old Shep.   Sir, I did;
No hireling slave, but in his palace bred,
I served him long.
    Œdi.   What was thy business there?
    Old Shep. For my life's better part I tended sheep.
    Œdi. And whither didst thou lead them?
    Old Shep.   To Cithæron,
And to the neighbouring plains.
    Œdi.   Behold this man:
            [*pointing to the* SHEPHERD *of Corinth.*
Dost thou remember to have seen him?

Old Shep.   Whom?
What hath he done?
  Œdi.   Him, who now stands before thee,
Callst thou to mind, or converse or connection
Between you in times past?
  Old Shep.   I can not say
I recollect it now.
  Shep. of Corinth. I do not wonder
He should forget me, but I will recall
Some facts of ancient date. He must remember
When on Cithæron we together fed
Our several flocks, in daily converse joined
From spring to autumn, and when winter bleak
Approached, retired. I to my little cot
Conveyed my sheep; he to the palace led
His fleecy care. Canst thou remember this?
  Old Shep. I do; but that is long, long since.
  Shep. of Corinth.   It is;
But say, good shepherd, canst thou call to mind
An infant whom thou didst deliver to me,
Requesting me to breed him as my own?
  Old Shep. Ha! wherefore askst thou this?
  Shep. of Corinth [*pointing to* ŒDIPUS]. Behold him
       here,
That very child.
  Old Shep.   Oh! say it not: away!
Perdition on thee!
  Œdi.   Why reprove him thus?
Thou art thyself to blame, old man.
  Old Shep.   In what
Am I to blame, my lord?
  Œdi.   Thou wilt not speak
Touching this boy.
  Old Shep. Alas! poor man, he knows not
What he hath said.
  Œdi.   If not by softer means
To be persuaded, force shall wring it from thee.

Old Shep. Treat not an old man harshly.

Œdi. [*to the* ATTENDANTS].   Bind his hands.

Old Shep. Wherefore, my lord? What wouldst thou
have me do?

Œdi. That child he talks of, didst thou give it to
him?

Old Shep. I did; and would to Heaven I then had
died!

Œdi. Die soon thou shalt, unless thou tellst it all.

Old Shep. Say, rather if I do.

Œdi.   This fellow means
To trifle with us, by his dull delay.

Old Shep. I do not; said I not I gave the child?

Œdi. Whence came the boy? Was he thy own, or who
Did give him to thee?

Old Shep.   From another hand
I had received him.

Œdi.   Say, what hand? From whom?
Whence came he?

Old Shep.   Do not—by the gods I beg thee,
Do not inquire!

Œdi.   Force me to ask again,
And thou shalt die!

Old Shep.   In Laius' palace born——

Œdi. Son of a slave, or of the king?

Old Shep.   Alas!
'Tis death for me to speak.

Œdi.   And me to hear;
Yet say it.

Old Shep. He was called the son of Laius;
But ask the queen, for she can best inform thee.

Œdi. Did she then give the child to thee?

Old Shep.   She did.

Œdi. For what?

Old Shep.   To kill him.

Œdi.   Kill her child! Inhuman
And barbarous mother!

Old Shep.   A dire oracle
Affrighted, and constrained her to it.
   Œdi.   Ha!
What oracle?
   Old Shep.   Which said, her son should slay
His parents.
   Œdi.   Wherefore gav'st thou then the infant
To this old shepherd?
   Old Shep.   Pity moved me to it:
I hoped he would have soon conveyed his charge
To some far-distant country; he, alas!
Preserved him but for misery and woe;
For, O my lord! if thou indeed art he,
Thou art of all mankind the most unhappy.
   Œdi. O me! at length the mystery's unravelled;
'Tis plain, 'tis clear; my fate is all determined.
Those are my parents who should not have been
Allied to me; she is my wife, e'en she
Whom Nature had forbidden me to wed;
I have slain him who gave me life; and now
Of thee, O light! I take my last farewell,
For Œdipus shall ne'er behold thee more.   [*Exeunt.*

CHORUS. *Strophe 1*

O hapless state of human race!
How quick the fleeting shadows pass
Of transitory bliss below,
Where all is vanity and woe!
By thy example taught, O prince! we see
Man was not made for true felicity.

Antistrophe 1

Thou, Œdipus, beyond the rest
Of mortals wert supremely blest;
Whom every hand conspired to raise,
Whom every tongue rejoiced to praise,

When from the Sphinx thy all-preserving hand
Stretched forth its aid to save a sinking land.

Strophe 2

Thy virtues raised thee to a throne,
And grateful Thebes was all thy own;
Alas! how changed that glorious name!
Lost are thy virtues and thy fame;
How couldst thou thus pollute thy father's bed?
How couldst thou thus thy hapless mother wed?

Antistrophe 2

How could that bed unconscious bear
So long the vile incestuous pair?
But time, of quick and piercing sight,
Hath brought the horrid deed to light;
At length Jocasta owns her guilty flame,
And finds a husband and a child the same.

Epode

Wretched son of Laius, thee
Henceforth may I never see,
But absent shed the pious tear,
And weep thy fate with grief sincere!
For thou didst raise our eyes to life and light,
To close them now in everlasting night.

MESSENGER, CHORUS

Messenger. Sages of Thebes, most honoured and re-
vered,
If e'er the house of Labdacus was dear
And precious to you, what will be your grief
When I shall tell the most disastrous tale
You ever heard, and to your eyes present
A spectacle more dreadful than they yet
Did e'er behold? Not the wide Danube's waves
Nor Phasis' streams can wash away the stains

Of this polluted palace; the dire crimes
Long time concealed at length are brought to light;
But those which spring from voluntary guilt
Are still more dreadful.

    Chor.   Nothing can be worse
Than that we know already; bringst thou more
Misfortunes to us?

    Mes.   To be brief, the queen,
Divine Jocasta's dead.

    Chor. Jocasta dead! Say, by what hand?

    Mes.   Her own;
And what's more dreadful, no one saw the deed.
What I myself beheld you all shall hear.
Inflamed with rage, soon as she reached the palace,
Instant retiring to the nuptial bed,
She shut the door, then raved and tore her hair,
Called out on Laius dead, and bade him think
On that unhappy son who murdered him
And stained his bed; then turning her sad eyes
Upon the guilty couch, she cursed the place
Where she had borne a husband from her husband,
And children from her child; what followed then
I know not, by the cries of Œdipus
Prevented, for on him our eyes were fixed
Attentive; forth he came, beseeching us
To lend him some sharp weapon, and inform him
Where he might find his mother and his wife,
His children's wretched mother and his own.
Some ill-designing power did then direct him
(For we were silent) to the queen's apartment;
Forcing the bolt, he rushed into the bed,
And found Jocasta, where we all beheld her,
Entangled in the fatal noose, which soon
As he perceived, loosing the pendant rope,
Deeply he groaned, and casting on the ground
His wretched body, showed a piteous sight
To the beholders; on a sudden, thence

Starting, he plucked from off the robe she wore
A golden buckle that adorned her side,
And buried in his eyes the sharpened point,
Crying, he ne'er again would look on her,
Never would see his crimes or miseries more,
Or those whom guiltless he could ne'er behold,
Or those to whom he now must sue for aid.
His lifted eyelids then, repeating still
These dreadful plaints, he tore ; while down his cheek
Fell showers of blood ! Such fate the wretched pair
Sustained, partakers in calamity,
Fallen from a state of happiness (for none
Were happier once than they) to groans and death,
Reproach and shame, and every human woe.

   Chor. And where is now the poor unhappy man?

   Mes. Open the doors, he cries, and let all Thebes
Behold his parents' murderer, adding words
Not to be uttered ; banished now, he says,
He must be, nor, devoted as he is
By his own curse, remain in this sad place.
He wants a kind conductor and a friend
To help him now, for 'tis too much to bear.
But you will see him soon, for lo ! the doors
Are opened, and you will behold a sight
That would to pity move his deadliest foe.

ŒDIPUS, MESSENGER, CHORUS

   Chor. Oh ! horrid sight ! more dreadful spectacle
Than e'er these eyes beheld ! what madness urged thee
To this sad deed ? What power malignant heaped
On thy poor head such complicated woe?
Unhappy man, alas ! I would have held
Some converse with thee, but thy looks affright me ;
I can not bear to speak to thee.

   Œdi.   O me!
Where am I? and whence comes the voice I hear?
Where art thou, Fortune?

Chor.   Changed to misery,
Dreadful to hear, and dreadful to behold.

Œdi. O cruel darkness! endless, hopeless night,
Shame, terrors, and unutterable woe!
More painful is the memory of my crimes
Than all the wounds my wild distraction made.

Chor. Thus doubly cursed, O prince! I wonder not
At thy affliction.

Œdi.   Art thou here, my friend?
I know thy voice; thou wouldst not leave the wretched;
Thou art my faithful, kind assistant still.

Chor. How couldst thou thus deprive thyself of sight?
What madness drove thee to the desperate deed?
What god inspired?

Œdi.   Apollo was the cause;
He was, my friends, the cause of all my woes;
But for these eyes—myself did quench their light—
I want not them; what use were they to me,
But to discover scenes of endless woe?

Chor. 'Tis but too true.

Œdi.   What pleasure now remains
For Œdipus? He can not joy in aught
To sight or ear delightful. Curse on him,
Whoe'er he was, that loosened my bound feet,
And saved me, in Cithæron's vale, from death!
I owe him nothing: had I perished then,
Much happier had it been for you, my friends,
And for myself.

Chor.   I too could wish thou hadst.

Œdi. I should not then have murdered Laius; then
I had not ta'en Jocasta to my bed;
But now I am a guilty wretch, the son
Of a polluted mother, father now
To my own brothers, all that's horrible
To Nature is the lot of Œdipus.

Chor. Yet must I blame this cruel act, for sure
The loss of sight is worse than death itself.

Œdi. I care not for thy counsel or thy praise;
For with what eyes could I have e'er beheld
My honoured father in the shades below,
Or my unhappy mother, both destroyed
By me? This punishment is worse than death,
And so it should be. Sweet had been the sight
Of my dear children—them I could have wished
To gaze upon; but I must never see
Or them, or this fair city, or the palace
Where I was born. Deprived of every bliss
By my own lips, which doomed to banishment
The murderer of Laius, and expelled
The impious wretch, by gods and men accursed:
Could I behold them after this? Oh no!
Would I could now with equal ease remove
My hearing too, be deaf as well as blind,
And from another entrance shut out woe!
To want our senses, in the hour of ill,
Is comfort to the wretched. O Cithæron!
Why didst thou e'er receive me, or received,
Why not destroy, that men might never know
Who gave me birth? O Polybus! O Corinth!
And thou, long time believed my father's palace,
Oh! what a foul disgrace to human nature
Didst thou receive beneath a prince's form!
Impious myself, and from an impious race.
Where is my splendour now? O Daulian path!
The shady forest, and the narrow pass
Where three ways meet, who drank a father's blood
Shed by these hands, do you not still remember
The horrid deed, and what, when here I came,
Followed more dreadful? Fatal nuptials, you
Produced me, you returned me to the womb
That bare me; thence relations horrible
Of fathers, sons, and brothers came; of wives,
Sisters, and mothers, sad alliance! all
That man holds impious and detestable.

But what in act is vile the modest tongue
Should never name. Bury me, hide me, friends,
From every eye; destroy me, cast me forth
To the wide ocean—let me perish there:
Do anything to shake off hated life.
Seize me; approach, my friends—you need not fear,
Polluted though I am, to touch me; none
Shall suffer for my crimes but I alone.

Chor. In most fit time, my lord, the noble Creon
This way advances; he can best determine
And best advise; sole guardian now of Thebes,
To him thy power devolves.

Œdi.   What shall I say?
Can I apply to him for aid whom late
I deeply injured by unjust suspicion?

CREON, ŒDIPUS, CHORUS

Creon. I come not, prince, to triumph o'er thy woes
With vile reproach; I pity thy misfortunes.
But, O my Thebans! if you do not fear
The censure of your fellow-citizens,
At least respect the all-creating eye
Of Phœbus, who beholds you thus exposing
To public view a wretch accursed, polluted,
Whom neither earth can bear, nor sun behold,
Nor holy shower besprinkle. Take him hence
Within the palace; those who are by blood
United should alone be witnesses
Of such calamity.

Œdi.   O Creon! thou,
The best of men, and I the worst, how kind
Thou art to visit me! Oh! by the gods
Let me entreat thee, since beyond my hopes
Thou art so good, now hear me; what I ask,
Concerns thee most,

Creon.   What is it thou desirest
Thus ardently?

Œdi. I beg thee, banish me
From Thebes this moment, to some land remote,
Where I may ne'er converse with man again.

Creon. Myself long since had done it, but the gods
Must be consulted first.

Œdi. Their will is known
Already, and their oracle declared
The guilty parricide should die.

Creon. It hath;
But, as it is, 'twere better to inquire
What must be done.

Œdi. For such a wretch as me
Wouldst thou again explore the will of Heaven?

Creon. Thy hapless fate should teach us to believe,
And reverence the gods.

Œdi. Now, Creon, list;
I beg thee, I conjure thee, let a tomb
Be raised, and all due honours paid to her
Who lies within: she was thy sister, Creon;
It is a duty which thou ow'st: for me,
I can not hope this city now will deign
To keep me here. O Creon! let me go,
And seek the solitary mountain's top,
My own Cithæron, by my parents doomed
Long since to be the grave of Œdipus;
Where would I die, as they decreed I should.
Alas! I can not, must not perish yet,
Till I have suffered evils worse than death,
For I was only saved to be unhappy;
But I must meet my fate, whate'er it be.
My sons are men, and wheresoever fortune
May place them, can not want the means of life;
They shall not burden thee; but O my friend!
What will become of my unhappy daughters,
With tenderest love, beneath a father's hand,
Cherished so long? Oh! take them to thy care,
Thou best of men! Oh! might I but embrace them,

But shed a tear o'er their disastrous fate,
Might I be suffered but to touch them here,
I should rejoice, and think I saw them still.
But hark! methinks e'en now I hear the voice
Of my dear daughters; hath the gracious Creon,
In pity to my woes, already brought
My children to me?—is it so?

Creon. It is:
Thy wishes are prevented; they are here.

Daughters of Œdipus, Œdipus, Creon, Chorus

Œdi. May Heaven reward thee for this goodness to
me,
And give thee much more bliss than I have known!
Now, my dear children, come toward me, come
Toward your father and your—brother; see
These sightless eyes, pierced by my own mad hands;
Behold that wretched father who begat you
Unknowingly on her who gave me birth;
I can not see you now—I can but weep
Your fate, to think what hours of wretchedness
You have to know hereafter. Whither now
Must my poor children fly? From every feast
Joyless with grief and shame, shall you return;
And when the time shall come when riper years
Should give you to the nuptial bed, who then,
Careless of fame, will let his child partake
The infamy of my abhorred race,
Sprung from a wretch accursed, who killed his father,
And from the womb that bare him did beget
You, my unhappy daughters? Such reproach
Must still be yours, to virgin solitude
Devoted ever, and a barren bed.
Son of Menœceus, thou alone art left
Their father now, for, oh! Jocasta's dead,
And I am—nothing. Do not then forsake
Thy kindred; nor, deserted and forlorn,

Suffer them still in penury and woe
To wander helpless, in their tender age:
Remember they have no support but thee.
O generous prince! have pity on them; give me
Thy friendly hand in promise of thy aid.
To you, my daughters, had your early years
Permitted, I had given my last advice;
Too young for counsel, all I ask of you
Is but to pray the gods that my sad life
May not be long; but yours, my children, crowned
With many days, and happier far than mine.

   Creon. It is enough; go in—thy grief transports thee
Beyond all bounds.

   Œdi.   'Tis hard; but I submit.

   Creon. The time demands it; therefore go.

   Œdi.   O Creon!
Knowst thou what now I wish?

   Creon.   What is it? Speak.

   Œdi. That I may quit this fatal place.

   Creon.   Thou ask'st
What Heaven alone can grant.

   Œdi.   Alas! to Heaven
I am most hateful.

   Creon.   Yet shalt thou obtain
What thou desirest.

   Œdi.   Shall I indeed?

   Creon.   Thou shalt;
I never say aught that I do not mean.

   Œdi. Then let me go: may I depart?

   Creon.   Thou mayst;
But leave thy children.

   Œdi.   Do not take them from me!

   Creon. Thou must not always have thy will. Already
Thou'st suffered for it.

   Chor.   Thebans, now behold
The great, the mighty Œdipus, who once
The Sphinx's dark enigma could unfold,

13

Who less to fortune than to wisdom owed,
In virtue as in rank to all superior,
Yet fallen at last to deepest misery.
Let mortals hence be taught to look beyond
The present time, nor dare to say, a man
Is happy till the last decisive hour
Shall close his life without the taste of woe.

THE ALCESTIS OF EURIPIDES

TRANSLATED BY

ARTHUR S. WAY

EURIPIDES, the son of Mnesarchides and Cleito, was born, 480 B. C., in Salamis, whither the Athenians had fled before the invading army of the Persians—tradition says upon the eve of the great battle that turned the tide in favour of Grecian liberty. The wealthy father—Aristophanes scores him for having made his money in trade—intended to train his son for the great national games, but Euripides soon put athletics aside for painting, and that again for literature. He took no part in public life—as did both Æschylus and Sophocles—was scholarly and almost a recluse, the friend of Socrates, and pupil of Prodicus, Protagoras, and Anaxagoras, and was the first Athenian to own a considerable private library. He married twice, both times unhappily, and left two sons. He is said to have been a bitter woman-hater in his old age. He produced his first play in 455 B. C., at which time Æschylus was dead, Sophocles had been before the public thirteen years, and Aristophanes, to be his greatest enemy, had not come into the world. But it was 441 B. C. before he was awarded a first prize in the contest. He received first prize only five times. He wrote ninety-two plays, eighteen of which have survived: "Alcestis," "Medea," "Hippolytus," "Hecuba," "Ion," "Suppliants," "Andromache," "Heraclidæ," "Troades," "Electra," "Helena," "Hercules Furens," "Phœnissæ," "Orestes," "Iphigeneia in Aulis," "Iphigeneia in Taurus," "Bacchæ," "Cyclops," a satyr-drama, and the doubtful play "Rhesus." Euripides was the most human of the three great tragedians, and perhaps he makes up in this what he may lose in comparison with Æschylus and Sophocles on the score of grandeur. He was very popular during his life, and at his death, which occurred in 406 B. C., at the court of the great literary patron, Archelaus of Macedonia, Sophocles and all Athens put on mourning for him, and the "Bacchæ," "Iphigeneia in Aulis," and perhaps "Iphigeneia in Taurus," were magnificently played at the theatre. He was Aristotle's favourite author, and has held a high place in the esteem of many ancient and modern writers.

APOLLO, being banished for a season from Olympus, and condemned to do service to a mortal, became herdsman of Admetus, King of Pheræ in Thessaly. Yet he loathed not his earthly taskmaster, but loved him, for that he was a just man, and hospitable exceedingly. Wherefore he obtained from the Fates this boon for Admetus, that, when his hour of death should come, they should accept in ransom for his life the life of whosoever should have before consented to die in his stead. Now when this was made known, none of them who were nearest by blood to the king would promise to be his ransom in that day. Then Alcestis his wife, the daughter of Pelias, King of Iolkos, pledged her to die for him. Of her love she did it, and for the honour of wifehood. And the years passed by, and the tale was told in many lands; and all men praised Alcestis, but Admetus bore a burden of sorrow, for day by day she became dearer to him, a wife wholly true, a mother most loving, and a lady to her thralls gentle exceedingly. But when it was known by tokens that the day was come, Admetus repented him sorely, but it availed not, for no mortal may recall a pledge once given to the gods. And on that day there came to the palace Apollo to plead with Death for Alcestis's sake; and a company of elders of Pheræ, to ask of her state and to make mourning for her. And when she was dead, ere she was borne forth to burial, came Herakles, son of Zeus, in his journeying, seeking the guest's right of meat and lodging, but not knowing aught of that which had come to pass. Of him was a great deliverance wrought, which is told herein.

DRAMATIS PERSONÆ

Apollo.
Death.
Chorus, composed of Elders of Pheræ.
Handmaid.
Alcestis, Daughter of Pelias, and Wife of Admetus.
Admetus, King of Pheræ.
Eumelus, Son of Admetus and Alcestis.
Herakles.
Pheres, Father of Admetus.
Servant, Steward of the Palace.
Guards, Attendants, Handmaids, and Mourners.

The scene throughout is in front of the palace of
Admetus at Pheræ.

ALCESTIS

———▸◆◂———

APOLLO. Halls of Admetus, where I stooped my pride
　　To brook the fare of serfs, yea I, a god—
　　The fault was fault of Zeus: he slew my son
Asklepius—hurled the levin through his heart.
Wroth for the dead, his smiths of heavenly fire
I slew, the Cyclopes; and, for blood-atonement,
Serf to a mortal man my father made me.
To this land came I, tended mine host's kine,
And warded still his house unto this day.
Righteous myself, I lighted on the righteous,
The son of Pheres: him I snatched from death,
Cozening the Fates: to me the Sisters pledged them
That imminent death Admetus should escape
If he for ransom gave another life.
To all he went—all near and dear—and asked
Gray sire, the mother that had given him life;
But, save his wife, found none that would consent
For him to die and never more see light.
Now in his arms upborne within yon home
She gaspeth forth her life: for on this day
Her weird it is to die and part from life.
I, lest pollution taint me in their house,
Go forth of yonder hall's beloved roof.　　[*Enter* DEATH.
Lo, yonder Death!—I see him nigh at hand,

Priest of the dead, who comes to hale her down
To Hades' halls—well hath he kept his time,
Watching this day, whereon she needs must die.
  Death. Ha, thou at the palace!—Wilt not make room,
    Phœbus?—thou wrestest the right yet again.
Thou removest the landmarks of gods of gloom.
  And thou makest their honours vain.
Did this not suffice thee, to thwart that doom
  Of Admetus, when, all by thy cunning beguiled
Were the Fates, that thou now must be warding the wife
  With thine hand made ready the bowstring to strain,
Though she pledged her from death to redeem with her
    life
              Her lord—she, Pelias' child?
  Apollo. Fear not: fair words and justice are with me.
  Death. Justice with thee! what needeth then the bow?
  Apollo. This?—'tis my wont to bear it evermore.
  Death. Yea, and to aid yon house in lawless wise.
  Apollo. Mine heart is heavy for my friend's mischance.
  Death. What, wilt thou wrest from me this second
    corpse?
  Apollo. Nay, not that other did I take by force.
  Death. Not?—why on earth then?—why not under-
    ground?
  Apollo. She was his ransom, she for whom thou comest.
  Death. Yea, and will hale her deep beneath the earth.
  Apollo. Take her and go: I trow I shall not bend thee—
  Death. To slay the victim due?—mine office this.
  Apollo. Nay, but to smite with death the ripe for death.
  Death. Ay, I discern thy plea—thy zeal, good sooth!
  Apollo. And may Alcestis never see old age?
  Death. Never:—should I not love mine honours too?
  Apollo. 'Tis soon or late—thou canst but take one life.
  Death. Yet mine the goodlier prize when die the
    young.
  Apollo. Think—royal obsequies if old she die!
  Death. Lo, Phœbus making laws to shield the rich!

Apollo. How sayst thou?—thou a sophist unawares!

Death. Would wealth not buy the boon of dying old?

Apollo. So then thou wilt not grant this grace to me?

Death. Nay surely—dost not know my wonted way?

Apollo. Hateful to mortals this, and loathed of gods.

Death. All things beyond thy rights thou canst not have.

Apollo. Surely thou shalt forbear, though ruthless thou,
So mighty a man to Pheres' halls shall come,
Sent of Eurystheus forth, the courser-car
From winter-dreary lands of Thrace to bring.
Guest-welcomed in Admetus' palace here,
By force yon woman shall he wrest from thee.
Yea, thou of me shalt have no thank for this,
And yet shalt do it, and shalt have mine hate.

[*Exit* APOLLO.

Death. Talk on, talk on: no profit shalt thou win.
This woman down to Hades' halls shall pass.
For her I go: my sword shall seal her ours:
For sacred to the nether gods is he,
He from whose head this sword hath shorn the hair.

[*Exit* DEATH.

Enter CHORUS, *dividing to right and left, so that the
sections answer one another*

Half-Chorus 1. What meaneth this hush afront of the hall?
The home of Admetus, why voiceless all?

Half-Chorus 2. No friend of the house who should speak of its plight
Is nigh, who should bid that we raise the keen
For the dead, or should tell us that yet on the light
Alcestis looketh, and liveth the queen,
The daughter of Pelias, the noblest, I ween,
        Yea, in all men's sight
The noblest of women on earth that have been.

Strophe 1

Half-Chorus 1. Or hearest thou mourning or sighing
    Or beating of hands,
    Or the wail of bereaved ones outcrying?
    No handmaid stands
    At the palace-gate.
O Healer, appear for the dying, appear as a bright bird flying
    'Twixt the surges of fate!
Half-Chorus 2. Ah, they would not be hushed, had the life of her flown!
Half-Chorus 1. Not forth of the door is the death-train gone.
Half-Chorus 2. Whence cometh thine hope, which I boast not mine own?
Half-Chorus 1. Would the king without pomp of procession have yielded the grave the possession
    Of so dear, of so faithful a one?

Antistrophe 1

Half-Chorus 2. Nor the cup in the gateway appeareth,
    From the spring that they bear
    To the gate that pollution feareth,
    Nor the severed hair
    In the porch for the dead,
Which the mourner in bitterness sheareth, neither beating of hands one heareth
    On maiden's head.
Half-Chorus 1. Yet surely is this the appointed day—
Half-Chorus 2. Ah! what wilt thou say?
Half-Chorus 1. Whereon of her doom she must pass to the tomb.
Half-Chorus 2. With a keen pang's smart hast thou stabbed mine heart.
Half-Chorus 1. It is meet, when the good are as flowers plucked away,

That in sorrow's gloom
Should the breast of the old tried friend have part.

CHORUS. *Strophe 2*

Though ye voyage all seas,
   Ye shall light on no lands,
Nor on Lycia's leas,
   Nor Ammonian sands,
Whence redemption shall come for the wretched, or loosing of Death's dread bands.

Doom's imminent slope
   Is a precipice-steep.
In no god is there hope,
   Though his altars should weep
With the crimson atonement, should veil them in clouds
of the hecatomb-sheep.

Antistrophe 2

Ah, once there was one!—
   Were life's light in the eyes
Of Phœbus's son,
   Then our darling might rise
From the mansions of darkness, through portals of Hades
return to our skies;

For he raised up the dead,
   Ere flashed from the heaven,
From Zeus' hand sped,
   That bolt of the levin.
But now what remaineth to wait for?—what hope of her
life is given?

No sacrifice more
   Unrendered remaineth:
No god, but the gore
   From his altars down-raineth:

Yet healing is none for our ills, neither balm that the
    spirit sustaineth.

Enter HANDMAID

But hither cometh of the handmaids one,
Weeping the while. What tidings shall I hear?
To grieve at all mischance unto thy lords
May be forgiven; but if thy lady lives
Or even now hath passed, fain would we know.
    Handmaid. She liveth, and is dead: both mayst thou say.
    Chorus. Ay so?—how should the same be dead and live?
    Handmaid. Even now she droopeth, gasping out her
      life.
    Chorus. Noble and stricken—how noble she thou losest!
    Handmaid. His depth of loss he knows not ere it come.
    Chorus. And hope—is no hope left her life to save?
    Handmaid. None—for the day foredoomed constrain-
      eth her.
    Chorus. Are all things meet, then, being done for her?
    Handmaid. Yea, ready is her burial-attire.
    Chorus. Let her be sure that glorious she dies
And noblest woman 'neath the sun's wide way.
    Handmaid. Noblest?—how not?—what tongue will
      dare gainsay?
What must the woman be who passeth her?
How could a wife give honour to her lord
More than by yielding her to die for him?
And this—yea, all the city knoweth this.
But what within she did, hear thou, and marvel.
For when she knew that the appointed day
Was come, in river-water her white skin
She bathed, and from the cedar-chests took forth
Vesture and jewels, and decked her gloriously,
And stood before the hearth, and prayed, and said:
" Queen, for I pass beneath the earth, I fall
Before thee now, and nevermore, and pray:—
Be mother to my orphans: mate with him

A loving wife, with her a noble husband.
Nor, as their mother dieth, so may they,
My children, die untimely, but with weal
In the home-land fill up a life of bliss."
To all the altars through Admetus' halls
She went, with wreaths she hung them, and she prayed,
Plucking the while the tresses of the myrtle,
Tearless, unsighing, and the imminent fate
Changed not the lovely rose-tint of her cheek.
Then to her bower she rushed, fell on the bed;
And there, oh, there she wept, and thus she speaks:
   "O couch, whereon I loosed the maiden zone
For this man, for whose sake I die to-day,
Farewell: I hate thee not.   Me hast thou lost,
Me only: loath to fail thee and my lord
I die: but thee another bride shall own,
Not more true-hearted; happier perchance."
Then falls thereon, and kisses: all the bed
Is watered with the flood of melting eyes.
But having wept her fill of many tears,
Drooping she goeth, reeling from the couch;
Yet oft, as forth the bower she passed, returned,
And flung herself again upon the couch.
And the babes, clinging to their mother's robes,
Were weeping: and she clasped them in her arms,
Fondling now this, now that, as one death-doomed.
And all the servants 'neath the roof were weeping,
Pitying their lady.   But to each she stretched
Her right hand forth; and none there was so mean
To whom she spake not and received reply.
Such are the ills Admetus' home within.
Now, had he died, he had ended: but in 'scaping,
He bears a pain that he shall ne'er forget.
   Chorus. Doth not Admetus groan for this affliction
Of such a noble wife to be bereft?
   Handmaid. Ay, weeps, and clasps his dear one in his
      arms,

And prays, "Forsake me not!"—asking the while
The impossible, for still she wanes and wastes,
Drooping her hand, a misery-burdened weight.
But yet, albeit hardly breathing now,
To the sun's rays fain would she lift her eyes,
As never more, but for the last time then
Destined to see the sun's beam and his orb.
But I will go and make thy presence known:
For 'tis not all that love so well their kings
As to stand by them, in afflictions loyal.
But from of old my lords were loved of thee.   [*Exit.*

Nine members of the CHORUS *chant successively:*

Chorus 1. O Zeus, for our lords is there naught but
     despair?
No path through the tangle of evils, no loosing of chains
     that have bound them?

Chorus 2. No tidings?—remaineth but rending of hair,
And the stricken ones turned to the tomb with the gar-
     ments of sorrow around them?

Chorus 3. Even so—even so! yet uplift we in prayer
Our hands to the gods, for that power from the days
     everlasting hath crowned them.

Chorus 4. O Healer-king,
Find thou for Admetus the balm of relief, for the captive
     deliverance!

Chorus 5. Vouchsafe it, vouchsafe it, for heretofore
     Hast thou found out a way; even now once more
     Pluck back our beloved from Hades' door,
     Strike down Death's hand red-reeking with gore!

Chorus 6. Woe's me! woe's me!—let the woe-dirge
     ring!
Ah, scion of Pheres, alas for thy lot, for love's long sev-
     erance!

Chorus 7. For such things on his sword might a man
     not fall,
Or knit up his throat in the noose 'twixt the heaven and
     the earth that quivereth?

Chorus 8. For his dear one—nay, but his dearest of all
Shall he see on this day lying dead, while her spirit by
    Lethe shivereth.
Chorus 9. O look! look yonder, where forth of the hall
She cometh, and he at her side whose life by her life she
    delivereth.

CHORUS, UNITED

Cry, land Pheraian, shrill the keen!
    Lift up thy voice to wail thy best
    There dying, and thy queenliest
Slow wasting to the gates unseen!

Tell me not this, that wedlock brings
    To them that wed more bliss than woe.
    I look back to the long-ago;
I muse on these unhappiest things.

Lo, here a king—he forfeiteth
    The truest heart, the noblest wife:
    And what shall be henceforth his life?
A darkened day, a living death.

Enter FEMALE ATTENDANTS *bearing* ALCESTIS, *accompanied by* ADMETUS *and* CHILDREN

Alcestis. O Sun, and the day's dear light,
And ye clouds through the wheeling heaven in the race
    everlasting flying!
Admetus. He seeth thee and me, two stricken ones,
Who wrought the gods no wrong, that thou shouldst die.
Alcestis. O land, O stately height
Of mine halls, and my bridal couch in Iolkos, my father-
    land, lying!
Admetus. Uplift thee, hapless love, forsake me not,
And pray the mighty gods in ruth to turn.
Alcestis. I see the boat with the oars twin-sweeping,
And, his hand on the pole as in haste aye keeping,

Charon the ferryman calleth, " What ho, wilt thou linger
    and linger?
Hasten—'tis thou dost delay me!" he crieth with beckon-
    ing finger.
   Admetus. Ah me! a bitter ferrying this thou namest!
O evil-starred, what woes endure we now!
   Alcestis. One haleth me—haleth me hence to the mansion
Of the dead! dost thou mark not the darkling expansion
Of the pinions of Hades, the blaze of his eyes 'neath their
    caverns out-glaring?
What wouldst thou?—Unhand me!—In anguish and pain
    by what path am I faring!
   Admetus. Woeful to them that love thee: most to me
And to thy babes, sad sharers in this grief.
   Alcestis. Let be—let me sink back to rest me:
    There is no strength left in my feet.
      Hades is near, and the night
      Is darkening down on my sight.
      Darlings, farewell: on the light
    Long may ye look :—I have blessed ye
    Ere your mother to nothingness fleet.
Admetus. Ah me! for thy word rusheth bitterness o'er me,
    Bitterness passing the anguish of death!
Forsake me not now, by the gods I implore thee,
    By the babes thou wilt orphan, O yield not thy breath!
Look up, be of cheer: if thou diest, before me
    Is nothingness.   Living, we aye live thine,
And we die unto thee; for our hearts are a shrine
Wherein for thy love passing word we adore thee!
   Alcestis. Admetus—for thou seest all my plight—
Fain would I speak mine heart's wish ere I die.
I, honouring thee, and setting thee in place
Before mine own soul still to see this light,
Am dying, unconstrained to die for thee.
I might have wed what man Thessalian
I would, have dwelt wealth-crowned in princely halls;
Yet would not live on, torn away from thee,

With orphaned children : wherefore spared I not
The gifts of youth still mine, wherein I joyed.
Yet she that bare, he that begat, forsook thee,
Though fair for death their time of life was come,
Yea, fair, to save their son and die renowned.
Their only one wert thou : no hope there was
To get them sons thereafter, hadst thou died.
So had I lived, and thou, to after days :
Thou wert not groaning, of thy wife bereaved,
Thy children motherless.   Howbeit this
Some god hath brought to pass : it was to be.
Let be :—remember thou what thank is due
For this : I never can ask full requital ;
For naught there is more precious than the life—
Yet justly due : for these thy babes thou lovest
No less than I, if that thine heart be right.
Suffer that they have lordship in mine home :
Wed not a stepdame to supplant our babes,
Whose heart shall tell her she is no Alcestis,
Whose jealous hand shall smite them, thine and mine.
Do not, ah ! do not this—I pray thee, I.
For the new stepdame hateth still the babes
Of her that's gone with more than viper-venom.
The boy—his father is his tower of strength
To whom to speak, of whom to win reply :
But, O my child, what girlhood will be thine ?
To thee what would she be, thy father's yoke-mate ?
What if with ill report she smirched thy name,
And in thy youth's flower marred thy marriage-hopes .
For thee thy mother ne'er shall deck for bridal,
Nor hearten thee in travail, O my child,
There, where naught gentler than the mother is.
For I must die, nor shall it be to-morn,
Nor on the third day comes on me this bane :
Straightway of them that are not shall I be.
Farewell, be happy.   Now for thee, my lord,
Abides the boast to have won the noblest wife,
14

For you, my babes, to have sprung from noblest mother.
   Chorus. Fear not; for I am bold to speak for him
This will he do, an if he be not mad.
   Admetus. It shall, it shall be, dread not thou: for thee
Living I had; and dead, mine only wife
Shalt thou be called: nor ever in thy stead
Shall bride Thessalian hail me as her lord.
None is there of a father so high-born,
None so for beauty peerless among women.
Children enough have I: I pray the gods
For joy in these—our joy in thee is naught.
Not for a year's space will I mourn for thee,
But long as this my life shall last, dear wife,
Loathing my mother, hating mine own sire,
For in word only, not in deed, they loved me.
Thou gav'st in ransom for my life thine all
Of precious, and didst save.   Do I not well
To groan, who lose such yokefellow in thee?
Revels shall cease, and gatherings at the wine,
Garlands, and song, which wont to fill mine house.
For never more mine hand shall touch the lyre:
Nor will I lift up heart to sing to flute
Of Libya: thou hast robbed my life of mirth.
And, wrought by craftsmen's cunning hands, thy form
Imaged, upon a couch outstretched shall lie,
Falling whereon, and clasping with mine hands,
Calling thy name, in fancy shall mine arms
Hold my belovèd, though I hold her not—
A chill delight, I wot—yet shall I lift
The burden from my soul.   In dreams shalt thou
Haunt me and gladden: sweet to see the loved,
Though but a fleeting presence night-revealed.
But, were the tongue and strain of Orpheus mine,
To witch Demeter's daughter and her lord,
And out of Hades by my song to win thee,
I had fared down: nor Pluto's hound had stayed me,
Nor spirit-wafter Charon at the oar,

Or ever I restored thy life to light.
Yet there look thou for me, whenso I die;
Prepare a home, as who shall dwell with me.
For in the selfsame cedar chest, wherein
Thou liest, will I bid them lay my bones
Outstretched beside thee: ne'er may I be severed,
No, not in death, from thee, my one true friend.

Chorus. Yea, I withal will mourn, as friend with friend
With thee for this thy wife, for she is worthy.

Alcestis. My children, ye yourselves have heard all this,
Have heard your father pledge him ne'er to wed
For your oppression and for my dishonour.

Admetus. Yea, now I say it, and I will perform.

Alcestis. On these terms take the children from mine
hand.

Admetus. I take them—precious gift from precious
hand.

Alcestis. Be to these babes a mother in my stead.

Admetus. Sore is their need, who are bereft of thee.

Alcestis. Darlings, I should have lived; and lo, I die.

Admetus. Ah me!—what shall I do, forlorn of thee?

Alcestis. Time shall bring healing—but the dead is
naught.

Admetus. Take me, ah, take me with thee to the grave!

Alcestis. Suffice it that one dies—she dies for thee.

Admetus. O Death, of what a wife dost thou bereave
me!

Alcestis. Dark—dark—mine eyes are drooping, heavy-
laden.

Admetus. Oh, I am lost if thou wilt leave me, wife!

Alcestis. No more—I am no more: as naught account
me.

Admetus. Uplift thy face: forsake not thine own children!

Alcestis. Sore loath do I—yet oh, farewell, my babes!

Admetus. Look unto them—oh, look!

Alcestis. I am no more.

Admetus. Ah, leav'st thou us?

Alcestis.   Farewell.   [*Dies.*

Admetus.   O wretch undone!

Chorus. Gone—gone!—No more is this Admetus' wife!

Eumelus. Woe for my lot!—to the tomb hath my
     mother descended, descended!

Never again, O my father, she seeth the light of the sun!

In anguish she leaves us forsaken: the story is ended, is
     ended,

  Of her sheltering love, and the tale of the motherless
     life is begun.

Look—look on her eyelids, her hands drooping nerveless!
     oh, hear me, oh, hear me!

  It is I—I beseech thee, my mother!—thine own little,
     own little bird!

It is I—oh, I cast me upon thee—thy lips are so near me,
     so near me,

  Unto mine am I pressing them, mother!—I plead for a
     word—but a word!

Admetus. With her who heareth not, nor seeth: ye

And I are stricken with a heavy doom.

     Eumelus. And I am but a little one, father—so young,
     and forsaken, forsaken,

  Forlorn of my mother—O hapless! a weariful lot shall
     be mine!

And thou, little maiden, my sister, the burden hast taken,
     hast taken,

  Which thy brother may bear not alone, and a weariful
     lot shall be thine.

O father, of long-living love was thy marriage uncher-
     ished, uncherished:

  Thou hast won not the goal of old age with the love of
     thy youth at thy side;

For, or ever she won to the fulness of days she hath per-
     ished, hath perished;

  And the home is a wreck and a ruin, for thou, O my
     mother, hast died!

Chorus. Admétus, this mischance thou needs must bear.
Nor first of mortals thou, nor shalt be last
To lose a noble wife; and, be thou sure,
From us, from all, this debt is due—to die.
Admetus. I know it: nowise unforeseen this ill
Hath swooped upon me: long I grieved to know it.
But—for to burial must I bear my dead—
Stay ye, and, tarrying, echo back my wail
To that dark god whom no drink-offerings move.
And all Thessalians over whom I rule
I bid take part in mourning for this woman,
With shaven head and sable-shrouding robe.
And ye which yoke the cars four-horsed, or steeds
Of single frontlet, shear with steel their manes.
Music of flutes the city through, or lyres,
Be none, while twelve moons round their circles out:
For dearer dead, nor kinder unto me
I shall not bury: worthy of mine honour
Is she, for she alone hath died for me.   [*Exit.*

CHORUS. *Strophe 1*

O Pelias' daughter, I hail thee:
    I waft thee eternal farewell
To thine home where the darkness must veil thee,
    Where in Hades unsunned thou shalt dwell.
Know, Dark-haired, thy gray Spirit-wafter
    Hath sped not with twy-plashing oar
Woman nobler, nor shall speed hereafter
        To Acheron's shore.

Antistrophe 1

For the seven-stringed shell, or for pæan
    Unharped, shall thy fame be a song,
When o'er Sparta the moon Karnean
    High rideth the whole night long.
And in Athens the wealthy and splendid
    Shall thy name on her bards' lips ring,

Such a theme hast thou left to be blended
    With the lays that they sing.

Strophe 2

O that the power were but in me,
    From the chambers of Hades, to light,
And from streams of Cocytus, to win thee
    With the oar of the river of night!
O dear among women, strong-hearted
    From Hades to ransom thy lord!
Never spirit in such wise departed.
    Light lie on thee, lady, the sward!
And, if ever thine husband shall mate him
    Again with a bride in thy stead,
I will loathe him, his children shall hate him,
    The babes of the dead.

Antistrophe 2

When his mother would not be contented
    To hide her from him in the tomb,
Nor his gray-haired father consented,
    Unholpen he looked on his doom.
Whom they bare—the hard-hearted!—they cared
        not,
    Though hoary their locks were, to save!
Thou art gone, for thy great love spared not
    Thy blossom of youth from the grave.
Ah, may it be mine, such communion
    Of hearts!—'tis vouchsafed unto few :—
Then ours should be sorrowless union
        Our life-days through.

Enter HERAKLES

Herakles. Strangers, who dwell in this Pheraian land,
Say, do I find Admetus in his home?
    Chorus. Herakles, in his home is Pheres' son.
Yet say, what brings thee to Thessalian land,

That thou shouldst come to this Pheraian town?

Herakles. A toil for King Eurystheus, lord of Tiryns.

Chorus. And whither journeyest? To what wanderings yoked?

Herakles. For Thracian Diomedes' four-horsed chariot.

Chorus. How canst thou? Sure he is unknown to thee!

Herakles. Unknown: to land Bistonian fared I never.

Chorus. Not save by battle may those steeds be won.

Herakles. Yet flinch I may not from the appointed toils.

Chorus. Thy life or his—a triumph or a grave.

Herakles. Not this the first time I have run such course.

Chorus. What profit is it if thou slay their lord?

Herakles. Those steeds shall I drive back to Tiryns' king.

Chorus. Hard task, to set the bit betwixt their jaws.

Herakles. That shall I, if their nostrils breathe not fire.

Chorus. Yea, but with ravening jaws do they rend men.

Herakles. Go to—thus banquet mountain beasts, not
horses.

Chorus. Nay, thou shalt see their cribs with gore be-
spattered.

Herakles. Whom boasteth he for father, he that reared
them?

Chorus. Ares, the king of Thracia's golden shield.

Herakles. Thou sayst: such toil my fate imposeth still,
Harsh evermore, uphillward straining aye,
If I must still in battle close with sons
Gotten of Ares; with Lykaon first,
And Kyknus then: and lo, I come to grapple—
The third strife this—with yon steeds and their lord.
But never man shall see Alkmene's child
Quailing before the hand of any foe.

Chorus. Lo, there himself, the ruler of the land,
Admetus, cometh forth his palace-hall.

Enter ADMETUS

Admetus. Hail, O thou sprung from Zeus' and Perseus'
blood!

Herakles. Admetus, hail thou too, Thessalia's king.

Admetus. Hale?—Would I were! Yet thy good heart I know.

Herakles. Wherefore, for mourning shaven, showst thou thus?

Admetus. This day must I commit to earth a corpse.

Herakles. Now Heaven forefend thou mournst for children dead!

Admetus. In mine home live the babes whom I begat.

Herakles. Sooth, death-ripe were thy sire, if he be gone.

Admetus. He liveth, and my mother, Herakles.

Herakles. Surely, O surely, not thy wife, Admetus?

Admetus. Twofold must be mine answer touching her.

Herakles. Or hath she died, sayst thou, or liveth yet?

Admetus. She is and she is not: here lies my sorrow.

Herakles. Nothing the more I know: dark sayings thine.

Admetus. Knowst not the doom whereon she needs must light?

Herakles. I know she pledged herself to die for thee.

Admetus. How lives she then, if she to this consented?

Herakles. Mourn not thy wife ere dead: abide the hour.

Admetus. Dead is the doomed, and no more is the dead.

Herakles. Diverse are these—to be and not to be.

Admetus. This, Herakles, thy sentence: that is mine.

Herakles. But now, why weep'st thou? What dear friend is dead?

Admetus. A woman—hers the memory we mourn.

Herakles. Some stranger born, or nigh of kin to thee?

Admetus. A stranger born; yet near and dear to us.

Herakles. How died a stranger then in house of thine?

Admetus. An orphan here she dwelt, her father dead.

Herakles. Would we had found thee mourning not, Admetus!

Admetus. Ay so?—what purpose lurketh 'neath thy word?

Herakles. On will I to another host's hearth-welcome.

Admetus. It can not be : may no such evil come!

Herakles. A burden unto mourners comes the guest.

Admetus. Dead are the dead—but enter thou mine house.

Herakles. 'Twere shame to banquet in the house of weeping.

Admetus. Aloof the guest-bowers are where we will lodge thee.

Herakles. Let me pass on, and have my thanks unmeasured.

Admetus. Unto another's hearth thou canst not go.

[*To an* ATTENDANT] Ho thou, lead on : open the guest-bowers looking

Away from these our chambers. Tell my stewards
To set on meat in plenty. Shut withal
The mid-court doors : it fits not that the guests,
The while they feast, hear wailings, and be vexed.

[*Exit* HERAKLES.

Chorus. What dost thou ?—such affliction at the door,
And guests for thee, Admetus? Art thou mad ?

Admetus. But had I driven him from my home and city

Who came my guest, then hadst thou praised me more ?
Nay, sooth ; for mine affliction so had grown
No less, and more inhospitable I ;
And to mine ills were added this beside,
That this my home were called " Guest-hating Hall."
Yea, and myself have proved him kindliest host
Whene'er to Argos' thirsty plain I fared.

Chorus. Why hide then the dread Presence in the house,

When came a friend ?—Thyself hast named him friend.

Admetus. Never had he been won to pass my doors,
Had he one whit of mine afflictions known.
To some, I wot, not wise herein I seem,
Nor wilt thou praise : but mine halls have not learned
To thrust away nor to dishonour guests.

CHORUS. *Strophe 1*

Halls thronged of the guests ever welcome, O dwelling
    Of a hero, forever the home of the free,
The lord of the lyre-strings sweet beyond telling,
    Apollo hath deignèd to sojourn in thee.
Amid thine habitations, a shepherd of sheep,
The flocks of Admetus he scorned not to keep,
While the shepherds' bridal-strains, soft-swelling
    From his pipe, pealed over the slant-sloped lea.

Antistrophe 1

And the spotted lynxes for joy of thy singing
    Mixed with thy flocks; and from Othrys' dell
Trooped tawny lions: the witchery-winging
    Notes brought dancing around thy shell,
Phœbus, the dappled fawn from the shadow
Of the tall-tressed pines tripping forth to the meadow,
Beating time to the chime of the rapture-ringing
    Music, with light feet tranced by its spell.

Strophe 2

Wherefore the flocks of my lord unnumbered
    By the Bœbian mere fair-rippling stray:
Where the steeds of the sun halt, darkness-cumbered,
    By Molossian marches, far away
The borders lie of his golden grain,
And his rolling stretches of pasture-plain;
And the havenless beach Ægean hath slumbered
    Under Pelion long 'neath the peace of his sway.

Antistrophe 2

And now, with the tears from his eyes fast-raining,
    Thrown wide are his palace-doors to the guest,
While newly his heart 'neath its burden is straining,
    For the wife that hath died in his halls distressed.
For to honour's heights are the high-born lifted,
And the good are with truest wisdom gifted;

And there broods on mine heart bright trust unwaning
  That the god-reverer shall yet be blest.

Admetus. O kindly presence of Pheraian men,
This corpse even now, with all things meet, my ser-
    vants
Bear on their shoulders to the tomb and pyre.
Wherefore, as custom is, hail ye the dead,
On the last journey as she goeth forth.
  Chorus. Lo, I behold thy sire with agèd foot
Advancing, and attendants in their hands
Bear ornaments to deck the dead withal.

  Enter PHERES, *with* ATTENDANTS, *bearing gifts*
  Pheres. I come in thine afflictions sorrowing, son:
A noble wife and virtuous hast thou lost,
None will gainsay: yet these calamities
We needs must bear, how hard to bear soever.
Receive these ornaments, and let her pass
Beneath the earth: well may the corpse be honoured
Of her who for thy life's sake died, my son;
Who made me not unchilded, left me not
Forlorn of thee to pine in woeful eld.
In all her sisters' eyes she hath crowned her life
With glory, daring such a deed as this.
O saviour of my son, who us upraisedst
In act to fall, all hail! May bliss be thine
Even in Hades. Thus to wed, I say,
Profiteth men—or nothing worth is marriage.
  Admetus. Bidden of me thou com'st not to this burial,
Nor count I thine the presence of a friend.
Thine ornaments she never shall put on;
She shall be buried needing naught of thine.
Thou grieve!—thou shouldst have grieved in my death-
    hour!
Thou stoodst aloof—the old, didst leave the young
To die—and wilt thou wail upon this corpse?

True father of my body thou wast not;
Nor she that said she bare me, and was called
My mother, gave me birth: of bondman blood
To thy wife's breast was I brought privily,
Put to the test, thou showedst who thou art,
And I account me not thy true-born son.
Peerless of men in soulless cowardice!
So old, and standing on the verge of life,
Yet hadst no will, yet hadst no heart to die
For thine own son!—Ye suffered her, a woman
Not of our house, whom I with righteous cause
Might count alone my mother and my father.
Yet here was honour, hadst thou dared the strife,
In dying for thy son.   A paltry space
To cling to life in any wise was left.
Then had I lived, and she, through days to come,
Nor I, left lorn, should thus mine ills bemoan.
Yet all that may the fortunate betide
Fell to thy lot; in manhood's prime a king:
Me hadst thou son and heir unto thine house,
So that thou wast not, dying, like to leave
A childless home for stranger folk to spoil.
Nor canst thou say that flouting thy gray hairs
I gave thee o'er to death, whose reverence
For thee was passing word—and this the thank
That thou and she that bear me render me!
Wherefore, make haste: beget thee other sons
To foster thy gray hairs, to compass thee
With death's observance, and lay out thy corpse.
Not I with this mine hand will bury thee.
For thee dead am I.   If I see the light—
Another saviour found—I call me son
To her, and loving fosterer of her age.
For naught the agèd pray for death's release,
Plaining of age and weary-wearing time.
Let death draw near—who then would die?   Not one:
No more is eld a burden unto them.

Chorus. Oh, hush! Suffice the affliction at the doors,
O son, infuriate not thy father's soul.

    Pheres. Son, whom, thinkst thou—some Lydian slave
      or Phrygian
Bought with thy money?—thus beratest thou?
What, knowst thou not that I Thessalian am,
Sprung from Thessalian sire, free man true-born?
This insolence passeth!—hurling malapert words
On me, not lightly thus shalt thou come off!
Thee I begat and nurtured, of mine house
The heir: no debt is mine to die for thee.
Not from our sires such custom we received
That sires for sons should die: no Greek law this.
Born for thyself wast thou, to fortune good
Or evil: all thy dues from us thou hast.
O'er many folk thou rulest; wide demesnes
Shall I leave thee: to me my fathers left them.
What is my wrong, my robbery of thee?
For me die thou not, I die not for thee.
Thou joy'st to see light—shall thy father joy not?
Sooth, I account our time beneath the earth
Long, and our life-space short, yet is it sweet.
Shamelessly hast thou fought against thy death:
Thy life is but transgression of thy doom
And murder of thy wife—*my* cowardice!
This from thee, dastard! worsted by a woman
Who died for thee, the glorious-gallant youth!
Cunning device hast thou devised to die
Never, cajoling still wife after wife
To die for thee!—and dost revile thy friends
Who will not so—and thou the coward, thou?
Peace! e'en bethink thee, if thou lov'st thy life,
So all love theirs. Thou, if thou speakest evil
Of us, shalt hear much evil, and that true.

    Chorus. Ye have said too much, thou now, and he
      before.
Refrain, old sire, from railing on thy son.

Admetus. Say on, say on ; I have said : if hearing truth
Gall thee, thou shouldst not have done me wrong.

Pheres. I had done more wrong, had I died for thee.

Admetus. What, for the young and old is death the
same?

Pheres. One life to live, not twain—this is our due.

Admetus. Have thy desire—one life outlasting Zeus.

Pheres. Dost curse thy parents, who hast had no wrong?

Admetus. Ay, whom I marked love-sick for dateless life.

Pheres. What?—art not burying her in thine own stead?

Admetus. A token, dastard, of thy cowardice.

Pheres. I did her not to death : thou canst not say it.

Admetus. Mayst thou feel thy need of me some day!

Pheres. Woo many women, that the more may die.

Admetus. This taunt strikes thee—'tis thou wast loath
to die.

Pheres. Sweet is yon sun-god's light, yea, it is sweet.

Admetus. Base is thy spirit, and unmeet for men.

Pheres. No agèd corpse thou bearest, inly laughing!

Admetus. Yet shalt thou die in ill fame, when thou
diest.

Pheres. Naught reck I of ill-speaking o'er my grave.

Admetus. Ah me! how full of shamelessness is eld!

Pheres. Not shameless she—but senseless hast thou
found her.

Admetus. Begone : leave me to bury this my dead.

Pheres. I go : her murderer will bury her.
Thou shalt yet answer for it to her kin.
Surely Akastus is no more a man,
If he of thee claim not his sister's blood.　[*Exit* PHERES.

Admetus. Avaunt, with her that kennelleth with thee!
Childless grow old, as ye deserve, while lives
Your child : ye shall not come beneath one roof
With me.　If need were to renounce by heralds
Thy fatherhood, I had renounced it now.
Let us—for we must bear the present ill—
Pass on, to lay our dead upon the pyre.

CHORUS

Alas for the loving and daring!
  Farewell to the noblest and best!
May Hermes conduct thee down-faring
  Kindly, and Hades to rest
Receive thee! If any atonement
  For ills even there may betide
To the good, O thine be enthronement
  By Hades' bride!

  [*Exeunt omnes in funeral procession.*

Enter SERVANT

Servant. Full many a guest, from many a land which
    came
Unto Admetus' dwelling, have I known,
Have set before them meat: but never guest
More pestilent received I to this hearth:
Who first, albeit he saw my master mourning,
Entered, and passed the threshold unashamed;
Then, nowise courteously received the fare
Found with us, though our woeful plight he knew,
But, what we brought not, hectoring bade us bring.
The ivy cup uplifts he in his hands,
And swills the darkling mother's fiery blood,
Till the wine's flame enwrapped him, heating him.
Then did he wreathe his head with myrtle sprays,
Dissonant-howling. Diverse strains were heard;
For he sang on, regardless all of ills
Darkening Admetus' house; we servants wept
Our mistress: yet we showed not to the guest
Eyes tear-bedewed, for so Admetus bade.
And now within the house must I be feasting
This guest—a lawless thief, a bandit rogue!
She from the house hath passed: I followed not,
Nor stretched the hand, nor wailed unto my mistress
Farewell, who was to me and all the household
A mother, for from ills untold she saved us,

Assuaging her lord's wrath. Do I not well
To loathe this guest, intruder on our griefs?

Enter HERAKLES

Herakles. Ho, fellow, why this solemn brooding look?
The servant should not lower upon the guest,
But welcome him with kindly-beaming cheer.
Thou, seeing here in presence thy lord's friend,
With visage sour and cloud of knitted brows
Receiv'st him, fretting o'er an alien grief.
Hither to me, that wiser thou mayst grow.
The lot of man—its nature knowest thou?
I trow not: how shouldst thou? Give ear to me.
From all mankind the debt of death is due,
Nor of all mortals is there one that knows
If through the coming morrow he shall live:
For trackless is the way of Fortune's feet,
Not to be taught, nor won by art of man.
This hearing then, and learning it from me,
Make merry, drink: the life from day to day
Account thine own, all else in Fortune's power.
Honour withal the sweetest of the gods
To men, the Cyprian queen—a gracious goddess!
These thoughts put by, and hearken to my words,
If words of wisdom unto thee they seem.
I trow it. Hence with sorrow overwrought;
Pass through yon doors and quaff the wine with me,
Thy brows with garlands bound. Full well I wot,
From all this lowering spirit prison-pent
Thine anchor shall Sir Beaker's plash upheave.
What, man!—the mortal must be mortal-minded.
So, for your solemn wights of knitted brows,
For each and all—if thou for judge wilt take me—
Life is not truly life, but mere affliction.
    Servant. All this we know: but now are we in
        plight
Not meet for laughter and for revelry.

Herakles. The woman dead is alien-born : grieve not
Exceeding much.   Yet live the household's lords.
    Servant. Live, quotha !—knowst thou not the house's
    ills ?
    Herakles. Yea, if thy master lied not unto me.
    Servant. Guest-fain he is—ah, guest-fain overmuch.
    Herakles. A stranger dead—and no guest-cheer for me?
    Servant. Oh, yea, an alien she—o'ermuch an alien !
    Herakles. Ha ! was he keeping some affliction back ?
    Servant. Go thou in peace : our lords' ills are for us.
    Herakles. Grief for a stranger such talk heralds not.
    Servant. Else had I not sore vexed beheld thy revelling.
    Herakles. How ! have I sorry handling of mine hosts?
    Servant. Thou cam'st in hour unmeet for welcoming,
For grief is on us ; and thou see'st shorn hair
And vesture of black robes.
    Herakles.   But who hath died?
Not of the children one, or gray-haired sire?
    Servant. Nay, but Admetus' wife is dead, O guest!
    Herakles. How sayst thou ?   Ha ! even then ye gave
    me welcome?
    Servant. For shame he could not thrust thee from
    his doors.
    Herakles. O hapless ! what a helpmeet hast thou lost !
    Servant. We have all perished, and not she alone.
    Herakles. I felt it, when I saw his tear-drowned eyes,
His shaven hair, and face : yet he prevailed,
Saying he bare a stranger-friend to burial.
I passed this threshold in mine heart's despite,
And drank in halls of him that loves the guest,
When thus his plight !   And am I revelling
With head wreath-decked?   That thou should'st ne'er
    have told,
When such affliction lay upon the home !
Where doth he bury her ?   Where shall I find her ?
    Servant. By the straight path that leads Larissa-ward
Shall see the hewn-stone tomb without the walls.
   15

Herakles. Oh, much-enduring heart and soul of mine,
Now show what son the Lady of Tiryns bare
Elektryon's child Alkmene, unto Zeus.
For I must save the woman newly dead,
And set Alcestis in this house again,
And render to Admetus good for good.
I go. The sable-vestured King of Corpses,
Death, will I watch for, and shall find, I trow,
Drinking the death-draught hard beside the tomb.
And if I lie in wait, and dart from ambush,
And seize, and with mine arms' coil compass him,
None is there shall deliver from mine hands
His straining sides, or e'er he yields his prey.
Yea, though I miss the quarry, and he come not
Unto the blood-clot, to the sunless homes
Down will I fare of Korê and her king,
And make demand. I doubt not I shall lead
Alcestis up, and give to mine host's hands,
Who to his halls received, nor drave me thence,
Albeit smitten with affliction sore,
But hid it, like a prince, respecting me.
Who is more guest-fain of Thessalians?
Who in all Hellas?—Oh, he shall not say
That one so princely showed a base man kindness.

[Exit.

Enter ADMETUS, *with* CHORUS *and* ATTENDANTS, *returning from the funeral*

Admetus.   Oh, hateful returning!
            Oh, hateful to see
          Drear halls full of yearning
            For the lost—ah me!
What aim or what rest have I?—silence or speech, of
what help shall they be?

            Would God I were dead!
            Oh, I came from the womb

To a destiny dread!
Ah, those in the tomb—
How I envy them! How I desire them, and long to abide
in their home!

To mine eyes nothing sweet
Is the light of the heaven,
Nor the earth to my feet;
Such a helpmeet is riven
By Death from my side, and my darling to Hades the
spoiler hath given.

Chorus.   Pass on thou, and hide thee
In thy chambers.

Admetus.   Ah woe!
Chorus.   Wail the griefs that betide thee:
How canst thou but so?
Admetus. O God!
Chorus. Thou hast passed through deep waters of
anguish—I know it, I know.
Admetus. Alas and alas!
Chorus.   No help bringeth this
To thy love in that place.
Admetus. Woe!
Chorus.   Bitter it is
The face of a wife well-belovèd for ever and ever to miss.
Admetus. Thou hast stricken mine heart
Where the wound will not heal.
What is worse than to part
From the loving and leal?
Would God I had wedded her not, home-bliss with Alces-
tis to feel!

Oh, I envy the lot
Of the man without wife,
Without child; single-wrought
Is the strand of his life:

No soul-crushing burden of sorrow, no strength-over-
mastering strife.

   But that children should sicken,
    That gloom of despair
   Over bride-beds should thicken,
    What spirit can bear,
When childless, unwedded, a man through life's calm
  journey might fare?

  Chorus. Thee Fortune hath met,
    Strong wrestler, and thrown;
    Yet no bounds hast thou set—
  Admetus. Woe's me!—
  Chorus.   To thy moan.
Oh, thy burden is heavy!
  Admetus. Alas!
  Chorus. Yet endure it: thou art not alone.
    Not thou art the first
    Of bereavèd ones.
  Admetus. Ah me!
  Chorus. Such tempest hath burst
    Upon many ere thee.
Unto each his mischance, when the surges roll up from
  Calamity's sea.
  Admetus. Oh, long grief and pain
    For belovèd ones passed!
    Why didst thou restrain
    When myself I had cast
Down into her grave, with the noblest to lie peace-lulled
  at the last?

   Not one soul, but two
    Had been Hades' prey,
   Souls utterly true
    Together for aye,
Which together o'er waves of the underworld mere had
  passed this day.

Chorus.　　　　Of my kin was there one,
　　　　　　　And the life's light failed
　　　　　　　In his halls of a son,
　　　　　　　One meet to be wailed,
His only belovèd : howbeit the manhood within him pre-
　　vailed ;
　　　　　　　And the ills heaven-sent
　　　　　　　As a man did he bear,
　　　　　　　Though by this was he bent
　　　　　　　Unto silvered hair,
Far on in life's path, without son for his remnant of weak-
　　ness to care.
Admetus.　　　Oh, how can I tread
　　　　　　　Thy threshold, fair home ?
　　　　　　　How shelter mine head
　　　　　　　'Neath my roof, now the doom
Of the gods' dice changeth ?—ah me, what change upon
　　all things is come !

　　　　　　　For with torches aflame
　　　　　　　Of the Pelian pine,
　　　　　　　And with bride-song I came
　　　　　　　In that hour divine,
Upbearing the hand of a wife—thine hand, O darling
　　mine !
　　　　　　　Followed revellers, raising
　　　　　　　Acclaim : ever broke
　　　　　　　From the lips of them praising,
　　　　　　　Of the dead as they spoke,
And of me, how the noble, the children of kings, Love
　　joined 'neath his yoke.

　　　　　　　But for bridal song
　　　　　　　Is the wail for the dead,
　　　　　　　And, for white-robed throng,
　　　　　　　Black vesture hath led
Me to halls where the ghost of delight lieth couched on
　　a desolate bed.

Chorus.　　　To the trance of thy bliss
　　　　　　　Sudden anguish was brought.
　　　　　Never lesson like this
　　　　　To thine heart had been taught:
Yet thy life hast thou won, and thy soul hast delivered
　from death:—is it naught?

　　　　　Thy wife hath departed:
　　　　　Love tender and true
　　　　Hast she left: stricken-hearted,
　　　　　Wherein is this new?
Hath Death not unyoked from the chariot of Love full
　many ere you?

　Admetus. Friends, I account the fortune of my wife
Happier than mine, albeit it seems not so.
For naught of grief shall touch her any more,
And glorious rest she finds from many toils.
But I, unmeet to live, my doom outrun,
Shall drag out bitter days: I know it now.
How shall I bear to enter this mine home?
Speaking to whom, and having speech of whom,
Shall I find joy of entering?—whither turn me?
The solitude within shall drive me forth,
Whenso I see my wife's couch tenantless,
And seats whereon she sat, and, 'neath the roof,
All foul the floor; when on my knees my babes
Falling shall weep their mother, servants moan
The peerless mistress from the mansion lost.
All this within: but from the world without
Shall bridals of Thessalians chase me: throngs
Where women gossip; for I shall not bear
On those companions of my wife to look.
And, if a foe I have, thus shall he scoff:
" Lo there who basely liveth—dared not die,
But whom he wedded gave, a coward's ransom,
And 'scaped from Hades.　Count ye him a man?

He hates his parents, though himself was loath
To die!" Such ill report, besides my griefs,
Shall mine be. Ah, what profit is to live,
O friends, in evil fame, in evil plight?

CHORUS. *Strophe 1*

Chorus. I have mused on the words of the wise,
　　Of the mighty in song;
I have lifted mine heart to the skies,
I have searched all truth with mine eyes;
　　But naught more strong
Than fate have I found: there is naught
　　In the tablets of Thrace,
Neither drugs whereof Orpheus taught,
Nor in all that Apollo brought
　　To Asklepius' race,
When the herbs of healing he severed, and out of their
anguish delivered
　　The pain-distraught.

Antistrophe 1

There is none other goddess beside,
　　To the altars of whom
No man draweth near, nor hath cried
To her image, nor victim hath died,
　　Averting her doom.
O goddess, more mighty for ill
　　Come not upon me
Than in days overpast: for his will
Even Zeus may in no wise fulfil
　　Unholpen of thee.
Steel is molten as water before thee, but never relenting
came o'er thee,
　　Who are ruthless still.

Strophe 2

Thee, friend, hath the goddess gripped: from her hands
    never wrestler hath slipped.
Yet be strong to endure: never mourning shall bring our
    beloved returning
        From the nethergloom up to the light.
      Yea, the heroes of gods begotten,
      They fade into darkness, forgotten
      In death's chill night.
    Dear was she in days ere we lost her,
    Dear yet, though she lie with the dead.
    None nobler shall Earth-mother foster
    Than the wife of thy bed.

Antistrophe 2

Not as mounds of the dead which have died, so account
    we the tomb of thy bride,
But oh, let the worship and honour that we render to
    gods rest upon her:
        Unto her let the wayfarer pray.
    As he treadeth the pathway that trendeth
    Aside from the highway, and bendeth
    At her shrine, he shall say:
    " Her life for her lord's was given;
    With the blest now abides she on high.
    Hail, queen, show us grace from thine
        heaven! "
    Even so shall they cry.

But lo, Alkmene's son, as seemeth, yonder,
Admetus, to thine hearth is journeying.

Enter HERAKLES, *leading a woman wholly veiled*

Herakles. Unto a friend behooveth speech outspoken,
Admetus, not to hide within the breast
Murmurs unvoiced. I came mid thine affliction.
Fair claim was mine to rank amid thy friends.

Thou told'st me not how lay thy wife a corpse:
Thou gavest me guest-welcome in thine home,
Making pretence of mourning for a stranger.
I wreathed mine head, I spilled unto the gods
Drink-offerings in a stricken house, even thine.
I blame thee, thus mishandled, yea, I blame thee.
Yet nowise is my will to gall thy grief.
But wherefore hither turning back I come,
This will I tell. Take, guard for me this maid,
Till, leading hitherward the Thracian mares,
I come from slaughter of Bistonia's lord.
But if—not that, for I would fain return—
I give her then, for service of thine halls.
Prize of hard toil unto mine hands she came:
For certain men I found but now arraying
An athlete-strife, toil-worthy, for all comers,
Whence I have won and bring this victor's meed.
Horses there were for them to take which won
The light foot's triumph; but for hero-strife,
Boxing and wrestling, oxen were the guerdon:
A woman made it richer. Shame it seemed
To hap thereon, and slip this glorious gain.
But, as I said, this woman be thy care:
For no thief's prize, but toil-achieved, I bring her.
Yea, one day thou perchance shalt say 'twas well.
 Admetus. Not flouting thee, nor counting among foes,
My wife's unhappy fate I hid from thee.
But this had been but grief uppiled on grief,
Hadst thou sped hence to be another's guest;
And mine own ills sufficed me to bewail.
But, for the woman—if in any wise
It may be, prince, bid some Thessalian guard her,
I pray thee, who hath suffered not as I.
In Pheræ many a friend and host thou hast.
Awaken not remembrance of my grief.
I could not, seeing her mine halls within,
Be tearless: add not hurt unto mine hurt.

Burdened enough am I by mine affliction.
Nay, in mine house where should a young maid lodge?—
For vesture and adorning speak her young—
What, 'neath the men's roof shall her lodging be?
And how unsullied, dwelling with young men?
Not easy is it, Herakles, to curb
The young: herein do I take thought for thee.
Or shall I ope to her my dead wife's bower?
How!—cause her to usurp my lost love's bed?
Twofold reproach I dread—from mine own folk,
Lest one should say that, traitor to her kindness,
I fall upon another woman's bed—
And of the dead, to me most reverence-worthy,
Needs must I take great heed. But, woman, thou,
Whoso thou art, know that thy body's stature
Is as Alcestis, and thy form as hers.
Ah me!—lead, for the gods' sake, from my sight
This woman!—Take not my captivity captive.
For, as I look on her, methinks I see
My wife: she stirs mine heart with turmoil: fountains
Of tears burst from mine eyes. O wretched I!
Now first I taste this grief's full bitterness.

    Chorus. In sooth thy fortune can I not commend:
Yet must we brook a god's gift, whoso cometh.

    Herakles. Oh, that such might I had as back to bring
To light thy wife from nethergloom abodes,
And to bestow this kindness upon thee!

    Admetus. Fain wouldst thou, well I know. But wherefore this?
It can not be the dead to light should come.

    Herakles. O'ershoot not now the mark, but bear all bravely.

    Admetus. Easier to exhort than suffer and be strong.

    Herakles. But what thy profit, though for aye thou moan?

    Admetus. I too know this; yet love constraineth me.

    Herakles. Love for the lost—ay, that draws forth the tear.

Admetus. She hath undone me more than words can tell.

Herakles. A good wife hast thou lost, who shall gainsay?

Admetus. So that this man hath no more joy in life.

Herakles. Time shall bring healing: now is thy grief young.

Admetus. Time—time?—Oh, yea, if this thy Time be Death!

Herakles. A wife, and yearning for new love, shall calm thee.

Admetus. Hush!—what sayst thou?—I could not think thereon!

Herakles. How?—wilt not wed, but widowed keep thy couch?

Admetus. Lives not the woman that shall couch with me.

Herakles. Lookst thou that this shall profit aught the dead?

Admetus. I needs must honour her where'er she be.

Herakles. Good—good—yet one with folly so might charge thee.

Admetus. So be it, so thou call me bridegroom never.

Herakles. I praise thee for that leal thou art to her.

Admetus. Death be my meed, if I betray her dead.

Herakles. Receive this woman now these halls within.

Admetus. Nay!—I beseech by Zeus that did beget thee!

Herakles. Yet shalt thou err if thou do not this thing.

Admetus. Yet shall mine heart be grief-stung, if I do it.

Herakles. Yield thou! this grace may prove perchance a duty.

Admetus. Oh, that in strife thou ne'er hadst won this maid!

Herakles. Yet thy friend's victory is surely thine.

Admetus. Well said: yet let the woman hence depart.

Herakles. Yea—if need be. First look well—need it be?

Admetus. Needs must—save thou wilt else be wroth with me.

Herakles. I too know what I do, insisting thus.

Admetus. Have then thy will: thy pleasure is my pain.

Herakles. Yet one day shalt thou praise me: only yield.

Admetus [*to* ATTENDANTS]. Lead ye her, if mine halls must needs receive.

Herakles. Not to thy servants' hands will I commit her.

Admetus. Thou lead her in then, if it seems thee good.

Herakles. Nay, but in thine hands will I place her—thine.

Admetus. I will not touch her!—Open stand my doors.

Herakles. Unto thy right hand only trust I her.

Admetus. O king, thou forcest me: I will not this!

Herakles. Be strong: stretch forth thine hand and touch thy guest.

Admetus. I stretch it forth, as to a headless Gorgon.

Herakles. Hast her?

Admetus.   I have.

Herakles.   Yea, guard her. Thou shalt call
The child of Zeus one day a noble guest.

> [*Raises the veil, and discloses* ALCESTIS.

Look on her, if in aught she seems to thee
Like to thy wife. Step forth from grief to bliss.

Admetus. What shall I say?—Gods! Marvel this un-hoped for!
My wife do I behold in very sooth,
Or doth some god-sent mockery-joy distract me?

Herakles. Not so; but this thou seest is thy wife.

Admetus. What if this be some phantom from the shades?

Herakles. No ghost-upraiser hast thou ta'en for guest.

Admetus. How?—whom I buried do I see—my wife?

Herakles. Doubt not: yet might'st thou well mistrust thy fortune.

Admetus. As wife, as living, may I touch, address her?

Herakles. Speak to her: all thou didst desire thou
  hast.
Admetus. O face, O form of my belovèd wife,
Past hope I have thee, who ne'er thought to see thee!
Herakles. Thou hast: may no god of thy bliss be
  jealous.
Admetus. O scion nobly-born of Zeus most high,
Blessings on thee! The Father who begat thee
Keep thee! Thou only hast restored my fortunes.
How didst thou bring her from the shades to light?
Herakles. I closed in conflict with the Lord of Spirits.
Admetus. Where, sayst thou, didst thou fight this
  fight with Death?
Herakles. From ambush by the tomb mine hands en-
  snared him.
Admetus. Now wherefore speechless standeth thus my
  wife?
Herakles. 'Tis not vouchsafed thee yet to hear her
  voice,
Ere to the powers beneath the earth she be
Unconsecrated, and the third day come.
But lead her in, and, just man as thou art,
Henceforth, Admetus, reverence still the guest.
Farewell. But I must go, and work the work
Set by the king, the son of Sthenelus.
Admetus. Abide with us, a sharer of our hearth.
Herakles. Hereafter this: now must I hasten on.
Admetus. Oh, prosper thou, and come again in peace!
Through all my realm I publish to my folk
That, for these blessings, dances they array,
And that atonement-fumes from altars rise.
For now to happier days than those o'erpast
Have we attained. I own me blest indeed.
Chorus. Oh, the works of the gods—in manifold forms
  they reveal them:
Manifold things unhoped-for the gods to accomplishment
  bring.

And the things that we looked for, the gods deign not to
 fulfil them ;
And the paths undiscerned of our eyes, the gods unseal
 them.
  So fell this marvellous thing.

            [*Exeunt omnes.*

THE MEDEA OF EURIPIDES

TRANSLATED BY

ARTHUR S. WAY

WHEN the Heroes, who sailed in the ship Argo to bring home the Golden Fleece, came to the land of Kolchis, they found that to win that treasure was a deed passing the might of mortal man, so terribly was it guarded by monsters magical, even fire-breathing bulls and an unsleeping dragon. But Aphrodite caused Medea the sorceress, daughter of Aietes the king of the land, to love Jason their captain, so that by her magic he overcame the bulls and the dragon. Then Jason took the Fleece, and Medea withal, for that he had pledged him to wed her in the land of Greece. But as they fled, Absyrtus her brother pursued them with a host of war, yet by Medea's devising was he slain. So they came to the land of Iolkos, and to Pelias, who held the kingdom which was Jason's of right. But Medea by her magic wrought upon Pelias's daughters so that they slew their father. Yet by reason of men's horror of the deed might not Jason and Medea abide in the land, and they came to Corinth. And there all men rejoiced for the coming of a hero so mighty in war and a lady renowned for wisdom unearthly, for that Medea was grandchild of the Sun-god. But after ten years, Kreon the king of the land spake to Jason, saying, "Lo, I will give thee my daughter to wife, and thou shalt reign after me, if thou wilt put away thy wife Medea ; but her and her two sons will I banish from the land." So Jason consented. And of this befell things strange and awful, which are told herein.

DRAMATIS PERSONÆ

NURSE OF MEDEA'S CHILDREN.
CHILDREN'S GUARDIAN.[1]
MEDEA.
CHORUS OF CORINTHIAN LADIES.
KREON, King of Corinth.
JASON.
AIGEUS, King of Athens.
MESSENGER.
CHILDREN OF MEDEA.

The Scene is in front of Jason's House at Corinth.

[1] *Pædagogus.*—A trusted servant, responsible for keeping the boys out of harm's way : he was present at their sports, accompanied them to and from school, and never let them be out of his sight.   A similar institution is familiar to Englishmen resident in India.

MEDEA

———▸◆◄———

Enter NURSE *of Medea's Children*

NURSE. Would God that Argo's hull had never
flown
    Through those blue Clashing Rocks to Kolchís-land!
Nor that in Pelion's glens had fallen ever
The axe-hewn pine, nor filled with oars the hands
Of hero-princes, who at Pelias' hest
Quested the Golden Fleece! My mistress then,
Medea, to Iolkos' towers had sailed not
With love for Jason thrilled through all her soul,
Nor had on Pelias' daughters wrought to slay
Their sire, nor now in this Corinthian land
Dwelt with her lord and children, gladdening
By this her exile them whose land received her;
Yea, and in all things serving Jason's weal,
Which is the chief salvation of the home,
When wife stands not at variance with her lord.
Now all is hatred: love is sickness-stricken.
For Jason, traitor to his babes and her,
My mistress, weddeth with a child of kings,
Daughter of Kreon ruler of the land.
And, slighted thus, Medea, hapless wife,
Cries on the oaths, invokes that mightiest pledge
Of the right hand, and calls the gods to witness
From Jason what requital she receives.

Foodless she lies, her frame to griefs resigned,
Wasting in tears all those long, weary hours
Since first she knew her outraged by her lord,
Never uplifting eye, nor turning ever
From earth her face; but like a rock or sea-wave
So hearkens she to friends that counsel her;
Saving at whiles, when, turning her white neck,
All to herself she wails her sire beloved,
Her land, her home, forsaking which she came
Hither with him who holds her now dishonoured.
Now knows she, hapless, by affliction's teaching,
How good is fatherland unforfeited.
She loathes her babes, joys not beholding them.
I fear her, lest some mischief she devise.
Grim is her spirit, one that will not brook
Mishandling: yea, I know her, and I dread
Lest through her heart she thrust the whetted knife,
Through the halls stealing silent to her bed,
Or slay the king and him that weds his child,
And get herself therefrom some worse misfortune;
For dangerous is she: who begins a feud
With her, not soon shall sing the triumph-song.
But lo, her boys, their racing-sport put by,
Draw near, unwitting of their mother's ills,
For the young heart loves not to brood in grief.

Enter CHILDREN'S GUARDIAN, *with boys*

Children's Guardian. O ancient chattel of my mistress'
    home,
Why at the gates thus lonely standest thou,
Thyself unto thyself discoursing ills?
How wills Medea to be left of thee?
    Nurse. O gray attendant of the sons of Jason,
The hearts of faithful servants still are touched
By ill-betiding fortunes of their lords.
For I have come to such a pass of grief,
That yearning took me hitherward to come

And tell to earth and heaven my lady's fortunes.

    Children's Guardian. Ceaseth not yet the hapless one
      from moan?

    Nurse. Cease!—her pain scarce begun, the midst far off!

    Children's Guardian. Ah, fool!—if one may say it of his
      lords—

Little she knoweth of the latest blow.

    Nurse. What is it, ancient? Grudge not thou to tell me.

    Children's Guardian. Naught: I repent me of the word
      that 'scaped me.

    Nurse. Nay, by thy beard, from fellow-thrall hide not—

Silence, if need be, will I keep thereof.

    Children's Guardian. I heard one saying—feigning not
      to hear,

As I drew near the marble thrones,[1] where sit

The ancients round Peirene's hallowed fount—

That Kreon, this land's lord, will shortly drive

These boys from soil Corinthian with their mother?

Howbeit, if the tale I heard be true

I know not; fain were I it were not so.

    Nurse. Will Jason brook his children suffering this,

What though he be estrangèd from their mother?

    Children's Guardian. The old ties in the race lag far
      behind

The new: no friend is he unto this house.

    Nurse. We are undone then, if we add fresh ill

To old, ere lightened be our ship of this.

    Children's Guardian. But thou—for 'tis not season that
      thy lady

Should know—keep silence, and speak not the tale.

    Nurse. Hear, babes, what father this is unto you!

I curse him—not: he is my master still:

But to his friends he stands convict of baseness.

    Children's Guardian. What man is not?—hast learned
      this only now,

That each man loves self better than his neighbour,

[1] So Mahaffy, adopted by Paley.

For just cause some, and some for greed of gain?
So, for a bride's sake, these their father loves not.
   Nurse. Pass in, dear children, for it shall be well.
But thou, keep these apart to the uttermost:
Bring them not nigh their mother angry-souled.
For late I saw her glare, as glares a bull
On these, as 'twere for mischief; nor her wrath,
I know, shall cease, until its lightning strike.
To foes may she work ill, and not to friends!

Medea (behind the scenes). O hapless I!—O miseries
      heaped on mine head!
   Ah me! ah me! would God I were dead!

Nurse. Lo, darlings, the thing that I told you!
   Lo the heart of your mother astir!
And astir is her anger: withhold you
   From her sight, come not nigh unto her.
Haste, get you within: O beware ye
   Of the thoughts as a wild-beast brood,
Of the nature too ruthless to spare ye
   In its desperate mood.

Pass ye within now, departing
   With all speed. It is plain to discern
How a cloud of lamenting, upstarting
   From its viewless beginnings, shall burn
In lightnings of fury yet fiercer.
   What deeds shall be dared of that soul,
So haughty, when wrong's goads pierce her,
   So hard to control?
         [*Exeunt* CHILDREN *with* GUARDIAN.

Medea (behind the scenes). Woe! I have suffered, have suffered, foul wrongs that may waken, may waken,
Mighty lamentings full well! O ye children accursed
   from the womb,

Hence to destruction, ye brood of a loathed óne forsaken,
    forsaken!
Hence with your father, and perish our home in the
    blackness of doom!

Nurse. Ah me, in the father's offences
        What part have the babes, that thine hate
    Should blast them?—forlorn innocences,
        How sorely I fear for your fate!
    Ah, princes—how fearful their moods are!—
        Long ruling, unschooled to obey—
    Unforgiving, unsleeping their feuds are.
        Better life's level way.

    Be it mine, if in greatness I may not,
        In quiet and peace to grow old.
    Sweeter name than " The Mean " shall ye say not;
        But to taste it is sweetness untold.
    But to men never weal above measure
        Availed : on its perilous height
    The gods in their hour of displeasure
        The heavier smite.

Enter CHORUS *of Corinthian Ladies*

Chorus. I have hearkened the voice of the daughter of
    Kolchis, the sound of the crying
Of the misery-stricken ; nor yet is she stilled. Now
    the tale of her tell,
Gray woman; for moaned through the porch from her
    chamber the wail of her sighing;
And I can not, I can not be glad while the home in afflic-
    tion is lying,
        The house I have loved so well.

Nurse. Home?—home there is none: it hath vanished
    away;
    For my lord to a bride of the princes is thrall;

And my lady is pining the livelong day
In her bower, and for naught that her friends' lips say
On her heart may the dews of comfort fall.

Medea (*behind the scenes*). Would God that the flame of the
 lightning from heaven descending, descending,
Might burn through mine head!—for in living wherein
 any more is my gain?
Alas and alas! Would God I might bring to an ending,
 an ending,
The life that I loathe, and behind me might cast all its
 burden of pain!

CHORUS. *Strophe*

O Zeus, Earth, Light, did ye hear her,
How waileth the woe-laden breath
Of the bride in unhappiest plight?
What yearning for vanished delight,
O passion-distraught, should have might
To cause thee to wish death nearer—
The ending of all things, death?

Make thou not for this supplication!
If thine husband hath turned and adored
New love, that estrangèd he is,
O harrow thy soul not for this.
It is Zeus that shall right thee, I wis.
Ah, pine not in over-vexation
Of spirit, bewailing thy lord!

Medea (*behind the scenes*). O Lady of Justice, O Artemis'
 Majesty, see it, O see it—
Look on the wrongs that I suffer, my oaths everlasting
 who tied
The soul of mine husband, that ne'er from the curse he
 might free it, nor free it
From your vengeance!—O may I behold him at last,
 even him and his bride,

Them, and these halls therewithal, all shattered in ruin,
  in ruin!—
    Wretches, who dare unprovoked to do to Medea de-
    spite!
O father, O city, whom erst I forsook, for undoing, undoing,
    And for shame, when the blood of my brother I spilt
    on the path of my flight!

Nurse. Do ye hear what she saith, and uplifteth her cry
  Unto Themis and Zeus, to the Suppliant's King,
Oath-steward of men that be born but to die?
Oh, my lady will lay not her anger by
  Soon, making her vengeance a little thing.

CHORUS. Antistrophe

If she would but come forth where we wait her,
  If she would but give ear to the sound
    Of our speech, that her spirit would learn
    From its fierceness of anger to turn,
    And her lust for revenge not burn!
Oh, ne'er may my love prove traitor,
  Never false to my friends be it found!

But go thou, and forth of the dwelling
  Thy mistress hitherward lead.
    Say to her that friends be we all.
    O hasten, ere mischief befall
    The lords of the palace-hall!
For her grief, like a tempest upswelling,
  Resistless shall ruinward speed.

Nurse. I will do it; but almost my spirit despaireth
    To win her; yet labour of love shall it be.
    But my queen on her thralls as a mad bull glareth,
    Or a lioness couched mid her whelps, whoso dareth
      With speech to draw near her, so tameless is she.

He should err not, who named the old singers in
 singing
Not cunning, but left-handed bards, for their lays
Did they frame for the mirth-tide, the festal in-
 bringing
Of the wine, and the feast, when the harp-strings are
 ringing
To sweeten with melody life's sweet days:

But the dread doom of mortals, the anguish heart-
 rending—
Never minstrel by music hath breathed on them
 peace,
Nor by song with his harp-notes in harmony blend-
 ing;
Albeit of these cometh death's dark ending
Unto many a home that is wrecked of these.

And yet were it surely a boon to bring healing
Of sorrow to mortals with song: but in vain
Mid the fulness of feasting ring voices clear-pealing,
And the banquet itself hath a glamour, concealing
From mortals their doom, flinging spells over pain.
                                        [*Exit* NURSE.

Chorus. I have heard it, the sigh-laden cry of the daughter
Of Kolchis, the woe-shrilling anguish of wailing
For the traitor to love who with false vows caught
 her,
Who in strength of her wrongs chideth Heaven,
 assailing
The Oath-queen of Zeus, who with cords all-
 prevailing
Forth haled her, and brought her o'er star-litten
 water,
Where the brine-mists hover o'er Pontus' Key,
Unto Hellas far over the boundless sea.

Enter MEDEA

Medea. Corinthian dames, I have come forth my doors
Lest ye should blame me. Many folk I know
Accounted haughty, some, for proud staid mien,[1]
Some, stranger-shy:[2] and some, that softly go,
Have gotten ill repute of indolence.
For justice sits not in the eyes of man,
Who, ere he hath discerned his neighbour's heart,
Hates him at sight, albeit nowise wronged.
The sojourner must learn the city's wont;
Nor praise I citizens-born, law to themselves,
Mannerless churls, which flout their fellow-folk.
But me—unlooked-for fell this blow on me,
And brake mine heart. Undone I am; have lost
All grace of life, and long to die, my friends.
For he that was mine all—thou know'st it well—[3]
My lord, of all men basest hath become.
Surely, of creatures that have life and wit,
We women are of all things wretchedest,
Who, first, must needs, as buys the highest bidder,
Thus buy a husband, and our body's master
So win—for deeper depth of ill is this.
Nay, risk is dire herein—or shall we gain
An evil lord or good? For change is shame
To woman, nor may she renounce her spouse.
And, coming to new customs, habits new,
Seer need she be, to know the thing unlearned,
What manner of man her couch's mate shall be.
But if we learn our lesson, if our lord
Dwell with us, plunging not against the yoke,
Happy our lot: if not—no help but death.
For the man, when at home they fret his soul,
Goes forth, and stays his loathing heart's disgust,
Unto a friend or age-mate turning him.

[1] Lit. "from their looks."
[2] Lit. "as being σεμνοί (reserved) when among strangers."
[3] Or, reading γιγνώσκειν—"For he, to know whom rightly was mine all."

We have but one, one heart to seek for comfort.
But we, say they, live an unperilled life
At home, while they do battle with the spear.
Falsely they deem: twice would I under shield
Stand, rather than bear childbirth peril once.
Yet thee and me the selfsame reasons touch not.
Thine is this city, thine a father's home;
Hast bliss of life and fellowship of friends.
But I, lone, cityless, and outraged thus
Of him who kidnapped me from foreign shores,
Mother nor brother have I, kinsman none,
For port of refuge from calamity.
Wherefore I fain would win of thee this boon:
If any path be found me, or device,
Whereby to avenge these wrongs upon mine husband,
On her who weds, on him who gives the bride,
Keep silence.   Woman quails at every peril,
Faint-heart to face the fray and look on steel;
But when in wedlock-rights she suffers wrong,
No spirit more bloodthirsty shall be found.
    Chorus. This will I; for 'tis just that thou, Medea,
Requite thy lord: no marvel thou dost grieve.
But I see Kreon, ruler of this land,
Advancing, herald of some new decree.

Enter KREON

    Kreon. Thee the black-lowering, wroth against thy lord,
Medea, bid I forth this land to fare
An exile, taking thy two sons with thee,
And make no tarrying: daysman of this cause
Am I, and homeward go I not again
Ere from the land's bounds I have cast thee forth.
    Medea. Ah me! undone am I in utter ruin!
My foes crowd sail pursuing: landing-place
Is none from surges of calamity.
Yet, howso wronged, one question will I ask—
For what cause, Kreon, dost thou banish me?

Kreon. I fear thee—need is none to cloak my words—
Lest on my child thou wreak some ill past cure.
And to this dread do many things conspire.
Wise art thou, cunning in much evil lore;
Chafed art thou, of thine husband's couch bereft:
I hear thou threatenest, so they bring me word,
To wreak on sire, on bridegroom, and on bride
Mischief. I guard mine head ere falls the blow.
Better be hated, woman, now of thee,
Than once relent, and sorely groan too late.

Medea. Not now first, Kreon—many a time ere now
Rumour hath wronged and wrought me grievous harm.
Ne'er should the man whose heart is sound of wit
Let teach his sons more wisdom than the herd.
They are burdened with unprofitable lore,
And spite and envy of other folk they earn.
For, if thou bring strange wisdom unto dullards,
Useless shalt thou be counted, and not wise:
And, grant thy name o'ertop the self-extolled
Wits, in the city odious shalt thou be.
Myself too in this fortune am partaker.
Of some my wisdom wins me jealousy,
Some count me idle; some, o'erbusy; some
Unsocial:—yet not over-wise am I.
And thou, thou fear'st me, lest I mar thy music.
Not such am I—O Kreon, dread not me—
That against princes I should dare transgress.
How hast thou wronged me? Thou hast given thy child
To whomso pleased thee. But—I hate mine husband:
And, doubtless, this in prudence hast thou done?
Nay, but I grudge not thy prosperity.
Wed ye, and prosper. But in this your land
Still let me dwell: for I, how wronged soe'er,
Will hold my peace, o'ermastered by the strong.

Kreon. Soft words to hear: but lurks mine heart
        within
Dread lest thou plottest mischief all the while;

And all the less I trust thee than before.
The vehement-hearted woman—yea, or man—
Is easier watched for than the silent-cunning.
But forth with all speed : plead me pleadings none.
For this is stablished : no device hast thou
To bide with us, who art a foe to me.

   Medea. Nay—by thy knees, and by the bride, thy
    child !

   Kreon. Thou wastest words ; thou never shalt prevail.

   Medea. Wilt drive me forth, respecting naught my
    prayers ?

   Kreon. Ay : more I love not thee than mine own
    house.

   Medea. Oh, how I call thee now to mind, my country !

   Kreon. Ay, dear to me is Corinth, next my children.

   Medea. Alas ! to mortals what a curse is love !

   Kreon. Blessing or curse, I trow, as fortune falls.

   Medea. Zeus, may the cause of this 'scape not thy ken !

   Kreon. Hence, passionate fool, and rid me of my
    trouble.

   Medea. Troubled am I, nor need I troubles new.

   Kreon. Soon shalt thou be by servants' hands thrust
    out.

   Medea. Nay—nay—not this, O Kreon, I beseech thee !

   Kreon. A coil thou wilt make, woman, as it seems.

   Medea. I will flee forth—not this the boon I crave.

   Kreon. Why restive then ?—why rid not Corinth of
    thee ?

   Medea. Suffer me yet to tarry this one day,
And somewhat for our exile to take thought,
And find my babes a refuge, since their sire
Cares naught to make provision for his sons.
Compassionate these : a father too art thou
Of children : meet it is thou show these grace.
Not for myself I fret, if I be banished :
For them in their calamity I mourn.

   Kreon. My spirit least of all is tyrannous.

Many a plan have my relentings marred:
And, woman, now I know I err herein,
Yet shalt thou win this boon. But I forewarn thee,
If thee the approaching Sun-god's torch behold
Within this country's confines with thy sons,
Thou diest—the word is said that shall not lie.
Now, if remain thou must, remain one day—
Too short for thee to do the deeds I dread.   [*Exit.*

Chorus. O hapless thou!
Woe's me for thy misery, woe for the trouble and anguish that meet thee!
Whitherward wilt thou turn thee?—what welcoming hand mid the strangers shall greet thee?
What home or what land to receive thee, deliverance from evils to give thee,
    Wilt thou find for thee now?
How mid surge of despair to o'erwhelm thee in ruin God's hand on thine helm
    Hath steered, O Medea, thy prow!

Medea. 'Tis ill done every way; who shall gainsay?
Yet nowise ill in this; deem not so yet.
Bridegroom and bride grim conflicts yet await;
Nor troubles light abide these marriage-makers.
Think'st thou that I had cringed to yon man ever,
Except to gain some gain, or work some wile?
Nor word nor touch of hand had I vouchsafed him.
But to such height of folly hath he come,
That, when he might forestall mine every plot
By banishment, this day of grace he grants me
To stay, wherein three foes will I lay dead,
The father, and the daughter, and mine husband.
And, having for them many paths of death,
Which first to take in hand I know not, friends;
Whether to set the bridal bower aflame,
Or through the heart to thrust the whetted knife,
Through yon halls stealing silent to their couch.

Yet one thing bars the way—if I be found
Crossing the threshold of the house and plotting,
Die shall I, and make mirth unto my foes.
Best the straight path, wherein my nature's cunning
Excels, by poisons to destroy them—yea.
Now, grant them dead: what city will receive me,
What host vouchsafe a land of refuge, home
Secure, and from the avenger shield my life?
There is none.　Tarrying then a little space,
If any tower of safety shall appear,
These deaths by guile and silence will I compass;
But if misfortune drive me desperate forth,
Myself will grip the sword—yea, though I die—
And slay, and dare the strong hand's reckless deed:
For, by the Queen of Night, whom I revere
Above all, and for fellow-worker chose,
Hekate, dweller by mine hearth's dark shrine,
Not one shall vex my soul, and rue it not.
Bitter and woeful bridal will I give them,
Bitter troth-plight and banishing of me.
Up, then!—spare naught of all thy sorcery-lore,
Medea, of thy plotting and contriving;
On to the dread deed!　Now is need of daring.
Look on my wrongs: thou must not make derision
For sons of Sisyphus, for Jason's bride—
Thou, sprung from royal father, from the Sun!
Thou know'st means.　Yea, our woman-nature 'tis—
Say they—to be most helpless for all good,
But fashioners most cunning of all ill.

CHORUS.　*Strophe 1*

Upward aback to their fountains the sacred rivers are
　　　stealing;
　Justice is turned to injustice, the order of old to con-
　　　fusion:
The thoughts of the hearts of men are treachery wholly,
　　　and reeling

From its ancient foundations, the faith of the gods is
become a delusion.
Changes—and changes!—the voice of the people shall
crown me with honour:
My life shall be sunlit with glory; for woman the old-
time story
Is ended, the slanders hoary no more shall as chains be
upon her.

Antistrophe 1

And the strains of the singers of old generations for
shame shall falter,
Which sang evermore of the treason of woman, her
faithlessness ever.
Alas, that our lips are not touched with the fire of song
from the altar
Of Phœbus, the Harper-king, of the inspiration-giver!
Else had I lifted my voice in challenge of song high-
ringing
Unto men: for the roll of the ages shall find for the
poet-sages
Proud woman-themes for their pages, heroines worthy
their singing.

Strophe 2

But thou from the ancient home didst sail over leagues
of foam,
On-sped by a frenzied heart, and the sea-gates sawest
dispart,
The Twin Rocks. Now, in the land
Of the stranger, thy doom is to waken
To a widowed couch, and forsaken
Of thy lord, and woe-overtaken,
To be cast forth shamed and banned.

Antistrophe 2

Disannulled is the spell of the oath: no shame for the
broken troth

17

In Hellas the wide doth remain, but heavenward its
    flight hath it ta'en.
        No home of a father hast thou
            For thine haven when trouble-storms lower.
            Usurped is thy bridal bower
            Of another, in pride of her power,
        Ill-starred, overqueening thee now.

Enter JASON

    Jason. Not now first, nay, but ofttimes have I marked
What desperate mischief is a froward spirit.
For in this land, this home, when thou might'st stay
Bearing unfractiously thy rulers' pleasure,
Banished thou art for wild and whirling words.
Me they vex not—cease never, an thou wilt,
Clamouring, " Jason is of men most base! "
But, for thy words against thy rulers' spoken,
Count it all gain—mere exile punishing thee.
For me—still strove I to appease the wrath
Of kings incensed : fain would I thou shouldst stay.
But thou rein'st not thy folly, speaking still
Evil of dignities; art therefore banished.
Yet, for all this, not wearied of my friends,
With so much forethought come I for thee, lady,
That, banished with thy babes, thou lack not gold,
Nor aught beside.   Full many an ill is brought
In exile's train.   Yea, though thou hatest me,
Ne'er can I harbour evil thought of thee.
    Medea. Caitiff of caitiffs !—blackest of reproaches
My tongue for thine unmanliness can frame—
Thou com'st to me—thou com'st, most hateful proved
To Heaven, to me, to all the race of men !
This is not daring, no, nor courage this,
To wrong thy friends, and blench not from their eyes,
But, of all plagues infecting men, the worst,
Even shamelessness.   And yet 'tis well thou cam'st,
For I shall ease the burden of mine heart

Reviling thee, and thou be galled to hear.
And with the first things first will I begin.
I saved thee, as they know, what Greeks soe'er
Entered with thee the selfsame Argo's hull,
Thee, sent to quell the flame-outbreathing bulls
With yoke-bands, and to sow the tilth of death.
The dragon, warder of the Fleece of Gold,
That sleepless kept it with his manifold coils,
I slew, and raised deliverance-light for thee.
Myself forsook my father and mine home,
And to Iolkos under Pelion came
With thee, more zealous in thy cause than wise,
And Pelias slew by his own children's hands—
Of all deaths worst—so cast out all thy ¹ fear.
And thus of me, basest of men, entreated,
For a new bride hast thou forsaken me,
Though I had borne thee children. Wert thou childless,
Not past forgiving were this marriage-craving.
But faith of oaths hath vanished. I know not
Whether thou deem'st the olden gods yet rule,
Or that new laws are now ordained for men ;
For thine heart speaks thee unto me forsworn.
Out on this right hand, which thou oft wouldst clasp—
These knees !—how vainly have we been embraced
By a base man, thus frustrate of our hopes !
Come, as a friend will I commune with thee—
Yet what fair dealing should I hope from thee ?—
Yet will I : questioned, baser shalt thou show.
Now, whither turn I ?—to my father's house,
Which, with my country, I for thee cast off ?
To Pelias' hapless daughters ?—Graciously
Their father's slayer would they welcome home !
For thus it is : a foe am I become
To mine own house. Whom I should ne'er have harmed,
For grace to thee I made mine enemies.
So then midst Hellas' daughters hast thou made me

¹ Or "Yea, cast out all their fear."

Blest in return for all : in thee have I—
O wretched I !—a wondrous spouse and leal,[1]
If from the land cast forth I pass to exile
Forlorn of friends, alone with children lone.
A proud reproach for our new bridegroom this—
In poverty thy babes, thy saviour, wander !
O Zeus, ah, wherefore hast thou given to men
Plain signs for gold which is but counterfeit,
But no assay-mark Nature-graven shows
On man's form, to discern the base withal?

    Chorus. Awful is wrath, and past all balm of healing,
When they that once loved clash in feud of hate.

    Jason. Needs must I be not ill at speech, meseems,
But, like the careful helmsman of a ship,
With close-reefed canvas run before the gale,
Woman, of thy tempestuous-railing tongue.
I—for thy kindness tower-high thou pilest—
Deem Kypris saviour of my voyaging,
Her, and none other or of gods or men.
A subtle wit thou hast—what need to force me
To tell the tale how Love, by strong compulsion
Of shafts unerring, made thee save my life?
Yet take I not account too strict thereof ;
For, in that thou didst save me, thou didst well.
Howbeit, more hast thou received than given
Of this my safety, as my words shall prove :—
First, then, in Hellas dwell'st thou, in the stead
Of land barbaric, knowest justice, learnest
To live by law without respect of force.
And all the Greeks have heard thy wisdom's fame.
Renown is thine : but if on earth's far bourn
Thou dwelledst yet, thou hadst not lived in story.
Now mine be neither gold-mine halls within,
Nor sweeter song be mine than Orpheus sang,
If my fair fortune be to fame unknown.

    [1] Or, reading κἄπιστον, " Woe's me !—a marvellous spouse beyond
belief."

No whit will I receive, nor offer thou.
No profit is there in a villain's gifts.
  Jason. In any wise I call the gods to witness
That all help would I give thee and thy sons;
But thy good likes thee not: thy stubborn pride
Spurns friends: I the more thy grief shall therefore be.
  Medea. Away!—impatience for the bride new-trapped
Consumes thee while thou loiterest at the doors!
Wed: for perchance—and God shall speed the word—
Thine shall be bridal thou wouldst fain renounce.

[Exit JASON.

CHORUS.   Strophe 1

Love bringeth nor glory nor honour to men when it
    cometh restraining
Not its unscanted excess; but if Kypris, in measure raining
  Her joy, cometh down, there is none other goddess so
      winsome as she.
Not upon me, O queen, do thou aim from thy bow all-
    golden
  The arrow desire-envenomed that none may avoid—
    not on me!

Antistrophe 1

But let Temperance shield[1] me, the fairest of gifts of the
    gods ever-living:
Nor ever with passion of jarring contention, nor feuds
    unforgiving,
  In her terrors may Love's Queen visit me, smiting with
      maddened unrest
For a couch mismated my soul; but the peace of the
    bride-bed be holden
  In honour of her, and her keen eyes choose for us bonds
      that be best.

Strophe 2

O fatherland, O mine home,
Not mine be the exile's doom!

---

[1] στέγοι (Verrall), vice manuscript στέργοι, "befriend."

Into poverty's pathways hard to be trod may my feet not
        be guided !
                Most piteous anguish were this.
By death—oh, by death ere then may the conflict of life
        be decided,
Ended be life's little day! To be thus from the home-
        land divided—
                No pang more bitter there is.

Antistrophe 2

            We have seen, and it needeth naught
            That of others herein we be taught:
For thee not a city, for thee not a friend hath compas-
        sionated
                When affliction most awful is thine.
But he, who regardeth not friends, accursed may he perish,
        and hated,
Who opes not his heart with sincerity's key to the hapless-
        fated—
                Never such shall be friend of mine!

Enter AIGEUS.

Aigeus. Medea, hail!—for fairer greeting-word
None knoweth to accost his friends withal.
        Medea. All hail thou also, wise Pandion's son,
Aigeus. Whence art thou journeying through this land?
        Aigeus. Leaving the ancient oracle of Phœbus.
        Medea. Why didst thou fare to earth's prophetic navel?
        Aigeus. To ask how seed of children might be mine.
        Medea. 'Fore Heaven !—aye childless is thy life till
        now ?
        Aigeus. Childless I am, by chance of some god's will.
        Medea. This, with a wife, or knowing not the couch ?
        Aigeus. Nay, not unyoked to wedlock's bed am I.
        Medea. Now what to thee spake Phœbus touching issue ?
        Aigeus. Deep words of wisdom not for man to inter-
        pret.

Medea. Without sin might I know the god's reply?

Aigeus. O yea—good sooth, it needs the wise heart most.

Medea. What said he? Say, if sin be not to hear.

Aigeus. The wine-skin's prominent foot I should not loose.

Medea. Till thou shouldst do what thing, or reach what land?

Aigeus. Till to the hearth ancestral back I came.

Medea. And thou, what wouldst thou sailing to this shore?

Aigeus. There is one Pittheus, King of Trœzen he—

Medea. A man most pious, Pelops' son, they say.

Aigeus. To him the god's response I fain would tell.

Medea. Yea—a wise man, and having skill herein.

Aigeus. Yea, and my best-belovèd spear-ally.

Medea. Now prosper thou, and win thine heart's desire.

Aigeus. Why droops thine eye?—why this wan-wasted hue?

Medea. Aigeus, of all men basest is mine husband.

Aigeus. What say'st thou? Clearly tell me thine heart's pain.

Medea. He wrongs me—Jason, nothing wronged of me.

Aigeus. What hath he done? More plainly tell it out.

Medea. Another wife he takes, his household's mistress.

Aigeus. Ha! hath he dared in truth this basest deed?

Medea. Yea: I am now dishonoured, once beloved.

Aigeus. Another love was this?—or hate of thee?

Medea. Love?—yea, of the highest—traitor he to love!

Aigeus. Away with him, if he be base as this!

Medea. His love was for affinity with princes.

Aigeus. Who giveth him his daughter? End the tale.

Medea. Kreon, who ruleth this Corinthian land.

Aigeus. Sooth, lady, reason was that thou shouldst
    grieve.
Medea. 'Tis death to me! Yea, also am I banished.
Aigeus. Of whom? A new ill this thou namest is.[1]
Medea. Kreon from Corinth driveth me an exile.
Aigeus. Doth Jason suffer this?—I praise it not.
Medea. In pretence, no: but to stand firm—not he!
But I beseech thee, touching this thy beard,
Clasping thy knees, and so become thy suppliant—
Pity, O pity me the evil-starred,
And see me not cast forth to homelessness:
Receive to a hearth-place in thy land and homes.
So by Heaven's blessing fruitful be thy love
In children, and in death thyself be blest.
Thou know'st not what good fortune thou hast found:
For I will end thy childlessness, will cause
Thy seed to grow to sons; such drugs I know.
    Aigeus. For many causes am I minded, lady,
This grace to grant thee: for the gods' sake first;
Then, for the seed of children thou dost promise;
For herein wholly extinct is Aigeus' name.
But thus it is—if to my land thou come,
I thy defence essay, in bounds of justice.
Howbeit of this do I forewarn thee, lady,
From this land will I not consent to lead thee.
But if thou reachest of thyself mine homes,
Safe shalt thou bide: to no man will I yield thee.
But from this land thou must thyself escape;
For blameless will I be to allies too.
    Medea. So be it. Yet, were oath-pledge given for this
To me, then had I all I would of thee.
    Aigeus. Ha! dost not trust me?—or at what dost
    stumble?
    Medea. I trust thee: but my foes are Pelias' house
And Kreon. Oath-bound, thou couldst never yield me

---

[1] Or, "Another's crime thou namest now," reading ἄλλου vice ἄλλο
(Verrall).

To these, when they would drag me from the land.
Hadst thou but promised, to the gods unpledged,[1]
Thou mightest turn their friend, might'st lightly yield
To herald-summons.   Strengthless is my cause:
Wealth is on their side, and a princely house.

Aigeus. Foresight exceeding, lady, in thy words![2]
Yet, if this be thy will, I draw not back;
Since for myself is this the safest course,
To have a plea to show unto thy foes;
And surer is thy part.   The Oath-gods name.

Medea. Swear by Earth's plain, and by my father's father
The Sun, and join the gods' whole race thereto.

Aigeus. That I will do or not do—what?   Say on.

Medea. That from thy land thyself wilt never cast me,
Nor, if a foe of mine would hale me thence,
Wilt, while thou liv'st, consenting yield me up.

Aigeus. By Earth, the Sun's pure majesty, and all
The Gods, I swear to abide by this thou hast said.

Medea. Enough.   For broken troth what penalty?

Aigeus. Whatso befalleth god-despising men.

Medea. Pass on thy way rejoicing: all is well.
I too will come with all speed to thy burg,
When mine intent is wrought, my wish attained.

[*Exit* AIGEUS.

Chorus. Now the Scion of Maia, the Wayfarer's King,
Bring thee safe to thine home, and the dream of thine
      heart,
The·sweet visions that wing thy feet, mayst thou bring
To accomplishment, Aigeus, for now this thing
      Hath taught me how noble thou art.

Medea. Zeus, Justice child of Zeus, and Light of the Sun,
Over my foes triumphant now, my friends,
Shall we become: our feet are on the path.
Now is there hope of vengeance on my foes.
For this man, there where lay my chiefest weakness,

[1] Reading ἀνώμοτος (737) and τάχ' (739).
[2] v.l. προθυμίαν: " Much eagerness to help thy words imply!" (ironical).

Hath for my plots a haven in storm appeared.
To him my bark's stern-hawser make I fast,
To Pallas' burg and fortress when I go.
And all my plots to thee now will I tell;
Nor look I that my words should pleasure thee—
One of mine household will I send to Jason,
And will entreat him to my sight to come;
And soft words, when he cometh, will I speak,
Saying, ".Thy will is mine," and, " It is well."
How that his royal marriage, my betrayal,
Is our advantage, and right well devised.
I will petition that my sons may stay—
Not for that I would leave on hostile soil
Children of mine for foes to trample on,
But the king's daughter so by guile to slay.
For I will send them bearing gifts in hand
Unto the bride, that they may not be banished,
A robe fine-spun, a golden diadem.
If she receive and don mine ornaments,
Die shall she wretchedly, and all who touch her,
With drugs so dread will I anoint my gifts.
Howbeit here I pass this story by,
And wail the deed that yet for me remains
To bring to pass; for I will slay my children,
Yea, mine: no man shall pluck them from mine hand.
Then, having brought all Jason's house to wrack,
I leave the land, fleeing my dear babes' blood,
And having dared a deed most impious.
For unendurable are mocks of foes.
Let all go: what is life to me? Nor country
Nor home have I, nor refuge from mine ills.
Then erred I, in the day when I forsook
My father's halls, by yon Greek's words beguiled,
Who with God's help shall render me requital.
For never living shall he see hereafter
The sons I bare him, nor shall he beget
Of his new bride a son, for doomed is she,

Wretch, to die wretchedly by drugs of mine.
Let none account me impotent, nor weak,
Nor meek of spirit!—Nay, in other sort,
Grim to my foes, and kindly to my friends,
For of such is the life most glorious.
    Chorus. Since thou hast made me partner of this tale—
Wishing to help thee, championing withal
The laws of men, I say, do thou not this.
    Medea. It can not be but so: yet reason is
That thou say this, who art not wronged as I.
    Chorus. Woman, wilt have the heart to slay thy sons?
    Medea. Yea: so mine husband's heart shall most be
      wrung.
    Chorus. But thou of wives most wretched shouldst
      become.
    Medea. So be it: wasted are all hindering words.
But ho! [*to the* NURSE] go thou and Jason bring to me—
Thou whom I use for every deed of trust.
And look thou tell none aught of mine intent,
If thine is loyal service, thou a woman.
                         [*Exit* MEDEA *and* NURSE.

CHORUS. *Strophe 1*

Oh, happy the race in the ages olden
    Of Erechtheus, the seed of the blest gods' line,
In a land unravaged, peace-enfolden,
    Aye quaffing of Wisdom's glorious wine,
Ever through air clear-shining brightly
As on wings uplifted pacing lightly,
Where they tell how Harmonia of tresses golden
    Bare the Pierid Muses, the stainless Nine.

Antistrophe 1

And the streams of Cephisus the lovely-flowing
    They tell how the Lady of Cyprus drew,
And in zephyr-wafts of the winds sweet-blowing
    Breathed far over the land their dew.

And she sendeth her Loves which, throned in glory
By Wisdom, fashion all virtue's story,
Over her tresses throwing, throwing,
    Roses in odorous wreaths aye new.

Re-enter MEDEA.

Strophe 2

How then should the hallowed city,
    The city of sacred waters,
        Which shields with her guardian hand
        All friends that would fare through her land,
        Receive a murderess banned,
Who had slaughtered her babes without pity,
    A pollution amidst of her daughters?

In thine heart's thoughts set it before thee—
    To murder the fruit of thy womb!
        O think what it meaneth to slay
        Thy sons—what a deed this day
        Thou wouldst do!—By thy knees we pray,
By heaven and earth we implore thee,
    Deal not to thy babes such a doom!

Antistrophe 2

O whence, and O whence wilt thou gain thee
    Such desperate hardihood
        That for spirit so fiendish shall serve,
        That shall strengthen thine heart, that shall nerve
        Thine hand, that it shall not swerve
From the ruthless deed that shall stain thee
    With horror of children's blood?

O how, when thine eyes thou art turning
    On thy little ones, wilt thou refrain
        The motherhood in thee, to feel
        No upwelling of tears?—Canst thou steel
        Thy breast when thy children kneel,

To crimson thine hand, with unyearning
Heart for thy darlings slain?

Enter JASON

Jason. Summoned I come : for, though thou be my foe,
This grace thou shalt not miss ; but I will hear
What new thing, lady, thou dost wish of me.
Medea. Jason, I ask thee to forgive the words
Late-spoken, and to bear with that my mood :
Well mayst thou, for remembrance of old loves.
Now have I called myself to account, and railed
Upon myself : " Wretch, wherefore am I mad?
And wherefore rage against good counsellors,
And am at feud with rulers of the land,
And with my lord, who works my veriest good,
Wedding a royal house, to raise up brethren
Unto my sons?   Shall I not cease from wrath?
What aileth me, when the gods proffer boons?
Have I not children?   Know I not that we
Are exiles from our own land, lacking friends?"
Thus musing, was I 'ware that I had nursed
Folly exceeding, anger without cause.
Now then I praise thee ; wise thou seem'st to me
In gaining us this kinship, senseless I,
Who in these counsels should have been thine ally,
Have furthered all, have decked the bridal couch,
And joyed to minister unto the bride.
But we are—women : needs not harsher word.
Yet evil shouldst thou not for evil render,
Nor pit against my folly folly of thine.
I yield, confessing mine unwisdom then,
But unto better counsels now am come.—
Children, my children, hither : leave the house.

Enter CHILDREN

Come forth, salute your father, and with me
Bid him farewell : be reconciled to friends

Ye, with your mother, from the hate o'erpast.
Truce is between us, rancour hath given place.
Clasp ye his right hand.—Woe for ambushed ills!
I am haunted by the shadow of hidden things!
Ah, children, will ye thus, through many a year
Living, still reach him loving arms? Ah me,
How swift to weep am I, how full of fear!
Feuds with your father ended—ah, so late!—
Have filled with tears these soft-relenting eyes.

    Chorus. And from mine eyes start tears of pale dismay.
Ah, may no evil worse than this befall!

    Jason. Lady, I praise this mood, yet blame not that:
'Tis nothing strange that womankind should rage
When the spouse trafficketh in alien marriage.
But now to better thoughts thine heart hath turned,
And thou, though late, upon the victor side
Hast voted: a wise woman's deed is this.—
And for you, children, not unheedfully
Your sire hath ta'en much forethought, so help Heaven.
For ye, I ween, in this Corinthian land
Shall with your brethren stand the foremost yet.
Grow ye in strength: the rest shall by your sire,
And whatso God is gracious, be wrought out.
You may I see to goodly stature grown,
In manhood's prime, triumphant o'er my foes.
Thou, why bedew'st thou with wan tears thine eyes,
Turning aback from them thy pallid cheek,
And dost not hear with gladness this my speech?

    Medea. 'Tis naught: but o'er these children broods
      mine heart.

    Jason. Fear not: all will I order well for them.

    Medea. This will I: 'Tis not I mistrust thy words;
But woman is but woman—born for tears.

    Jason. Why, helpless one, dost make moan over these?

    Medea. I bare them. When thou prayedst life for
      them,
Pity stole o'er me, whispering, "Shall this be?"

But that for which thou cam'st to speech of me
In part is said; to speak the rest is mine:[1]
Since the king pleaseth forth the land to send me,
For me too this is best—I know it well—
That I bide not, a stumbling-block to thee
And the land's lords, whose house's foe I seem,
So fare I forth to exile from this land.
But, that my sons by thine hand may be reared,
Entreat thou Kreon that they be not banished.

Jason. Prevail I may not, yet must I essay.

Medea. Nay then, thy bride bid thou to pray her sire
That thy sons be not banished from this land.

Jason. Yea, surely; and, I trow, her shall I win,
If of her sister women she is one.

Medea. I too will bear a part in thine endeavour;
For I will send her gifts unmatched for beauty
Of all that men see now, I know, by far,
A robe fine-spun, a golden diadem;
Our sons to bear them. Now must an attendant
With all speed hither bring the ornaments.
Blessings shall hers be, not one, but untold,
Who winneth thee for lord, a peerless spouse,
Who owneth ornaments which once the Sun,
My father's father, gave unto his offspring!—
Take in your hands, my sons, these bridal gifts,
And to the happy princess-bride bear ye
And give: with gifts shall she be satisfied.

Jason. But, fond one, why make void thine hands of
these?
Deem'st thou a royal house hath lack of robes,
Or gold, deem'st thou? Keep these and give them not.
For, if my wife esteems me aught, my wish
Will she prefer to treasures, well I wot.

---

[1] Verrall here says, "There is no apparent reason for the emphatic pronoun" (ἐγώ). Is it not that the object of the interview was twofold, first, to ask Jason's pardon—that had now been spoken by him; secondly, to introduce a proposal of her own, involving independent action on her part?

Medea. Nay, speak not so : gifts sway the gods, they
  say.
Gold weigheth more with men than words untold.
Hers fortune is; God favoureth now her cause;
Young is her power. Life would I give for ransom
Of my sons' banishment, not gold alone.—
Now, children, enter ye the halls of wealth.
Unto your sire's new wife, my lady-queen,
Make supplication, pray ye be not exiled,
Giving mine ornaments. Most importeth this,
That she into her hands receive my gifts.
Haste ye, and to your mother bring glad tidings
Of good success in that she longs to win.

  [*Exeunt* JASON *and* CHILDREN.

CHORUS. *Strophe 1*

Now for the life of the children mine hope hath been
  turned to despairing.
No hope any more! On the slaughterward path even
  now are they faring!
The bride shall receive it, the diadem-garland that beareth
  enfolden
    Doom for the hapless mid glittering sheen:
And to set the adorning of Hades about her tresses golden
    She shall take it her hands between.

Antistrophe 1

For its glamour of beauty, its splendour unearthly, shall
  swiftly persuade her
To bedeck her with robe and with gold-wrought crown:
  she shall soon have arrayed her
In attire as a bride in the presence of phantoms from
  Hades uprisen;
    In such dread gin shall her feet be ta'en:
In the weird of death shall the hapless be whelmed, and
  from doom's dark prison
    Shall she steal forth never again.

Strophe 2

And thou, wretch, bridegroom accursed, who art fain of a
   princely alliance,
        Blasting thou bringest—unknowing, unthink-
          ing!—
Of life on thy sons, and thy bride shall to foul death plight
   her affiance.
        How far from thy fortune of old art thou
          sinking!

Antistrophe 2

And amid my lamentings I mourn for thine anguish, O
   hapless mother
        Of children, who makest thee ready to slaugh-
          ter
Thy babes, to avenge thee on him who would lawlessly
   wed with another,
        Would forsake thee to dwell with a prince's
          daughter.

Enter CHILDREN'S GUARDIAN, *with* CHILDREN

Children's Guardian. Mistress, remission for thy sons
   of exile!
Thy gift the princess-bride with joy received
In hand; and there is peace unto thy sons.
   Medea. Alas!
   Children's Guardian. Why dost thou stand confounded
   mid good hap?
Now wherefore turnest thou thy face away,
And dost not hear with gladness this my speech?
   Medea. Woe's me!
   Children's Guardian. This cry is to the tidings not
   attuned.
   Medea. Woe yet again!
   Children's Guardian.   Can I have brought ill hap
Unwitting—erred in deeming these glad tidings?
   Medea. As they are, are thy tidings: thee I blame not.

Children's Guardian. Why down-drooped is thine eye?
    Why flow thy tears?
Medea. Needs must they, ancient; for these things the
    gods
And I withal—O fool!—have ill contrived.
Children's Guardian. Fear not: thy children yet shall
    bring thee home.
Medea. Others ere then shall wretched I send home.
Children's Guardian. Not thou alone art severed from
    thy sons.
Submissively must mortals bear mischance.
    Medea. This will I: but within the house go thou,
And for my children's daily needs prepare.
                        [*Exit* CHILDREN'S GUARDIAN.
O children, children, yours a city is,
And yours a home, where, leaving wretched me,
Dwell shall ye, of your mother aye bereft.
I shall go exiled to another land,
Ere I have joyed in you, have seen your bliss,
Ere I have decked for you the couch, the bride,
The bridal bower, and held the torch on high.
O me accursed in this my ruthless mood!
For naught, for naught, my babes, I nurtured you,
And all for naught I laboured, travail-worn,
Bearing sharp anguish in your hour of birth.
Ah for the hopes—unhappy!—all mine hopes
Of ministering hands about mine age,
Of dying folded round with loving arms,
All men's desire!   But now—'tis past—'tis past,
That sweet imagining!   Forlorn of you
A bitter life and woeful shall I waste.
Your mother never more with loving eyes
Shall ye behold, passed to another life.
Woe! woe! why gaze your eyes on me, my darlings?
Why smile to me the latest smile of all?
Alas! what shall I do?—Mine heart is failing
As I behold my children's laughing eyes!

Women, I can not! farewell, purposes
O'erpast! I take my children from the land.
What need to wring the father's heart with ills
Of these, to gain myself ills twice so many?
Not I, not I!—Ye purposes, farewell!
Yet—yet—what ails me? Would I earn derision,
Letting my foes slip from mine hand unpunished?
I must dare this. Out on my coward mood
That from mine heart let loose relenting words!
Children, pass ye within.   [*Exeunt* CHILDREN.
               Now, whoso may not
Sinless be present at my sacrifice,
On his head be it: mine hand faltereth not.
Oh! oh!
O heart, mine heart, do not—do not this deed!
Let them be, wretched heart, spare thou thy babes!
There dwelling with me shall they gladden thee.—
No!—by the nether fiends that dwell with Hades,
Never shall this betide, that I will leave
My children for my foes to trample on.
They needs must die. And, since it needs must be,
Even I will slay them—I, who gave them life.
All this is utter doom—she shall not 'scape!
Yea, on her head the wreath is; in my robes
The princess-bride is perishing—I know it.
But—for I fare on journey most unhappy,
And shall speed these on yet unhappier—
I would speak to my sons.
          Re-enter CHILDREN
              Give, O my babes,
Give to your mother the right hand to kiss.
O dearest hand, O lips most dear to me,
O form and noble feature of my children,
Blessing be on you—there!—for all things here
Your sire hath reft. O sweet, O sweet embrace!
O children's rose-leaf skin, O balmy breath!
Away, away! Strength faileth me to gaze

On you, but I am overcome of evil. [*Exeunt* CHILDREN.
Now, now, I learn what horrors I intend :.
But passion overmastereth sober thought :
And this is cause of direst ills to men.

CHORUS

I

Full oft ere this my soul hath scaled
    Lone heights of thought, empyreal steeps,
    Or plunged far down the darkling deeps,
Where woman's feebler heart hath failed.

Yet wherefore failed? Should woman find
    No inspiration thrill her breast,
    Nor welcome ever that sweet guest
Of Song, that uttereth Wisdom's mind?

Alas! not all! Few, few are they—
    Perchance amid a thousand one
    Thou shouldest find—for whom the sun
Of poesy makes an inner day.

II

Now this I say—calm bliss, that ne'er
    Knew love's wild fever of the blood,
    The pains, the joys, of motherhood,
Passeth all parents' joy-blent care.

The childless, they that never prove
    If sunshine comes, or cloud, to men
    With babes, far lie beyond their ken
The toils, the griefs, of parent-love.

But they whose halls with laughter sweet
    Of children ring—I mark them aye
    Care-fretted, travailing alway
To win their loved ones nurture meet.

III

One toils with love more strong than death:
  Yet—yet—who knoweth whether he
  A wise man or a fool shall be
To whom he shall his wealth bequeath?

But last, but worst, remains to tell:
  For though ye get you wealth enow,
  And though your sons to manhood grow,
Fair sons and good—if Death the fell,

To Hades vanishing, bears down
  Your children's lives, what profit is
  That Heaven hath laid, with all else, this
Upon mankind, this sorrow's crown?

Medea. Friends, long have I, abiding Fortune's hap,
Expected what from yonder shall befall.
And lo! a man I see of Jason's train
Hitherward coming, and my eager heart
Foretelleth him the herald of new ills.

Enter MESSENGER

Messenger. O thou who hast wrought an awful deed
    and lawless,
Flee, O Medea, flee, nor once leave thou
The sea-wain, or the car that scours the plain.
Medea. Now what hath happed that calleth for such
    flight?
Messenger. Dead is the princess even now, and dead
Kreon her father, by thy poison-drugs.
Medea. A glorious tale thou tellest: thou henceforth
Art of my benefactors and my friends.
Messenger. What say'st?—Of sound mind art thou, and
    not mad?
Who, hearing of the havoc of the hearth
Of kings, art glad, and hast no fear for this?
Medea. Oh, yea; I too with words of controversy

Could answer thee—yet be not hasty, friend,
But tell how died they : thou shouldst gladden me
Doubly, if these most horribly have perished.

    Messenger. When, with their father, came thy children
        twain,
And passed into the halls for marriage decked,
Glad were we thralls who sorrowed for thy woes.
And straightway buzzed from ear to ear the tale
Of truce to old feuds 'twixt thy lord and thee.
The hand one kisseth, one the golden head
Of those thy sons : myself by joy on-drawn
Followed thy children to the women's bowers.
Now she which had our worship in thy stead,
Ere she beheld thy chariot-yoke of sons,
Aye upon Jason turned her yearning gaze.
But then her veil before her eyes she cast,
And swept aback the scorn of her white neck,
Loathing thy sons' approach : but now thy lord,
To turn the maiden's wrath and spite aside,
Thus spake : " Nay, be not hostile to thy friends :
Cease from thine anger, turn thine head again,
Accounting friends whomso thy spouse accounts.
Their gifts receive, and plead thou with thy sire
To pardon these their exile—for my sake."
She, when she saw the attire, could not refrain,
But yielded her lord all.   And ere their father
Far from her bower with those thy sons had gone,
She took the rich-wrought robes and clad herself,
Circling her ringlets with the golden crown,
And by a shining mirror ranged her tresses,
Smiling at her own phantom image there.
Then, rising from her seat, she paced adown
The halls with mincing tread of ivory feet,
Exulting in the gifts, and oftentimes
Sweeping her glance from neck to ankle-hem.
But then was there a fearful sight to see.
Suddenly changed her colour : reeling back

With trembling limbs she goes; and scarce in time
Drops on the couch to fall not on the ground.
Then a gray handmaid, deeming peradventure
That frenzy was of Pan or some god sent,
Raised the prayer-cry, before she saw the foam
White-frothing from her lips, or marked how rolled
Her eyeballs, and her face's bloodless hue.
Then a scream, unaccordant, long and loud,
She shrilled forth. Straight to her father's chambers one
Darted, and one unto her new-made spouse,
To tell the bride's mischance: and all the roof
Echoed with multitudinous-hurrying feet.
And a swift athlete's straining limbs had won
By this the goal of the six-plethra course:
Then she from trance all speechless of closed eyes
Awoke—ah, wretch!—with horrible-shrilling shriek:
For like two charging hosts her agony came—
The golden coil about her head that lay
'Gan spurt a marvellous stream of ravening fire;
While the fine robes, the gift thy children brought,
Devoured the white flesh of the unhappy one.
Upstarting from her seat she flees, all flame,
Shaking her hair, her head, this way and that,
To cast from her the crown; but firmly fixed
The gold held fast its clasp: the fire, whene'er
She shook her locks, with doubled fury blazed.
Then misery-vanquished falls she on the floor,
Past recognising, save for a father, marred.
No more was seen her eyes' imperial calm,
No more her comely features; but the gore
Dripped from her head's crown flecked with blended fire.
The flesh-flakes from her bones, like the pine's tears,
'Neath that mysterious drug's devourings melted—
Dread sight—and came on all folk fear to touch
The corpse: her hideous fate had we for warning.
But, ignorant of all, her wretched sire,
Suddenly entering, falls upon her corpse,

And straightway wailed and clasped the body round,
And kissed it, crying: "Oh, my hapless child,
What god thus horribly hath thee destroyed?
Who maketh this old sepulchre bereft
Of thee? Ah me, would I might die with thee!"
But, when from wailing and from moans he ceased,
Fain would he have upraised his agèd frame,
Yet clave, as ivy clings to laurel boughs,
To those fine robes: then was a ghastly wrestling:
For, while he laboured to upraise his knee,
She strained against him: if by force he haled,
Then from the bones he tare his agèd flesh.
At last refrained he, and gave up the ghost,
Ill-starred, who could no more withstand his bane.
There lie the corpses, child by agèd sire
Clasped—such affliction tears, not words, must mourn.
And of thy part no word be said by me—
Thyself from punishment wilt find escape.
But man's lot now, as oft, I count a shadow,
Nor fear to say that such as seem to be
Wise among men and cunning in speech-lore,
Even these are chargeable with deepest folly;
For among mortals happy man is none.
In Fortune's flood-tide might a man become
More prosperous than his neighbour: happy?—no!

[Exit.

Chorus. Meseems the gods with many an ill this day
Will compass Jason—yea, and rightfully.
But O the pity of thy calamity,
Daughter of Kreon, who to Hades' halls
Hast passed, because with thee would Jason wed!
Medea. Friends, my resolve is taken, with all speed
To slay my children, and to flee this land,
And not to linger and to yield my sons
To death by other hands more merciless.
They needs must die: and, since it needs must be,
Even I will give them death, who gave them life.

MEDEA.

Photogravure from a painting by Nathanael Sichel.

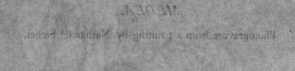

Up, gird thee for the fray, mine heart! Why loiter
To do the dread ill deeds that must be done?
Come, wretched hand of mine, grasp thou the sword;
Grasp it—move toward life's bitter starting-post,
And turn not craven: think not on thy babes,
How dear they are, how thou didst bear them: nay,
For this short day do thou forget thy sons,
Thereafter mourn them.   For, although thou slay,
Yet dear they are, and I a wretched woman.

                                    [*Exit* MEDEA.

CHORUS.   *Strophe*

O Earth, O all-revealing splendour
    Of the Sun, look down on a woman accurst,
    Or ever she slake the murder-thirst
Of a mother whose hands would smite the tender
                    Fruit of her womb.
Look down, for she sprang of thy lineage golden,
And by terror of men is the gods' seed holden [1]
                    And the shadow of doom.
But thou, O heaven-begotten glory,
Restrain her, refrain her: the wretched, the gory
Erinnys by demons dogged, we implore thee,
                    Cast forth of the home!

Antistrophe

For naught was the childbirth-travail wasted;
    For naught didst thou bear them, the near and the
                    dear,
    O thou who hast fled through the Pass of Fear,
From the dark-blue Clashing Crags who hast hasted,
                    Speeding thy flight!
Alas for her!—wherefore hath grim Wrath stirred her
Through depths of her soul, that ruthless murder
                    Her wrongs must requite?
For stern upon mortals the vengeance falleth
For kin's blood spilt; from the earth it calleth,

                    [1] Conjecturing πίτνει for manuscript πίτνειν.

A voice from the gods, and the slayers appalleth
On whose homes it shall light.

[*Children's cries behind the scenes.*]

Child 1. What shall I do?—How flee my mother's hands?

Child 2. I know not, dearest brother. Death is here!

Chorus. Ah, the cry!—dost thou hear it?—the children's cry!

Wretch!—woman of cursèd destiny!

Shall I enter?—My heart crieth, "Rescue the children
from murder drawn nigh!"

Child 1. Yea, for the gods' sake, help! Sore is our
need—

Child 2. For now we are hemmed in by the sword's
death-toils!

CHORUS

Wretch! of what rock is thy breast?—of what steel is
the heart of thee moulded,
That the babes thou hast borne, with the selfsame hands
that with love have enfolded
These, thou hast set thee to slay?
Of one have I heard that laid hands on her loved ones of
old, one only,
Even Ino distraught of the gods, when Zeus' bride drave
her, lonely
And lost, from her home to stray:
And she fell—ah, wretch!—on the brink as she stood
Of the sea-scaur: guilt of her children's blood
Dragged downward her feet to the salt sea-flood,
And she died with her children twain.
What ghastlier horror remains to be wrought?
O bride-bed of women, with anguish fraught,
What scathe upon mortals ere now hast thou brought,
What manifold bane!

Enter JASON

Jason. Women, which stand anear unto this roof—
Is she within the halls, she who hath wrought

Dread deeds, Medea, or in flight passed thence?
For either must she hide her 'neath the earth,
Or lift on wings her frame to heaven's far depths,
Or taste the vengeance of a royal house.
How, trusts she, having murdered the land's lords,
Scatheless herself from these halls forth to flee?
Yet not for her care I, but for my sons.
Whom she hath wronged shall recompense her wrong:
But I to save my childen's life am come,
Lest to my grief the kinsmen of the dead
Avenge on them their mother's impious murder.

> *Chorus.* Wretch, thou know'st not what depth of woe
> thou hast reached,

Jason, or thou hadst uttered not such words.

> *Jason.* What now?—and is she fain to slay me too?
> *Chorus.* Thy sons are dead, slain by the mother's hand.
> *Jason.* Ah me!—what sayst thou?—thou hast killed
> me, woman!
> *Chorus.* Thy children are no more: so think of them.
> *Jason.* How?—slew them?—Where?—within, without,
> the halls?
> *Chorus.* Open, and thou shalt see thy children's
> corpses.
> *Jason.* Shoot back the bolts with all speed, serving-
> men!

Unbar, that I may see this twofold woe—
The dead, and her, with slaughter to requite her.

MEDEA *appears in mid air in a chariot drawn by dragons*

> *Medea.* Why shakest thou these doors and wouldst
> unbar,

Seeking thy dead and me who wrought the deed?
Cease this essay. If thou wouldst aught of me,
Say what thou wilt: thine hand shall touch me never.
Such chariot hath my father's sire, the Sun,
Given me, a defence from foeman's hand.

> *Jason.* O thing abhorred! O woman hatefullest

To gods, to me, to all the race of men,
Thou that couldst thrust the sword into the babes
Thou bar'st, and me hast made a childless ruin!
Thus hast thou wrought, yet look'st thou on the sun
And earth, who hast dared a deed most impious?
Now ruin seize thee!—clear I see, who saw not
Then, when from halls and land barbarian
To a Greek home I bare thee, utter bane,
Traitress to sire and land that nurtured thee!
Thy guilt's curse-bolt on me the gods have launched;
For thine own brother by his hearth thou slewest
Ere thou didst enter fair-prowed Argo's hull.
With such deeds thou begannest. Wedded then
To this man, and the mother of my sons,
For wedlock-right's sake hast thou murdered them.
There is no Grecian woman that had dared
This—yet I stooped to marry thee, good sooth,
Rather than these, a hateful bride and fell,
A tigress, not a woman, harbouring
A fiercer nature than Tyrrhenian Scylla.
But—for untold revilings would not sting
Thee, in my nature is such hardihood—
Avaunt, thou miscreant stained with thy babes' blood!
For me remains to wail my destiny,
Who of my new-wed bride shall have no joy,
And to the sons whom I begat and nurtured
Living I shall not speak—lost, lost to me!

Medea. I might have lengthened out long controversy
To these thy words, if Father Zeus knew not
How I have dealt with thee and thou with me.
'Twas not for thee to set my couch at naught
And live a life of bliss, bemocking me!
Nor for thy princess, and thy marriage-kinsman,
Kreon, unscathed to banish me this land!
Wherefore a tigress call me, an thou wilt,
Or Scylla, haunter of Tyrrhenian shore;
For thine heart have I wrung, as well behooved.

Jason. Ha! but thou sorrowest too, thou shar'st mine ills!

Medea. Oh, yea: yet grief is gain, so thou laugh not.

Jason. O children mine, what miscreant mother had ye!

Medea. O sons, destroyed by your own father's lust!

Jason. Sooth, 'twas no hand of mine that murdered them.

Medea. Nay, but thine insolence and thy new-forged bonds.

Jason. How, claim the right for wedlock's sake to slay them!

Medea. A light affliction count'st thou this to woman?

Jason. So she be wise—in thy sight naught were good.

Medea. These live no more: this, this shall cut thine heart!

Jason. They live—ah me!—avengers on thine head.

Medea. The gods know who began this misery.

Jason. Yea, verily, thy spirit abhorred they know.

Medea. Abhorred art thou; I loathe thy bitter tongue.

Jason. And I thine—yet were mutual riddance easy.

Medea. How then?—what shall I do?—fain would I this.

Jason. Yield me my dead to bury and bewail.

Medea. Never: with this hand will I bury them,
To Mountain Here's precinct bearing them,
That never foe may do despite to them,
Rifling their tomb. This land of Sisyphus
Will I constrain with solemn festival
And rites to atone for this unhallowed murder.
But I—I go unto Erechtheus' land,
With Aigeus to abide, Pandion's son.
Thou, as is meet, foul wretch, shalt foully die,
By Argo's wreckage smitten on the skull,
Now thou hast seen this bridal's bitter ending.

Jason. Now the Fury-avenger of children smite thee,
And Justice that looketh on murder requite thee!

Medea. What god or what spirit will heed thy request,
Caitiff forsworn, who betrayest the guest?

Jason. Avaunt, foul thing by whose deed thy children
have died!

Medea. Go hence to thine halls, thence lead to the
grave thy bride!

Jason. I go, a father forlorn of the two sons reft from
his home!

Medea. Not yet dost thou truly mourn: abide till thine
old age come.

Jason. O children beloved above all!

Medea. Of their mother beloved, not of thee.

Jason. Yet she slew them!

Medea. That thou mightest fall in the net that
thou spreadest for me.

Jason. Woe's me! I yearn with my lips to press
My sons' dear lips in my wretchedness.

Medea. Ha! now art thou calling upon them, now
wouldst thou kiss,
Who rejectedst them then?

Jason. For the gods' sake grant me but this,
The sweet soft flesh of my children to feel!

Medea. No—wasted in air is all thine appeal.

Jason. O Zeus, dost thou hear it, how spurned I am?—
What outrage I suffer of yonder abhorred
Child-murderess, yonder tigress-dam?
Yet out of mine helplessness, out of my shame,
I bewail my belovèd, I call to record
High Heaven, I bid God witness the word,
That my sons thou hast slain, and withholdest me
That mine hands may not touch them, nor bury their clay!
Would God I had gotten them never, this day
To behold them destroyed of thee!

Chorus. All dooms be of Zeus in Olympus; 'tis his to
reveal them.
Manifold things unhoped-for the gods to accomplishment bring.

And the things that we looked for, the gods deign not to
    fulfil them;
And the paths undiscerned of our eyes, the gods unseal
    them.
        So fell this marvellous thing.

                           [*Exeunt omnes.*

ΑΡΙΣΤΟΦΑΝΗΣ
ΦΙΛΙΠΠΙΔΟΥ
ΑΘΗΝΑΙΟΣ

THE CLOUDS OF ARISTOPHANES

TRANSLATED BY

WILLIAM JAMES HICKIE

ARISTOPHANES, the greatest of Attic comedians, and one of the greatest of all times, was born about 450 B. C. Very little is known of his life. He is supposed not to have been of pure Attic blood, and his father is said to have been a property-holder of Ægina. He had three sons—Philippus, Araros, and Nicostratos—who were all comic poets. Throughout his life Aristophanes championed the cause of the aristocratic element of Athenian society. He bitterly opposed, and in turn held up to the highest ridicule, everything that savoured in the least of demagogism or popular sophistry. He began his career with "The Banqueters," in 427 B. C., and continued to produce popular plays until his death, about 385 B. C. Of the fifty or more plays that he is said to have written, eleven have been preserved : "The Acharnians," "The Knights," "The Clouds," "The Wasps," "The Peace," "The Birds," "Lysistrata," "The Thesmophoriazusæ," "The Frogs," "The Ecclesiazusæ," and "Plutus." From the beginning of his public career Aristophanes was the sworn enemy of Euripides, and after the death of the latter "The Frogs" was written (405 B. C.) to extol Æschylus by belittling the life and art of Euripides.

DRAMATIS PERSONÆ

STREPSIADES.
PHIDIPPIDES.
SERVANT OF STREPSIADES.
DISCIPLES OF SOCRATES.
SOCRATES.
CHORUS OF CLOUDS.
JUST CAUSE.
UNJUST CAUSE.
PASIAS.
AMYNIAS.
WITNESS.
CHÆREPHON.

SCENE: The interior of a sleeping-apartment; STREP-
SIADES, PHIDIPPIDES, and two servants are in their beds;
a small house is seen at a distance. Time: midnight.

THE CLOUDS

STREPSIADES (*sitting up in his bed*). Ah me! ah me! O King Jupiter, of what a terrible length the nights are! Will it never be day? And yet long since I heard the cock. My domestics are snoring. But they would not have done so heretofore. May you perish then, O war! for many reasons, because I may not even punish my domestics. Neither does this excellent youth awake through the night; but takes his ease, wrapped up in five blankets. Well, if it is the fashion, let us snore wrapped up. [*Lies down, and then snores immediately, starts up again.*]

But I am not able, miserable man, to sleep, being tormented by my expenses, and my stud of horses, and my debts, through this son of mine. He, with his long hair, is riding horses and driving curricles, and dreaming of horses; while I am driven to distraction, as I see the moon bringing on the twentieths; for the interest is running on.—Boy! light a lamp, and bring forth my tablets, that I may take them and read to how many I am indebted, and calculate the interest. [*Enter Boy with a light and tablets.*] Come, let me see, what do I owe? Twelve minae to Pasias. Why twelve minae to Pasias? Why did I borrow them? When I bought the blood horse. Ah me, unhappy! Would that it had had its eye knocked out with a stone first!

THE CLOUDS

STREPSIADES (*sitting up in his bed*). Ah me! ah me! O King Jupiter, of what a terrible length the nights are! Will it never be day? And yet long since I heard the cock. My domestics are snoring; but they would not have done so heretofore! May you perish then, O war! for many reasons; because I may not even punish my domestics. Neither does this excellent youth awake through the night; but takes his ease, wrapped up in five blankets. Well, if it is the fashion, let us snore wrapped up. [*Lies down, and then almost immediately starts up again.*]

But I am not able, miserable man, to sleep, being tormented by my expenses, and my stud of horses, and my debts, through this son of mine. He, with his long hair, is riding horses and driving curricles, and dreaming of horses; while I am driven to distraction, as I see the moon bringing on the twentieths; for the interest is running on.—Boy! light a lamp, and bring forth my tablets, that I may take them and read to how many I am indebted, and calculate the interest. [*Enter boy with a light and tablets.*] Come, let me see; what do I owe? Twelve minæ to Pasias. Why twelve minæ to Pasias? Why did I borrow them? When I bought the blood-horse. Ah me, unhappy! Would that it had had its eye knocked out with a stone first!

Phidippides (*talking in his sleep*). You are acting unfairly, Philo! Drive on your own course.

Strep. This is the bane that has destroyed me; for even in his sleep he dreams about horsemanship.

Phid. How many courses will the war-chariots run?

Strep. Many courses do you drive me, your father.— But what debt came upon me after Pasias? Three minæ to Amynias for a little chariot and pair of wheels.

Phid. Lead the horse home, after having given him a good rolling.

Strep. O foolish youth, you have rolled me out of my possessions; since I have been cast in suits, and others say that they will have surety given them for the interest.

Phid. (*awaking*). Pray, father, why are you peevish, and toss about the whole night?

Strep. A bailiff out of the bedclothes is biting me.

Phid. Suffer me, good sir, to sleep a little.

Strep. Then, do you sleep on; but know that all these debts will turn on your head. [PHIDIPPIDES *falls asleep again.*] Alas! would that the match-maker had perished miserably, who induced me to marry your mother. For a country life used to be most agreeable to me, dirty, un-trimmed, reclining at random, abounding in bees, and sheep, and oil-cake. Then I, a rustic, married a niece of Megacles, the son of Megacles, from the city, haughty, luxurious, and Cœsyrafied. When I married her, I lay with her redolent of new wine, of the cheese-crate, and abundance of wool; but she, on the contrary, of ointment, saffron, wanton-kisses, extravagance, gluttony, and of Colias and Genetyllis. I will not indeed say that she was idle; but she wove. And I used to show her this cloak by way of pretext, and say, "Wife, you weave at a great rate."

SERVANT *re-enters*

Servant. We have no oil in the lamp.

Strep. Ah me! why did you light the thirsty lamp? Come hither, that you may weep!

Ser. For what, pray, shall I weep?

Strep. Because you put in one of the thick wicks. [SERVANT *runs out.*]—After this, when this son was born to us, to me, forsooth, and to my excellent wife, we squabbled then about the name: for she was for adding ἵππος to the name, Xanthippus, or Charippus, or Callippides; but I was for giving him the name of his grandfather, Phidonides. For a time therefore we disputed; and then at length we agreed, and called him Phidippides. She used to take this son and fondle him, saying, "When you, being grown up, shall drive your chariot to the city, like Megacles, with a xystis." But I used to say, "Nay, rather, when dressed in a leathern jerkin, you shall drive your goats from Phelleus, like your father. He paid no attention to my words, but poured a horse-fever over my property. Now, therefore, by meditating the whole night, I have discovered one path for my course extraordinarily excellent; to which if I persuade this youth I shall be saved. But first I wish to awake him. How then can I awake him in the most agreeable manner?—How? Phidippides, my little Phidippides?

Phid. What, father?

Strep. Kiss me, and give me your right hand!

Phid. There. What's the matter?

Strep. Tell me, do you love me?

Phid. Yes, by this Equestrian Neptune.

Strep. Nay, do not by any means mention this Equestrian to me, for this god is the author of my misfortunes. But, if you really love me from your heart, my son, obey me.

Phid. In what then, pray, shall I obey you?

Strep. Reform your habits as quickly as possible; and go and learn what I advise.

Phid. Tell me now, what do you prescribe?

Strep. And will you obey me at all?

Phid. By Bacchus, I will obey you.

Strep. Look this way then! Do you see this little door and little house?

Phid. I see it. What then, pray, is this, father?

Strep. This is a thinking-shop of wise spirits. There dwell men who in speaking of the heavens persuade people that it is an oven, and that it encompasses us, and that we are the embers. These men teach, if one give them money, to conquer in speaking, right or wrong.

Phid. Who are they?

Strep. I do not know the name accurately. They are minute philosophers, noble and excellent.

Phid. Bah! they are rogues; I know them. You mean the quacks, the pale-faced wretches, the bare-footed fellows, of whose number are the miserable Socrates and Chærephon.

Strep. Hold! hold! be silent! Do not say anything foolish. But, if you have any concern for your father's patrimony, become one of them, having given up your horsemanship.

Phid. I would not, by Bacchus, if even you were to give me the pheasants which Leogoras rears!

Strep. Go, I entreat you, dearest of men, go and be taught.

Phid. Why, what shall I learn?

Strep. They say that among them are both the two causes—the better cause, whichever that is, and the worse: they say that the one of these two causes, the worse, prevails, though it speaks on the unjust side. If therefore you learn for me this unjust cause, I would not pay to any one, not even an obolus of these debts, which I owe at present on your account.

Phid. I can not comply; for I should not dare to look upon the knights, having lost all my colour.

Strep. Then, by Ceres, you shall not eat any of my goods! neither you, nor your draught-horse, nor your blood-horse ; but I will drive you out of my house to the crows.

Phid. My uncle Megacles will not permit me to be without a horse. But I'll go in, and pay no heed to you.

[*Exit* PHIDIPPIDES.

Strep. Though fallen, still I will not lie prostrate : but having prayed to the gods, I will go myself to the think-ing-shop and get taught. How, then, being an old man, and having a bad memory, and dull of comprehension, shall I learn the subtleties of refined disquisitions?—I must go. Why thus do I loiter and not knock at the door ? [*Knocks at the door.*] Boy ! little boy !

Disciple (*from within*). Go to the devil ! Who is it that knocked at the door ?

Strep. Strepsiades, the son of Phidon, of Cicynna.

Dis. You are a stupid fellow, by Jove ! who have kicked against the door so very carelessly, and have caused the miscarriage of an idea which I had con-ceived.

Strep. Pardon me ; for I dwell afar in the country. But tell me the thing which has been made to miscarry.

Dis. It is not lawful to mention it, except to disciples.

Strep. Tell it, then, to me without fear ; for I here am come as a disciple to the thinking-shop.

Dis. I will tell you ; but you must regard these as mysteries. Socrates lately asked Chærephon about a flea, how many of its own feet it jumped ; for after hav-ing bit the eyebrow of Chærephon it leaped away on to the head of Socrates.

Strep. How, then, did he measure this ?

Dis. Most cleverly. He melted some wax, and then took the flea and dipped its feet in the wax ; and then a pair of Persian slippers stuck to it when cooled. Having gently loosened these, he measured back the distance.

Strep. O King Jupiter ! what subtlety of thought !

Dis. What then would you say if you heard another contrivance of Socrates ?

Strep. Of what kind? Tell me, I beseech you!

Dis. Chærephon the Sphettian asked him whether he thought gnats buzzed through the mouth or the breech.

Strep. What, then, did he say about the gnat?

Dis. He said the intestine of the gnat was narrow, and that the wind went forcibly through it, being slender, straight to the breech; and then that the rump, being hollow where it is adjacent to the narrow part, resounded through the violence of the wind.

Strep. The rump of gnats then is a trumpet! Oh, thrice happy he for his sharp-sightedness! Surely a defendant might easily get acquitted who understands the intestine of the gnat.

Dis. But he was lately deprived of a great idea by a lizard.

Strep. In what way? Tell me.

Dis. As he was investigating the courses of the moon and her revolutions, then as he was gaping upward a lizard in the darkness dropped upon him from the roof.

Strep. I am amused at a lizard's having dropped on Socrates.

Dis. Yesterday evening there was no supper for us.

Strep. Well. What then did he contrive for provisions?

Dis. He sprinkled fine ashes on the table, and bent a little spit, and then took it as a pair of compasses and filched a cloak from the Palæstra.

Strep. Why then do we admire that Thales? Open, open quickly the thinking-shop, and show to me Socrates as quickly as possible. For I desire to be a disciple. Come, open the door. [*The door of the thinking-shop opens, and the pupils of* SOCRATES *are seen all with their heads fixed on the ground, while* SOCRATES *himself is seen suspended in the air in a basket.*] O Hercules, from what country are these wild beasts?

Dis. What do you wonder at? To what do they seem to you to be like?

Strep. To the Spartans who were taken at Pylos. But why in the world do these look upon the ground?

Dis. They are in search of the things below the earth.

Strep. Then they are searching for roots. Do not, then, trouble yourselves about this; for I know where there are large and fine ones. Why, what are these doing, who are bent down so much?

Dis. These are groping about in darkness under Tartarus.

Strep. Why then does their rump look toward heaven?

Dis. It is getting taught astronomy alone by itself. [*Turning to the pupils.*] But go in, lest he meet with us.

Strep. Not yet, not yet; but let them remain, that I may communicate to them a little matter of my own.

Dis. It is not permitted to them to remain without in the open air for a very long time.   [*The pupils retire.*

Strep. (*discovering a variety of mathematical instruments*). Why, what is this, in the name of heaven? Tell me.

Dis. This is Astronomy.

Strep. But what is this?

Dis. Geometry.

Strep. What then is the use of this?

Dis. To measure out the land.

Strep. What belongs to an allotment?

Dis. No, but the whole earth.

Strep. You tell me a clever notion; for the contrivance is democratic and useful.

Dis. (*pointing to a map*). See, here's a map of the whole earth. Do you see? this is Athens.

Strep. What say you? I don't believe you; for I do not see the Dicasts sitting.

Dis. Be assured that this is truly the Attic territory.

Strep. Why, where are my fellow-tribesmen of Cicynna?

Dis. Here they are. And Euboea here, as you see, is stretched out a long way by the side of it to a great distance.

Strep. I know that; for it was stretched by us and Pericles. But where is Lacedæmon?

Dis. Where is it? Here it is.

Strep. How near it is to us! Pay great attention to this, to remove it very far from us.

Dis. By Jupiter, it is not possible.

Strep. Then you will weep for it. [*Looking up and discovering* SOCRATES.] Come, who is this man who is in the basket?

Dis. Himself.

Strep. Who's " Himself "?

Dis. Socrates.

Strep. O Socrates! Come, you sir, call upon him loudly for me.

Dis. Nay, rather, call him yourself; for I have no leisure. [*Exit* DISCIPLE.

Strep. Socrates! my little Socrates!

Socrates. Why callest thou me, thou creature of a day?

Strep. First tell me, I beseech you, what you are doing.

Soc. I am walking in the air, and speculating about the sun.

Strep. And so you look down upon the gods from your basket, and not from the earth?

Soc. For I should never have rightly discovered things celestial if I had not suspended the intellect, and mixed the thought in a subtle form with its kindred air. But if, being on the ground, I speculated from below on things above, I should never have discovered them. For the earth forcibly attracts to itself the meditative moisture. Water-cresses also suffer the very same thing.

Strep. What do you say?—Does meditation attract the moisture to the water-cresses? Come then, my little Socrates, descend to me, that you may teach me those things, for the sake of which I have come. [SOCRATES *lowers himself and gets out of the basket.*]

Soc. And for what did you come?

Strep. Wishing to learn to speak; for, by reason of usury, and most ill-natured creditors, I am pillaged and plundered, and have my goods seized for debt.

Soc. How did you get in debt without observing it?

Strep. A horse-disease consumed me—terrible at eating. But teach me the other one of your two causes, that which pays nothing; and I will swear by the gods, I will pay down to you whatever reward you exact of me.

Soc. By what gods will you swear? for, in the first place, gods are not a current coin with us.

Strep. By what do you swear? By iron money, as in Byzantium?

Soc. Do you wish to know clearly celestial matters, what they rightly are?

Strep. Yes, by Jupiter, if it be possible!

Soc. And to hold converse with the Clouds, our divinities?

Strep. By all means.

Soc. (*with great solemnity*). Seat yourself, then, upon the sacred couch.

Strep. Well, I am seated!

Soc. Take, then, this chaplet.

Strep. For what purpose a chaplet?—Ah me! Socrates, see that you do not sacrifice me like Athamas!

Soc. No; we do all these to those who get initiated.

Strep. Then what shall I gain, pray?

Soc. You shall become in oratory a tricky knave, a thorough rattle, a subtle speaker.—But keep quiet.

Strep. By Jupiter! you will not deceive me; for if I am besprinkled, I shall become fine flour.

Soc. It becomes the old man to speak words of good omen, and to hearken to my prayer.—O sovereign King, immeasurable Air, who keepest the earth suspended, and thou bright Æther, and ye august goddesses, the Clouds sending thunder and lightning, arise, appear in the air, O mistresses, to your deep thinker!

Strep. Not yet, not yet, till I wrap this around me, lest

I be wet through. To think of my having come from home without even a cap, unlucky man!

Soc. Come then, ye highly honoured Clouds, for a display to this man. Whether ye are sitting upon the sacred snow-covered summits of Olympus, or in the gardens of Father Ocean form a sacred dance with the Nymphs, or draw in golden pitchers the streams of the waters of the Nile, or inhabit the Mæotic lake, or the snowy rock of Mimas, hearken to our prayer, and receive the sacrifice, and be propitious to the sacred rites. [*The following song is heard at a distance, accompanied by loud claps of thunder.*]

Chorus. Eternal Clouds! let us arise to view with our dewy, clear-bright nature, from loud-sounding Father Ocean to the wood-crowned summits of the lofty mountains, in order that we may behold clearly the far-seen watch-towers, and the fruits, and the fostering, sacred earth, and the rushing sounds of the divine rivers, and the roaring, loud-sounding sea; for the unwearied eye of Æther sparkles with glittering rays. Come, let us shake off the watery cloud from our immortal forms and survey the earth with far-seeing eye.

Soc. O ye greatly venerable Clouds, ye have clearly heard me when I called. [*Turning to* STREPSIADES.] Did you hear the voice, and the thunder which bellowed at the same time, feared as a god?

Strep. I too worship you, O ye highly honoured, and am inclined to reply to the thundering, so much do I tremble at them and am alarmed. And whether it be lawful, or be not lawful, I have a desire just now to ease myself.

Soc. Don't scoff, nor do what these poor-devil-poets do, but use words of good omen, for a great swarm of goddesses is in motion with their songs.

Cho. Ye rain-bringing virgins, let us come to the fruitful land of Pallas, to view the much-loved country of Cecrops, abounding in brave men; where is reverence for sacred rites not to be divulged; where the house that receives the initiated is thrown open in holy mystic rites;

and gifts to the celestial gods; and high-roofed temples, and statues; and most sacred processions in honour of the blessed gods; and well-crowned sacrifices to the gods, and feasts, at all seasons; and with the approach of spring the Bacchic festivity, and the rousings of melodious choruses, and the loud-sounding music of flutes.

Strep. Tell me, O Socrates, I beseech you, by Jupiter, who are these that have uttered this grand song? Are they some heroines?

Soc. By no means; but heavenly Clouds, great divinities to idle men; who supply us with thought and argument, and intelligence, and humbug, and circumlocution, and ability to hoax, and comprehension.

Strep. On this account therefore my soul, having heard their voice, flutters, and already seeks to discourse subtilely, and to quibble about smoke, and having pricked a maxim with a little notion, to refute the opposite argument. So that now I eagerly desire, if by any means it be possible, to see them palpably.

Soc. Look, then, hither, toward Mount Parnes; for now I behold them descending gently.

Strep. Pray where? Show me.

Soc. See! there they come in great numbers through the hollows and thickets; there, obliquely.

Strep. What's the matter? for I can't see them.

Soc. By the entrance.

Enter CHORUS

Strep. Now at length with difficulty I just see them.

Soc. Now at length you assuredly see them, unless you have your eyes running pumpkins.

Strep. Yes, by Jupiter! O highly honoured Clouds, for now they cover all things.

Soc. Did you not, however, know, nor yet consider, these to be goddesses?

Strep. No, by Jupiter! but I thought them to be mist, and dew, and smoke.

20

Soc. For you do not know, by Jupiter! that these feed very many sophists, Thurian soothsayers, practisers of medicine, lazy-long-haired-onyx-ring-wearers, song-twisters for the cyclic dances, and meteorological quacks. They feed idle people who do nothing, because such men celebrate them in verse.

Strep. For this reason, then, they introduced into their verses "the dreadful impetuosity of the moist, whirling-bright clouds"; and "the curls of hundred-headed Typho"; and "the hard-blowing tempests"; and then, "aërial, moist"; "crooked-clawed birds, floating in air"; and "the showers of rain from dewy Clouds." And then, in return for these, they swallow "slices of great, fine mullets, and bird's-flesh of thrushes."

Soc. Is it not just, however, that they should have their reward, on account of these?

Strep. Tell me, pray, if they are really Clouds, what ails them, that they resemble mortal women? For they are not such.

Soc. Pray, of what nature are they?

Strep. I do not clearly know: at any rate they resemble spread-out fleeces, and not women, by Jupiter! not a bit; for these have noses.

Soc. Answer, then, whatever I ask you.

Strep. Then say quickly what you wish.

Soc. Have you ever, when you looked up, seen a cloud like to a centaur, or a panther, or a wolf, or a bull?

Strep. By Jupiter, have I! But what of that?

Soc. They become all things, whatever they please. And then if they see a person with long hair, a wild one of these hairy fellows, like the son of Xenophantes, in derision of his folly, they liken themselves to centaurs.

Strep. Why, what, if they should see Simon, a plunderer of the public property, what do they do?

Soc. They suddenly become wolves, showing up his disposition.

Strep. For this reason, then, for this reason, when they

yesterday saw Cleonymus the recreant, on this account they became stags, because they saw this most cowardly fellow.

Soc. And now too, because they saw Clisthenes, you observe, on this account they became women.

Strep. Hail therefore, O mistresses! And now, if ever ye did to any other, to me also utter a voice reaching to heaven, O all-powerful queens.

Cho. Hail, O ancient veteran, hunter after learned speeches! And thou, O priest of most subtle trifles! tell us what you require? For we would not hearken to any other of the present meteorological sophists, except to Prodicus; to him, on account of his wisdom and intelligence; and to you, because you walk proudly in the streets, and cast your eyes askance, and endure many hardships with bare feet, and in reliance upon us lookest supercilious.

Strep. O Earth, what a voice! how holy, and dignified, and wondrous!

Soc. For, in fact, these alone are goddesses; and all the rest is nonsense.

Strep. But come, by the Earth, is not Jupiter, the Olympian, a god?

Soc. What Jupiter? Do not trifle. There is no Jupiter.

Strep. What do you say? Who rains, then? For first of all explain this to me.

Soc. These, to be sure. I will teach you it by powerful evidence. Come, where have you ever seen him raining at any time without Clouds? And yet he ought to rain in fine weather, and these to be absent.

Strep. By Apollo, of a truth you have rightly confirmed this by your present argument. And yet, before this, I really thought that Jupiter caused the rain. But tell me who it is that thunders. This makes me tremble.

Soc. These, as they roll, thunder.

Strep. In what way? you all-daring man!

Soc. When they are full of much water, and are compelled to be borne along, being necessarily precipitated when full of rain, then they fall heavily upon each other and burst and clap.

Strep. Who is it that compels them to be borne along? is it not Jupiter?

Soc. By no means, but æthereal Vortex.

Strep. Vortex? It had escaped my notice that Jupiter did not exist, and that Vortex now reigned in his stead. But you have taught me nothing as yet concerning the clap and the thunder.

Soc. Have you not heard me, that I said that the Clouds, when full of moisture, dash against each other, and clap by reason of their density?

Strep. Come, how am I to believe this?

Soc. I'll teach you from your own case. Were you ever, after being stuffed with broth at the Panathenaïc festival, then disturbed in your belly, and did a tumult suddenly rumble through it?

Strep. Yes, by Apollo! and immediately the little broth plays the mischief with me, and is disturbed, and rumbles like thunder, and grumbles dreadfully: at first gently pappax, pappax; and then it adds papa-pappax; and finally, it thunders downright papapappax, as they do.

Soc. Consider, therefore, how you have trumpeted from a little belly so small: and how is it not probable that this air, being boundless, should thunder loudly?

Strep. For this reason, therefore, the two names also, Trump and Thunder, are similar to each other. But teach me this, whence comes the thunderbolt blazing with fire, and burns us to ashes when it smites us, and singes those who survive. For indeed Jupiter evidently hurls this at the perjured.

Soc. Why, how then, you foolish person, and savouring of the dark ages and antediluvian, if his manner is to smite the perjured, does he not blast Simon, and Cleonymus, and Theorus? And yet they are very perjured. But he smites his own temple, and Sunium the promontory of Athens, and the tall oaks. Wherefore? for indeed an oak does not commit perjury.

Strep. I do not know; but you seem to speak well. For what, pray, is the thunderbolt?

Soc. When a dry wind, having been raised aloft, is inclosed in these Clouds, it inflates them within, like a bladder; and then, of necessity, having burst them, it rushes out with vehemence by reason of its density, setting fire to itself through its rushing and impetuosity.

Strep. By Jupiter, of a truth I once experienced this exactly at the Diasian festival! I was roasting a haggis for my kinsfolk, and through neglect I did not cut it open; but it became inflated, and then suddenly bursting, befouled my eyes, and burned my face.

Cho. O mortal, who hast desired great wisdom from us! How happy will you become among the Athenians and among the Greeks, if you be possessed of a good memory, and be a deep thinker, and endurance of labour be implanted in your soul, and you be not wearied either by standing or walking, nor be exceedingly vexed at shivering with cold, nor long to break your fast, and you refrain from wine, and gymnastics, and the other follies, and consider this the highest excellence, as is proper a clever man should, to conquer by action and counsel, and by battling with your tongue.

Strep. As far as regards a sturdy spirit, and care that makes one's bed uneasy, and a frugal and hard-living and savory-eating belly, be of good courage and don't trouble yourself; I would offer myself to hammer on, for that matter.

Soc. Will you not, pray, now believe in no god, except what we believe in—this Chaos, and the Clouds, and the Tongue—these three?

Strep. Absolutely I would not even converse with the others, not even if I met them; nor would I sacrifice to them, nor make libations, nor offer frankincense.

Cho. Tell us then boldly, what we must do for you? for you shall not fail in getting it, if you honour and admire us, and seek to become clever.

Strep. O mistresses, I request of you then this very small favour, that I be the best of the Greeks in speaking by a hundred stadia.

Cho. Well, you shall have this from us, so that henceforward from this time no one shall get more opinions passed in the public assemblies than you.

Strep. Grant me not to deliver important opinions; for I do not desire these, but only to pervert the right for my own advantage, and to evade my creditors.

Cho. Then you shall obtain what you desire; for you do not covet great things. But commit yourself without fear to our ministers.

Strep. I will do so in reliance upon you, for necessity oppresses me, on account of the blood-horses, and the marriage that ruined me. Now, therefore, let them use me as they please. I give up this my body to them to be beaten, to be hungered, to be troubled with thirst, to be squalid, to shiver with cold, to flay into a leathern bottle, if I shall escape clear from my debts, and appear to men to be bold, glib of tongue, audacious, impudent, shameless, a fabricator of falsehoods, inventive of words, a practised knave in lawsuits, a law-tablet, a thorough rattle, a fox, a sharper, a slippery knave, a dissembler, a slippery fellow, an impostor, a gallows-bird, a blackguard, a twister, a troublesome fellow, a licker-up of hashes. If they call me this, when they meet me, let them do to me absolutely what they please. And if they like, by Ceres! let them serve up a sausage out of me to the deep thinkers.

Cho. This man has a spirit not void of courage, but prompt. Know, that if you learn these matters from me, you will possess among mortals a glory as high as heaven.

Strep. What shall I experience?

Cho. You shall pass with me the most enviable of mortal lives the whole time.

Strep. Shall I then ever see this?

Cho. Yea, so that many be always seated at your gates, wishing to communicate with you and come to a conference with you, to consult with you as to actions and affidavits of many talents, as is worthy of your abilities. [*To* SOCRATES.] But attempt to teach the old man by degrees whatever you purpose, and scrutinize his intellect, and make trial of his mind.

Soc. Come now, tell me your own turn of mind; in order that, when I know of what sort it is, I may now, after this, apply to you new engines.

Strep. What? By the gods, do you purpose to besiege me?

Soc. No; I wish to briefly learn from you if you are possessed of a good memory.

Strep. In two ways, by Jove! If anything be owing to me, I have a very good memory; but if I owe, unhappy man, I am very forgetful.

Soc. Is the power of speaking, pray, implanted in your nature?

Strep. Speaking is not in me, but cheating is.

Soc. How, then, will you be able to learn?

Strep. Excellently, of course.

Soc. Come, then, take care that, whenever I propound any clever dogma about abstruse matters, you catch it up immediately.

Strep. What then? Am I to feed upon wisdom like a dog?

Soc. This man is ignorant and brutish.—I fear, old man, lest you will need blows. Come, let me see; what do you do if any one beat you?

Strep. I take the beating; and then, when I have waited a little while, I call witnesses to prove it; then, again, after a short interval, I go to law.

Soc. Come, then, lay down your cloak.

Strep. Have I done any wrong?

Soc. No; but it is the rule to enter naked.

Strep. But I do not enter to search for stolen goods.

Soc. Lay it down. Why do you talk nonsense?

Strep. Now tell me this, pray. If I be diligent and learn zealously, to which of your disciples shall I become like?

Soc. You will no way differ from Chærephon in intellect.

Strep. Ah me, unhappy! I shall become half-dead.

Soc. Don't chatter; but quickly follow me hither with smartness.

Strep. Then give me first into my hands a honeyed cake; for I am afraid of descending within, as if into the cave of Trophonius.

Soc. Proceed; why do you keep poking about the door? [*Exeunt* SOCRATES and STREPSIADES.

Cho. Well, go in peace, for the sake of this your valour. May prosperity attend the man, because, being advanced into the vale of years, he imbues his intellect with modern subjects, and cultivates wisdom! [*Turning to the audience.*]

Spectators, I will freely declare to you the truth, by Bacchus, who nurtured me! So may I conquer, and be accounted skilful, as that, deeming you to be clever spectators, and this to be the cleverest of my comedies, I thought proper to let you first taste that comedy, which gave me the greatest labour. And then I retired from the contest defeated by vulgar fellows, though I did not deserve it. These things, therefore, I object to you, a learned audience, for whose sake I was expending this labour. But not even thus will I ever willingly desert the discerning portion of you. For since what time my Modest Man and my Rake were very highly praised here by an audience, with whom it is a pleasure even to hold converse, and I (for I was still a virgin, and it was not lawful for me as yet to have children) exposed my offspring, and another girl took it up and owned it, and you generously reared and educated it, from this time I have had sure pledges of your good will toward me. Now, therefore, like that well-known Electra, has this comedy come seeking, if haply it meet with an audience so clever, for it will recognise, if it should see, the lock of its brother. But see how modest she is by nature, who, in the first place, has come, having stitched to her no leathern phallus hanging down, red at the top, and thick, to set the boys a laughing; nor yet jeered the bald-headed, nor danced the cordax; nor does the old man who speaks the verses beat the person near him with his staff, keeping out of sight wretched ribaldry; nor has she rushed in with torches, nor does she shout ἰού, ἰού; but has come relying on herself and her verses. And I, although so excellent a poet, do not give myself airs, nor do I seek to deceive you by twice and thrice bringing forward the same pieces; but I am always clever at introducing new fashions, not at all resembling each other, and all of them clever; who struck Cleon in the belly when at the height of his power, and could not bear to attack him afterward when he was down. But these scribblers, when once Hyperbolus has given them a handle, keep ever trampling on this wretched man and his mother. Eupolis, indeed, first of all craftily introduced his Maricas, having basely, base fellow, spoiled by altering my play of the Knights, having added to it, for the sake of the cordax, a drunken old woman, whom Phrynichus long ago poetized, whom the whale was for devouring. Then again Hermippus made verses on Hyperbolus; and now all others press hard upon Hyperbolus, imitating my simile of the eels. Whoever, therefore, laughs at these, let him not take pleasure in my attempts; but if you are delighted with me and my inventions, in times to come you will seem to be wise.

I first invoke, to join our choral band, the mighty Jupiter, ruling on high, the monarch of gods; and the potent master of the trident, the fierce upheaver of earth and briny sea; and our father of great renown, most august Æther, life-supporter of all: and the horse-guider, who fills the plain of the earth with exceeding bright beams, a mighty deity among gods and mortals.

Most clever spectators, come, give us your attention; for having been injured, we blame you to your faces. For though we benefit the state most of all the gods, to us alone of deities you do not offer sacrifice nor yet pour libations, who watch over you. For if there should be any expedition without prudence, then we either thunder or drizzle small rain. And then, when you were for choosing as your general the Paphlagonian tanner, hateful to the gods, we contracted our brows and were enraged; and thunder burst through the lightning; and the Moon forsook her usual paths; and the Sun immediately drew in his wick to himself, and declared he would not give you light, if Cleon should be your general. Nevertheless you chose him. For they say that ill counsel is in this city; that the gods, however, turn all these your mismanagements to a prosperous issue. And how this also shall be advantageous, we will easily teach you. If you should convict the cormorant Cleon of bribery and embezzlement, and then make fast his neck in the stocks, the affair will turn out for the state to the ancient form again, if you have mismanaged in any way, and to a prosperous issue.

Hear me again, King Phœbus, Delian Apollo, who inhabitest the high-peaked Cynthian rock! and thou, blessed goddess, who inhabitest the all-golden house of Ephesus, in which Lydian damsels greatly reverence thee; and thou, our national goddess, swayer of the ægis, Minerva, guardian of the city! and thou, reveller Bacchus, who, inhabiting the Parnassian rock, sparklest with torches, conspicuous among the Delphic Bacchanals!

When we had got ready to set out hither, the Moon met us, and commanded us first to greet the Athenians and their allies; and then declared that she was angry, for that she had suffered dreadful things, though she benefits you all, not in words, but openly. In the first

place, not less than a drachma every month for torches;
so that also all, when they went out of an evening, were
wont to say, "Boy, don't buy a torch, for the moonlight
is beautiful." And she says she confers other benefits on
you, but that you do not observe the days at all correctly,
but confuse them up and down; so that she says the gods
are constantly threatening her, when they are defrauded
of their dinner, and depart home, not having met with the
regular feast according to the number of the days. And
then, when you ought to be sacrificing, you are inflicting
tortures and litigating. And often, while we gods are
observing a fast, when we mourn for Memnon or Sarpe-
don, you are pouring libations and laughing. For which
reason Hyperbolus, having obtained by lot this year to
be Hieromnemon, was afterward deprived by us gods of
his crown: for thus he will know better that he ought to
spend the days of his life according to the Moon.

Enter SOCRATES

Soc. By Respiration, and Chaos, and Air, I have not
seen any man so boorish, nor so impracticable, nor so
stupid, nor so forgetful; who, while learning some little
petty quibbles, forgets them before he has learned them.
Nevertheless I will certainly call him out here to the light.
Where is Strepsiades? Come forth with your couch.

Strep. (*from within*). The bugs do not permit me to
bring it forth.

Soc. Make haste and lay it down; and give me your
attention.

Enter STREPSIADES

Strep. Very well.

Soc. Come now; what do you now wish to learn first of
those things in none of which you have ever been instructed?
Tell me. About measures, or rhythms, or verses?

Strep. I should prefer to learn about measures; for it
is but lately I was cheated out of two chœnices by a meal-
huckster.

Soc. I do not ask you this, but which you account the most beautiful measure : the trimetre or the tetrametre?

Strep. I think nothing superior to the semisextarius.

Soc. You talk nonsense, man.

Strep. Make a wager then with me, if the semisextarius be not a tetrametre.

Soc. Go to the devil! how boorish you are and dull of learning. Perhaps you may be able to learn about rhythms.

Strep. But what good will rhythms do me for a living?

Soc. In the first place, to be clever at an entertainment, understanding what rhythm is for the war-dance, and what, again, according to the dactyle.

Strep. According to the dactyle? By Jove, but I know it!

Soc. Tell me, pray.

Strep. What else but this finger? Formerly, indeed, when I was yet a boy, this here!

Soc. You are boorish and stupid.

Strep. For I do not desire, you wretch, to learn any of these things.

Soc. What then?

Strep. That, that, the most unjust cause.

Soc. But you must learn other things before these : namely, what quadrupeds are properly masculine.

Strep. I know the males, if I am not mad—κριὸς, τράγος, ταῦρος, κύων, ἀλεκτρυών.

Soc. Do you see what you are doing? You are calling both the female and the male ἀλεκτρυὼν in the same way.

Strep. How, pray? come, tell me.

Soc. How? The one with you is ἀλεκτρυὼν, and the other is ἀλεκτρυὼν also.

Strep. Yea, by Neptune! how now ought I to call them?

Soc. The one ἀλεκτρύαινα, and the other ἀλέκτωρ.

Strep. ᾽Αλεκτρύαινα? Capital, by the Air! So that, in return for this lesson alone, I will fill your κάρδοπος full of barley-meal on all sides.

Soc. See! see! there again 's another blunder! You make κάρδοπος, which is feminine, to be masculine.

Strep. In what way do I make κάρδοπος masculine?

Soc. Most assuredly; just as if you were to say Κλεώνυμος.

Strep. How, pray? Tell me.

Soc. Κάρδοπος with you is tantamount to Κλεώνυμος.

Strep. Good sir, Cleonymus had no kneading-trough, but kneaded his bread in a round mortar. How ought I to call it henceforth?

Soc. How? Call it καρδόπη, as you call Σωστράτη.

Strep. Καρδόπη, in the feminine?

Soc. For so you speak it rightly.

Strep. But that would make it καρδόπη, Κλεωνύμη.

Soc. You must learn one thing more about names, what are masculine, and what of them are feminine.

Strep. I know what are female.

Soc. Tell me, pray.

Strep. Lysilla, Philinna, Clitagora, Demetria.

Soc. What names are masculine?

Strep. Thousands: Philoxenus, Melesias, Amynias.

Soc. But, you wretch! these are not masculine.

Strep. Are they not males with you?

Soc. By no means: for how would you call to Amynias, if you met him?

Strep. How would I call? Thus: "Come hither, come hither, Amynia!"

Soc. Do you see? you call Amynias a woman.

Strep. Is it not then with justice, who does not serve in the army? But why should I learn these things, that we all know?

Soc. It is no use, by Jupiter! Having reclined yourself down here—

Strep. What must I do?

Soc. Think out some of your own affairs.

Strep. Not here, pray, I beseech you; but, if I must, suffer me to excogitate these very things on the ground.

Soc. There is no other way. [*Exit* SOCRATES.

Strep. Unfortunate man that I am! what a penalty shall I this day pay to the bugs!

Cho. Now meditate and examine closely; and roll yourself about in every way, having wrapped yourself up; and quickly, when you fall into a difficulty, spring to another mental contrivance. But let delightful sleep be absent from your eyes.

Strep. Attatai! attatai!

Cho. What ails you? why are you distressed?

Strep. Wretched man, I am perishing! The Corinthians, coming out from the bed, are biting me, and devouring my sides, and drinking up my life-blood, and tearing away my flesh, and digging through my vitals, and will annihilate me.

Cho. Do not now be very grievously distressed.

Strep. Why, how, when my money is gone, my complexion gone, my life gone, and my slipper gone? And furthermore in addition to these evils, with singing the night-watches, I am almost gone myself.

Re-enter SOCRATES

Soc. Ho you! what are you about? Are you not meditating?

Strep. I? Yea, by Neptune!

Soc. And what, pray, have you thought?

Strep. Whether any bit of me will be left by the bugs.

Soc. You will perish most wretchedly.

Strep. But, my good friend, I have already perished.

Soc. You must not give in, but must wrap yourself up; for you have to discover a device for abstracting, and a means of cheating. [*Walks up and down while* STREPSIADES *wraps himself up in the blankets.*]

Strep. Ah me! would, pray, some one would throw over me a swindling contrivance from the sheep-skins.

Soc. Come now; I will first see this fellow, what he is about. Ho you! are you asleep?

Strep. No; by Apollo, I am not!

Soc. Have you got anything?

Strep. No; by Jupiter, certainly not!

Soc. Nothing at all?

Strep. Nothing, except what I have in my right hand.

Soc. Will you not quickly cover yourself up, and think of something?

Strep. About what? for do you tell me this, O Socrates!

Soc. Do you, yourself, first find out and state what you wish.

Strep. You have heard a thousand times what I wish. About the interest; so that I may pay no one.

Soc. Come then, wrap yourself up, and having given your mind play with subtilty, revolve your affairs by little and little, rightly distinguishing and examining.

Strep. Ah me, unhappy man!

Soc. Keep quiet; and if you be puzzled in any one of your conceptions, leave it and go; and then set your mind in motion again, and lock it up.

Strep. (*in great glee*). O dearest little Socrates!

Soc. What, old man?

Strep. I have got a device for cheating them of the interest.

Soc. Exhibit it.

Strep. Now tell me this, pray; if I were to purchase a Thessalian witch, and draw down the moon by night, and then shut it up, as if it were a mirror, in a round crest-case, and then carefully keep it—

Soc. What good, pray, would this do you?

Strep. What? If the moon were to rise no longer anywhere, I should not pay the interest.

Soc. Why so, pray?

Strep. Because the money is lent out by the month.

Soc. Capital! But I will again propose to you another clever question. If a suit of five talents should be entered against you, tell me how you would obliterate it.

Strep. How? how? I do not know; but I must seek.

Soc. Do not then always revolve your thoughts about yourself; but slack away your mind into the air, like a cock-chafer tied with a thread by the foot.

Strep. I have found a very clever method of getting rid of my suit, so that you yourself would acknowledge it.

Soc. Of what description?

Strep. Have you ever seen this stone in the chemists' shops, the beautiful and transparent one, from which they kindle fire?

Soc. Do you mean the burning-glass?

Strep. I do. Come, what would you say, pray, if I were to take this, when the clerk was entering the suit, and were to stand at a distance, in the direction of the sun, thus, and melt out the letters of my suit?

Soc. Cleverly done, by the Graces!

Strep. Oh! how I am delighted, that a suit of five talents has been cancelled!

Soc. Come now, quickly seize upon this.

Strep. What?

Soc. How, when engaged in a lawsuit, you could overturn the suit, when you were about to be cast, because you had no witnesses.

Strep. Most readily and easily.

Soc. Tell me, pray.

Strep. Well now, I'll tell you. If, while one suit was still pending, before mine was called on, I were to run away and hang myself.

Soc. You talk nonsense.

Strep. By the gods would I! for no one will bring an action against me when I am dead.

Soc. You talk nonsense. Begone; I can't teach you any longer.

Strep. Why so? Yea, by the gods, O Socrates!

Soc. You straightway forget whatever you learn. For, what now was the first thing you were taught? Tell me.

Strep. Come, let me see: nay, what was the first?

What was the first? Nay, what was the thing in which we knead our flour? Ah me! what was it?

Soc. Will you not pack off to the devil, you most forgetful and most stupid old man?

Strep. Ah me, what then, pray, will become of me, wretched man? For I shall be utterly undone, if I no not learn to ply the tongue. Come, O ye Clouds, give me some good advice.

Cho. We, old man, advise you, if you have a son grown up, to send him to learn in your stead.

Strep. Well, I have a fine, handsome son, but he is not willing to learn. What must I do?

Cho. But do you permit him?

Strep. Yes, for he is robust in body, and in good health, and is come of the high-plumed dames of Cœsyra. I will go for him, and if he be not willing, I will certainly drive him from my house. [*To* SOCRATES.] Go in and wait for me a short time. [*Exit.*

Cho. Do you perceive that you are soon about to obtain the greatest benefits through us alone of the gods? For this man is ready to do everything that you bid him. But you, while the man is astounded and evidently elated, having perceived it, will quickly fleece him to the best of your power. [*Exit* SOCRATES.] For matters of this sort are somehow accustomed to turn the other way.

Enter STREPSIADES *and* PHIDIPPIDES

Strep. By Mist, you certainly shall not stay here any longer! but go and gnaw the columns of Megacles.

Phid. My good sir, what is the matter with you, O father? You are not in your senses, by Olympian Jupiter!

Strep. See, see! "Olympian Jupiter!" What folly! To think of your believing in Jupiter, as old as you are!

Phid. Why, pray, did you laugh at this?

Strep. Reflecting that you are a child, and have antiquated notions. Yet, however, approach, that you may know more; and I will tell you a thing, by learning which you will be a man. But see that you do not teach this to any one.

Phid. Well, what is it?

Strep. You swore now by Jupiter.

Phid. I did.

Strep. Seest thou, then, how good a thing is learning? There is no Jupiter, O Phidippides!

Phid. Who then?

Strep. Vortex reigns, having expelled Jupiter.

Phid. Bah! Why do you talk foolishly?

Strep. Be assured that it is so.

Phid. Who says this?

Strep. Socrates the Melian, and Chærephon, who knows the footmarks of fleas.

Phid. Have you arrived at such a pitch of frenzy, that you believe madmen?

Strep. Speak words of good omen, and say nothing bad of clever men and wise; of whom, through frugality, none ever shaved or anointed himself, or went to a bath to wash himself; while you squander my property in bathing, as if I were already dead. But go as quickly as possible and learn instead of me.

Phid. What good could any one learn from them?

Strep. What, really? Whatever wisdom there is among men. And you will know yourself, how ignorant and stupid you are. But wait for me here a short time.

[*Runs off.*

Phid. Ah me! what shall I do, my father being crazed? Shall I bring him into court and convict him of lunacy, or shall I give information of his madness to the coffin-makers?

Re-enter STREPSIADES *with a cock under one arm and a hen under the other*

Strep. Come, let me see; what do you consider this to be? tell me.

Phid. Alectryon.

Strep. Right. And what this?

Phid. Alectryon.

Strep. Both the same? You are very ridiculous. Do not do so, then, for the future; but call this ἀλεκτρύαινα, and this one ἀλέκτωρ.

Phid. Ἀλεκτρύαινα! Did you learn these clever things by going in just now to the Titans?

Strep. And many others too; but whatever I learned on each occasion I used to forget immediately, through length of years.

Phid. Is it for this reason, pray, you have also lost your cloak?

Strep. I have not lost it; but have studied it away.

Phid. What have you made of your slippers, you foolish man?

Strep. I have expended them, like Pericles, for needful purposes. Come, move, let us go. And then if you obey your father, go wrong if you like. I also know that I formerly obeyed you, a lisping child of six years old, and bought you a go-cart at the Diasia, with the first obolus I received from the Heliæa.

Phid. You will assuredly some time at length be grieved at this.

Strep. It is well done of you that you obeyed. Come hither, come hither, O Socrates! come forth, for I bring to you this son of mine, having persuaded him against his will.

Enter SOCRATES

Soc. For he is still childish, and not used to the baskets here.

Phid. You would yourself be used to them if you were hanged.

Strep. A mischief take you! do you abuse your teacher?

Soc. "Were hanged" quoth 'a! how sillily he pronounced it, and with lips wide apart! How can this youth ever learn an acquittal from a trial or a legal summons, or persuasive refutation? And yet Hyperbolus learned this at the cost of a talent.

Strep. Never mind; teach him. He is clever by nature. Indeed, from his earliest years, when he was a little fellow only so big, he was wont to form houses and carve ships within-doors, and make little wagons of leather, and make frogs out of pomegranate-rinds, you can't think how cleverly. But see that he learns those two causes; the better, whatever it may be; and the worse, which, by maintaining what is unjust, overturns the better. If not both, at any rate the unjust one by all means.

Soc. He shall learn it himself from the two causes in person.   [*Exit* SOCRATES.

Strep. I will take my departure. Remember this now, that he is to be able to reply to all just arguments. [*Exit* STREPSIADES, *and enter* JUST CAUSE *and* UNJUST CAUSE.

Just Cause. Come hither! show yourself to the spectators, although being audacious.

Unjust Cause. Go whither you please; for I shall far rather do for you, if I speak before a crowd.

Just. You destroy me? Who are you?

Unj. A cause.

Just. Ay, the worse.

Unj. But I conquer you, who say that you are better than I.

Just. By doing what clever trick?

Unj. By discovering new contrivances.

Just. For these innovations flourish by the favour of these silly persons.

Unj. No; but wise persons.

Just. I will destroy you miserably.

Unj. Tell me, by doing what?

Just. By speaking what is just.

Unj. But I will overturn them by contradicting them; for I deny that justice even exists at all.

Just. Do you deny that it exists?

Unj. For come, where is it?

Just. With the gods.

Unj. How, then, if justice exists, has Jupiter not perished, who bound his own father?

Just. Bah! this profanity now is spreading! Give me a basin.

Unj. You are a dotard and absurd.

Just. You are debauched and shameless.

Unj. You have spoken roses of me.

Just. And a dirty lickspittle.

Unj. You crown me with lilies.

Just. And a parricide.

Unj. You don't know that you are sprinkling me with gold.

Just. Certainly not so formerly, but with lead.

Unj. But now this is an ornament to me.

Just. You are very impudent.

Unj. And you are antiquated.

Just. And through you, no one of our youths is willing to go to school; and you will be found out some time or other by the Athenians, what sort of doctrines you teach the simple-minded.

Unj. You are shamefully squalid.

Just. And you are prosperous. And yet formerly you were a beggar, saying that you were the Mysian Tele-phus, and gnawing the maxims of Pandeletus out of your little wallet.

Unj. Oh, the wisdom—

Just. Oh, the madness—

Unj. Which you have mentioned.

Just. And of your city, which supports you who ruin her youths.

Unj. You sha'n't teach this youth, you old dotard.

Just. Yes, if he is to be saved, and not merely to prac-tise loquacity.

Unj. (*to* PHIDIPPIDES). Come hither, and leave him to rave.

Just. You shall howl, if you lay your hand on him.

Cho. Cease from contention and railing. But show to us, you, what you used to teach the men of former times, and you, the new system of education; in order that, having heard you disputing, he may decide and go to the school of one or the other.

Just. I am willing to do so.

Unj. I also am willing.

Cho. Come now, which of the two shall speak first?

Unj. I will give him the precedence; and then, from these things which he adduces, I will shoot him dead with new words and thoughts. And at last, if he mutter, he shall be destroyed, being stung in his whole face and his two eyes by my maxims, as if by bees.

Cho. Now the two, relying on very dexterous arguments and thoughts, and sententious maxims, will show which of them shall appear superior in argument. For now the whole crisis of wisdom is here laid before them; about which my friends have a very great contest. But do you, who adorned our elders with many virtuous manners, utter the voice in which you rejoice, and declare your nature.

Just. I will, therefore, describe the ancient system of education, how it was ordered, when I flourished in the advocacy of justice, and temperance was the fashion. In the first place it was incumbent that no one should hear the voice of a boy uttering a syllable; and next, that those from the same quarter of the town should march in good order through the streets to the school of the harp-master, naked, and in a body, even if it were to snow as thick as meal. Then again, their master would teach them, not sitting cross-legged, to learn by rote a song, either " Παλλάδα περσέπολιν δεινὰν," or " τηλέπορόν τι βόαμα," raising to a higher pitch the harmony which our fathers transmitted to us. But if any of them were to play the buffoon, or turn any quavers, like these difficult turns the present artists make after the manner of Phrynis, he used to be thrashed, being beaten with many

blows, as banishing the Muses. And it behooved the
boys, while sitting in the school of the Gymnastic-master,
to cover the thigh, so that they might exhibit nothing in-
decent to those outside; then, again, after rising from the
ground, to sweep the sand together, and to take care not
to leave an impression of the person for their lovers.
And no boy used in those days to anoint himself below
the navel; so that their bodies wore the appearance of
blooming health. Nor used he to go to his lover, having
made up his voice in an effeminate tone, prostituting himself with his eyes. Nor used it to be allowed when one
was dining to take the head of a radish, or to snatch from
their seniors dill or parsley, or to eat fish, or to giggle, or
to keep the legs crossed.

Unj. Aye, antiquated and Dipolia - like, and full of
grasshoppers, and of Cecydes, and of the Buphonian
festival!

Just. Yet certainly these are those principles by which
my system of education nurtured the men who fought at
Marathon. But you teach the men of the present day,
from their earliest years, to be wrapped up in himatia;
so that I am choked, when at the Panathenaia a fellow,
holding his shield before his person, neglects Tritogenia,
when they ought to dance. Wherefore, O youth, choose,
with confidence, me, the better cause, and you will learn
to hate the Agora, and to refrain from baths, and to be
ashamed of what is disgraceful, and to be enraged if any
one jeer you, and to rise up from seats before your seniors
when they approach, and not to behave ill toward your
parents, and to do nothing else that is base, because you
are to form in your mind an image of Modesty: and not
to dart into the house of a dancing woman, lest, while
gaping after these things, being struck with an apple by
a wanton, you should be damaged in your reputation:
and not to contradict your father in anything; nor by
calling him Iapetus, to reproach him with the ills of age,
by which you were reared in your infancy.

Unj. If you shall believe him in this, O youth, by Bacchus, you will be like the sons of Hippocrates, and they will call you a booby.

Just. Yet certainly shall you spend your time in the gymnastic schools, sleek and blooming; not chattering in the market-place rude jests, like the youths of the present day; nor dragged into court for a petty suit, greedy, pettifogging, knavish; but you shall descend to the Academy and run races beneath the sacred olives along with some modest compeer, crowned with white reeds, redolent of yew, and careless ease, and of leaf-shedding white poplar, rejoicing in the season of spring, when the plane-tree whispers to the elm. If you do these things which I say, and apply your mind to these, you will ever have a stout chest, a clear complexion, broad shoulders, a little tongue, large hips, little lewdness. But if you practise what the youths of the present day do, you will have, in the first place, a pallid complexion, small shoulders, a narrow chest, a large tongue, little hips, great lewdness, a long psephism; and this deceiver will persuade you to consider everything that is base to be honourable, and what is honourable to be base; and, in addition to this, he will fill you with the lewdness of Antimachus.

Cho. O thou that practisest most renowned high-towering wisdom! how sweetly does a modest grace attend your words! Happy, therefore, were they who lived in those days, in the times of former men! In reply, then, to these, O thou that hast a dainty-seeming Muse, it behooveth thee to say something new; since the man has gained renown. And it appears you have need of powerful arguments against him, if you are to conquer the man, and not incur laughter.

Unj. And yet I was choking in my heart, and was longing to confound all these with contrary maxims. For I have been called among the deep thinkers the "worse cause," on this very account, that I first contrived how to speak against both law and justice : and this art is worth more than ten thousand staters, that one should choose the worse cause, and nevertheless be victorious. But mark how I will confute the system of education on which he relies, who says, in the first place, that he will not permit you to be washed with warm water. And yet, on what principle do you blame the warm baths?

Just. Because it is most vile, and makes a man cowardly.

Unj. Stop! For immediately I seize and hold you by the waist without escape. Come, tell me, which of the sons of Jupiter do you deem to have been the bravest in soul, and to have undergone most labours?

Just. I consider no man superior to Hercules.

Unj. Where, pray, did you ever see cold Heraclean baths? And yet, who was more valiant than he?

Just. These are the very things which make the bath full of youths always chattering all day long, but the palæstras empty.

Unj. You next find fault with their living in the market-place; but I commend it. For if it had been bad, Homer would never have been for representing Nestor as an orator; nor all the other wise men. I will return, then, from thence to the tongue, which this fellow says our youths ought not to exercise, while I maintain they should. And, again, he says they ought to be modest: two very great evils. For tell me to whom you have ever seen any good accrue through modesty; and confute me by your words.

Just. To many. Peleus, at any rate, received his sword on account of it.

Unj. A sword? Marry, he got a pretty piece of luck, the poor wretch! while Hyperbolus, he of the lamps, got more than many talents by his villainy, but, by Jupiter, no sword!

Just. And Peleus married Thetis, too, through his modesty.

Unj. And then she went off, and left him; for he was

not lustful, nor an agreeable bedfellow to spend the night with. Now a woman delights in being wantonly treated. But you are an old dotard. For (*to* PHIDIPPIDES) consider, O youth, all that attaches to modesty, and of how many pleasures you are about to be deprived—of women, of games at cottabus, of dainties, of drinking-bouts, of giggling. And yet, what is life worth to you if you be deprived of these enjoyments? Well, I will pass from thence to the necessities of our nature. You have gone astray, you have fallen in love, you have been guilty of some adultery, and then have been caught. You are undone, for you are unable to speak. But if you associate with me, indulge your inclination, dance, laugh, and think nothing disgraceful. For if you should happen to be detected as an adulterer, you will make this reply to him, "that you have done him no injury": and then refer him to Jupiter, how even he is overcome by love and women. And yet, how could you, who are a mortal, have greater power than a god?

Just. But what if he should suffer the radish through obeying you, and be depillated with hot ashes? What argument will he be able to state, to prove that he is not a blackguard?

Unj. And if he be a blackguard, what harm will he suffer?

Just. Nay, what could he ever suffer still greater than this?

Unj. What then will you say, if you be conquered by me in this?

Just. I will be silent: what else can I do?

Unj. Come now, tell me; from what class do the advocates come?

Just. From the blackguards.

Unj. I believe you. What then? from what class do tragedians come?

Just. From the blackguards.

Unj. You say well. But from what class do the public orators come?

Just. From the blackguards.

Unj. Then have you perceived that you say nothing to the purpose? And look which class among the audience is the more numerous.

Just. Well now, I'm looking.

Unj. What, then, do you see?

Just. By the gods, the blackguards to be far more numerous. This fellow, at any rate, I know; and him yonder; and this fellow with the long hair.

Unj. What, then, will you say?

Just. We are conquered. Ye blackguards, by the gods, receive my cloak, for I desert to you. [*Exeunt the* TWO CAUSES, *and re-enter* SOCRATES *and* STREPSIADES.

Soc. What then? Whether do you wish to take and lead away this your son, or shall I teach him to speak?

Strep. Teach him, and chastise him: and remember that you train him properly; on the one side able for petty suits; but train his other jaw able for the more important causes.

Soc. Make yourself easy; you shall receive him back a clever sophist.

Strep. Nay, rather, pale and wretched. [*Exeunt* SOCRATES, STREPSIADES, *and* PHIDIPPIDES.

Cho. Go ye, then: but I think that you will repent of these proceedings. We wish to speak about the judges, what they will gain, if at all they justly assist this Chorus. For in the first place, if you wish to plough up your fields in spring, we will rain for you first; but for the others afterward. And then we will protect the fruits, and the vines, so that neither drought afflict them, nor excessive wet weather. But if any mortal dishonour us who are goddesses, let him consider what evils he will suffer at our hands, obtaining neither wine nor anything else from his farm. For when his olives and vines sprout, they shall be cut down; with such slings will we smite them. And if we see him making brick, we will rain; and we will smash the tiles of his roof with round hailstones. And if he himself, or any one of his kindred or friends, at any time marry, we will rain the whole night; so that he will probably wish rather to have been even in Egypt than to have judged badly.

Enter STREPSIADES *with a meal-sack on his shoulder*

Strep. The fifth, the fourth, the third, after this the second; and then, of all days what I most fear, and dread, and abominate, immediately after this there is the Old and New. For every one, to whom I happen to be indebted, swears, and says he will ruin and utterly destroy me, having made his deposits against me; though I only ask what is moderate and just—" My good sir, one part don't take just now; the other part put off, I pray; and the other part remit "; they say that thus they will never get back their money, but abuse me, as that I am unjust, and say that they will go to law with me. Now therefore let them go to law, for it little concerns me, if Phidippides has learned to speak well. I shall soon know by knocking at the thinking-shop. [*Knocks at the door.*] Boy, I say! Boy, boy!

Enter SOCRATES

Soc. Good-morning, Strepsiades.

Strep. The same to you. But first accept this present; for one ought to compliment the teacher with a fee. And tell me about my son, if he has learned that cause, which you just now brought forward.

Soc. He has learned it.

Strep. Well done, O Fraud, all-powerful queen!

Soc. So that you can get clear off from whatever suit you please.

Strep. Even if witnesses were present when I borrowed the money?

Soc. Yea, much more! even if a thousand be present.

Strep. Then I will shout with a very loud shout: Ho! weep, you petty-usurers, both you and your principals, and your compound interests! for you can no longer do me any harm, because such a son is being reared for me in this house, shining with a double-edged tongue, my guardian, the preserver of my house, a mischief to my enemies, ending the sadness of the great woes of his father. Him do thou run and summon from within to me. [SOCRATES *goes into the house.*] O child! O son! come forth from the house! hear your father!

Re-enter SOCRATES *leading in* PHIDIPPIDES

Soc. Lo, here is the man!

Strep. O my dear, my dear!

Soc. Take your son and depart.　　　[*Exit* SOCRATES.

Strep. Oh, oh, my child! Huzza! Huzza! how I am delighted at the first sight of your complexion! Now, indeed, you are, in the first place, negative and disputatious to look at, and this fashion native to the place plainly appears, the "What do you say?" and the seeming to be injured when, I well know, you are injuring and inflicting a wrong; and in your countenance there is the Attic look. Now, therefore, see that you save me, since you have also ruined me.

Phid. What, pray, do you fear?

Strep. The Old and New.

Phid. Why, is any day old and new?

Strep. Yes; on which they say that they will make their deposits against me.

Phid. Then those that have made them will lose them; for it is not possible that two days can be one day.

Strep. Can not it?

Phid. Certainly not; unless the same woman can be both old and young at the same time.

Strep. And yet it is the law.

Phid. For they do not, I think, rightly understand what the law means.

Strep. And what does it mean?

Phid. The ancient Solon was by nature the commons' friend.

Strep. This surely is nothing whatever to the Old and New.

Phid. He therefore made the summons for two days, for the Old and New, that the deposits might be made on the first of the month.

Strep. Why, pray, did he add the old day?

Phid. In order, my good sir, that the defendants, being present a day before, might compromise the matter of their own accord; but if not, that they might be worried on the morning of the new moon.

Strep. Why, then, do the magistrates not receive the deposits on the new moon, but on the Old and New?

Phid. They seem to me to do what the forestallers do: in order that they may appreciate the deposits as soon as possible, on this account they have the first pick by one day.

Strep. (*turning to the audience*). Bravo! ye wretches, why do you sit senseless, the gain of us wise men, being blocks, ciphers, mere sheep, jars heaped together? Wherefore I must sing an encomium upon myself and this my son, on account of our good fortune.—"O happy Strepsiades! how wise you are yourself, and how excellent is the son whom you are rearing!" my friends and fellow-tribesmen will say of me, envying me, when you prove victorious in arguing causes.—But first I wish to lead you in and entertain you. [*Exeunt* STREPSIADES *and* PHIDIPPIDES.

Pasias (*entering with his summons-witness*). Then, ought a man to throw away any part of his own property? Never! but it were better then at once to put away blushes, rather than now to have trouble; since I am now dragging you to be a witness, for the sake of my own money; and further, in addition to this, I shall become an enemy to my fellow-tribesman. But never, while I live, will I disgrace my country, but will summon Strepsiades—

Strep. (*from within*). Who's there?

Enter STREPSIADES

Pas. For the Old and New.

Strep. I call you to witness, that he has named it for two days. For what matter do you summon me?

Pas. For the twelve minæ, which you received when you were buying the dapple-gray horse.

Strep. A horse?—Do you not hear? I, whom you all know to hate horsemanship!

Pas. And, by Jupiter! you swore by the gods too, that you would repay it.

Strep. Ay, by Jove! for then my Phidippides did not yet know the irrefragable argument.

Pas. And do you now intend, on this account, to deny the debt?

Strep. Why, what good should I get else from his instruction?

Pas. And will you be willing to deny these upon oath of the gods?

Strep. What gods?

Pas. Jupiter, Mercury, and Neptune.

Strep. Yes, by Jupiter! and would pay down, too, a three-obol piece besides to swear.

Pas. Then may you perish some day for your impudence!

Strep. This man would be the better for it if he were cleansed by rubbing with salt.

Pas. Ah me, how you deride me!

Strep. He will contain six choæ.

Pas. By great Jupiter and the gods, you certainly shall not do this to me with impunity!

Strep. I like your gods amazingly; and Jupiter, sworn by, is ridiculous to the knowing ones.

Pas. You will assuredly suffer punishment, some time or other, for this. But answer and dismiss me, whether you are going to repay me my money, or not.

Strep. Keep quiet now, for I will presently answer you distinctly.   [*Runs into the house.*

Pas. (*to his summons-witness*). What do you think he will do?

Witness. I think he will pay you.

Re-enter STREPSIADES *with a kneading-trough*

Strep. Where is this man who asks me for his money? Tell me what is this?

Pas. What this is? a κάρδοπος.

Strep. And do you then ask me for your money, being such an ignorant person? I would not pay, not even an obolus, to any one who called the καρδόπη κάρδοπος.

Pas. Then won't you pay me?

Strep. Not, as far as I know. Will you not then pack off as fast as possible from my door?

Pas. I will depart; and be assured of this, that I will make deposit against you, or may I live no longer!

Strep. Then you will lose it besides, in addition to your twelve minæ. And yet I do not wish you to suffer this, because you named the κάρδοπος foolishly. [*Exeunt* PASIAS *and* WITNESS, *and enter* AMYNIAS.

Amynias. Ah me! ah me!

Strep. Ha! whoever is this, who is lamenting? Surely it was not one of Carcinus's deities that spoke.

Amyn. But why do you wish to know this, who I am? —a miserable man.

Strep. Then follow your own path.

Amyn. O harsh fortune! O Fates, breaking the wheels of my horses! O Pallas, how you have destroyed me!

Strep. What evil, pray, has Tlepolemus ever done you?

Amyn. Do not jeer me, my friend; but order your son to pay me the money which he received; especially as I have been unfortunate.

Strep. What money is this?

Amyn. That which he borrowed.

Strep. Then you were really unlucky, as I think.

Amyn. By the gods, I fell while driving my horses.

Strep. Why, pray, do you talk nonsense, as if you had fallen from an ass?

Amyn. Do I talk nonsense if I wish to recover my money?

Strep. You can't be in your senses yourself.

Amyn. Why, pray?

Strep. You appear to me to have had your brains shaken as it were.

Amyn. And you appear to me, by Hermes, to be going to be summoned, if you will not pay me the money?

Strep. Tell me now, whether you think that Jupiter always rains fresh rain on each occasion, or that the sun draws from below the same water back again?

Amyn. I know not which; nor do I care.

Strep. How then is it just that you should recover your money, if you know nothing of meteorological matters?

Amyn. Well, if you are in want, pay me the interest of my money.

Strep. What sort of animal is this interest?

Amyn. Most assuredly the money is always becoming more and more every month and every day as the time slips away.

Strep. You say well. What then? Is it possible that you consider the sea to be greater now than formerly?

Amyn. No, by Jupiter, but equal: for it is not fitting that it should be greater.

Strep. And how then, you wretch, does this become no way greater, though the rivers flow into it, while you seek to increase your money?—Will you not take yourself off from my house? Bring me the goad.

Enter SERVANT *with a goad*

Amyn. I call you to witness these things.

Strep. (*beating him*). Go! why do you delay? Won't you march, Mr. Blood-horse?

Amyn. Is not this an insult, pray?

22

Strep. Will you move quickly? [*Pricks him behind with the goad.*] I'll lay on you, goading you behind, you outrigger? Do you fly? [AMYNIAS *runs off.*] I thought I should stir you, together with your wheels and your two-horse chariots.   [*Exit* STREPSIADES.

Cho. What a thing it is to love evil courses! For this old man, having loved them, wishes to withhold the money that he borrowed. And he will certainly meet with something to-day, which will perhaps cause this sophist to suddenly receive some misfortune, in return for the knaveries he has begun. For I think that he will presently find what has been long boiling up, that his son is skilful to speak opinions opposed to justice, so as to overcome all with whomsoever he holds converse, even if he advance most villainous doctrines; and perhaps, perhaps his father will wish that he were even speechless.

Strep. (*running out of the house pursued by his son*). Hollo! Hollo! O neighbours and kinsfolk and fellow-tribesmen, defend me, by all means, who am being beaten! Ah me, unhappy man, for my head and jaw! Wretch! do you beat your father?

Phid. Yes, father.

Strep. You see him owning that he beats me.

Phid. Certainly.

Strep. O wretch, and parricide, and house-breaker!

Phid. Say the same things of me again, and more. Do you know that I take pleasure in being much abused?

Strep. You blackguard!

Phid. Sprinkle me with roses in abundance.

Strep. Do you beat your father?

Phid. And will prove too, by Jupiter! that I beat you with justice.

Strep. O thou most rascally! Why, how can it be just to beat a father?

Phid. I will demonstrate it, and will overcome you in argument.

Strep. Will you overcome me in this?

Phid. Yea, by much and easily. But choose which of the two Causes you wish to speak.

Strep. Of what two Causes?

Phid. The better, or the worse?

Strep. Marry, I did get you taught to speak against justice, by Jupiter, my friend, if you are going to persuade me of this, that it is just and honourable for a father to be beaten by his sons!

Phid. I think I shall certainly persuade you; so that, when you have heard, not even you yourself will say anything against it.

Strep. Well, now, I am willing to hear what you have to say.

Cho. It is your business, old man, to consider in what way you shall conquer the man; for, if he were not relying upon something, he would not be so licentious. But he is emboldened by something; the boldness of the man is evident. Now you ought to tell to the Chorus from what the contention first arose. And this you must do by all means.

Strep. Well, now, I will tell you from what we first began to rail at one another. After we had feasted, as you know, I first bade him take a lyre, and sing a song of Simonides, "The Shearing of the Ram." But he immediately said it was old-fashioned to play on the lyre, and sing while drinking, like a woman grinding parched barley.

Phid. For ought you not then immediately to be beaten and trampled on, bidding me sing, just as if you were entertaining cicadæ?

Strep. He expressed, however, such opinions then too within, as he does now; and he asserted that Simonides was a bad poet. I bore it at first, with difficulty, indeed, yet nevertheless I bore it. And then I bade him at least take a myrtle-wreath and recite to me some portion of Æschylus; and then he immediately said, "Shall I consider Æschylus the first among the poets, full of empty

sound, unpolished, bombastic, using rugged words?"
And hereupon you can't think how my heart panted.
But, nevertheless, I restrained my passion, and said, "At
least recite some passage of the more modern poets, of
whatever kind these clever things be." And he immediately sang a passage of Euripides, how a brother, O
averter of ill! debauched his uterine sister. And I bore
it no longer, but immediately assailed him with many
abusive reproaches. And then, after that, as was natural,
we hurled word upon word. Then he springs upon me;
and then he was wounding me, and beating me, and throttling me, and killing me.

Phid. Were you not therefore justly beaten, who do
not praise Euripides, the wisest of poets?

Strep. He the wisest! Oh, what shall I call you?
But I shall get beaten again.

Phid. Yes, by Jupiter, with justice!

Strep. Why, how with justice? Who, O shameless
fellow, reared you, understanding all your wishes, when
you lisped what you meant? If you said bryn, I, understanding it, used to give you to drink. And when you
asked for mamman, I used to come to you with bread.
And you used no sooner to say caccan, than I used to
take and carry you out of doors, and hold you before me.
But you now, throttling me who was bawling and crying
out because I wanted to ease myself, had not the heart to
carry me forth out of doors, you wretch; but I did it
there, while I was being throttled.

Cho. I fancy the hearts of the youths are panting to
hear what he will say. For if, after having done such
things, he shall persuade him by speaking, I would not
take the hide of the old folks, even at the price of a chick-
pea. It is thy business, thou author and upheaver of new
words, to seek some means of persuasion, so that you shall
seem to speak justly.

Phid. How pleasant it is to be acquainted with new
and clever things, and to be able to despise the established

laws! For I, when I applied my mind to horsemanship alone, used not to be able to utter three words before I made a mistake; but now, since he himself has made me cease from these pursuits, and I am acquainted with subtle thoughts, and arguments, and speculations, I think I shall demonstrate that it is just to chastise one's father.

Strep. Ride, then, by Jupiter! since it is better for me to keep a team of four horses, than to be killed with beating.

Phid. I will pass over to that part of my discourse where you interrupted me; and first I will ask you this: Did you beat me when I was a boy?

Strep. I did, through good-will and concern for you.

Phid. Pray tell me, is it not just that I also should be well inclined toward you in the same way, and beat you, since this is to be well inclined—to give a beating? For why ought your body to be exempt from blows, and mine not? And yet I too was born free. The boys weep, and do you not think it right that a father should weep? You will say that it is ordained by law that this should be the lot of boys. But I would reply, that old men are boys twice over; and that it is the more reasonable that the old should weep than the young, inasmuch as it is less just that they should err.

Strep. It is nowhere ordained by law that a father should suffer this.

Phid. Was it not then a man like you and me, who first proposed this law, and by speaking persuaded the ancients? Why then is it less lawful for me also in turn to propose henceforth a new law for the sons, that they should beat their fathers in turn? But as many blows as we received before the law was made, we remit; and we concede to them our having been well thrashed without return. Observe the cocks and these other animals, how they punish their fathers; and yet, in what do they differ from us, except that they do not write decrees?

Strep. Why then, since you imitate the cocks in all things, do you not both eat dung and sleep on a perch?

Phid. It is not the same thing, my friend; nor would it appear so to Socrates.

Strep. Therefore do not beat me; otherwise you will one day blame yourself.

Phid. Why, how?

Strep. Since I am justly entitled to chastise you; and you to chastise your son, if you should have one.

Phid. But if I should not have one, I shall have wept for nothing, and you will die laughing at me.

Strep. To me, indeed, O comrades, he seems to speak justly; and I think we ought to concede to them what is fitting. For it is proper that we should weep, if we do not act justly.

Phid. Consider still another maxim.

Strep. No; for I shall perish if I do.

Phid. And yet perhaps you will not be vexed at suffering what you now suffer.

Strep. How, pray? for inform me what good you will do me by this.

Phid. I will beat my mother, just as I have you.

Strep. What do you say? what do you say? This other, again, is a greater wickedness.

Phid. But what if, having the worst Cause, I shall conquer you in arguing, proving that it is right to beat one's mother?

Strep. Most assuredly, if you do this, nothing will hinder you from casting yourself and your Worse Cause into the pit along with Socrates.—These evils have I suffered through you, O Clouds! having intrusted all my affairs to you.

Cho. Nay, rather, you are yourself the cause of these things, having turned yourself to wicked courses.

Strep. Why, pray, did you not tell me this, then, but excited with hopes a rustic and aged man?

Cho. We always do this to him whom we perceive to

be a lover of wicked courses, until we precipitate him into misfortune, so that he may learn to fear the gods.

Strep. Ah me! it is severe, O Clouds! but it is just; for I ought not to have withheld the money which I borrowed.—Now, therefore, come with me, my dearest son, that you may destroy the blackguard Chærephon and Socrates, who deceived you and me.

Phid. I will not injure my teachers.

Strep. Yes, yes, reverence Paternal Jove.

Phid. "Paternal Jove," quoth'a! How antiquated you are! Why, is there any Jove?

Strep. There is.

Phid. There is not, no; for Vortex reigns, having expelled Jupiter.

Strep. He has not expelled him; but I fancied this, on account of this Vortex here. Ah me, unhappy man! when I even took you who are of earthenware for a god.

Phid. Here rave and babble to yourself. [*Exit* PHIDIPPIDES.

Strep. Ah me, what madness! How mad, then, I was, when I ejected the gods on account of Socrates! But, O dear Hermes, by no means be wroth with me, nor destroy me; but pardon me, since I have gone crazy through prating. And become my adviser, whether I shall bring an action and prosecute them, or whatever you think.— You advise me rightly, not permitting me to get up a lawsuit, but as soon as possible to set fire to the house of the prating fellows. Come hither, come hither, Xanthias! Come forth with a ladder, and with a mattock, and then mount upon the thinking-shop, and dig down the roof, if you love your master, until you tumble the house upon them. [XANTHIAS *mounts upon the roof.*] But let some one bring me a lighted torch, and I'll make some of them this day suffer punishment, even if they be ever so much impostors.

1st Dis. (*from within*). Hollo! hollo!

Strep. It is your business, O torch, to send forth abundant flame.   [*Mounts upon the roof.*

1st Dis. What are you doing, fellow?

Strep. What am I doing? why, what else, than chopping logic with the beams of your house? [*Sets the house on fire.*

2d Dis. (*from within*). Ah me! who is setting fire to our house?

Strep. That man, whose cloak you have taken.

3d Dis. (*from within*). You will destroy us! you will destroy us!

Strep. For I also wish this very thing; unless my mattock deceive my hopes, or I should somehow fall first and break my neck.

Soc. (*from within*). Hollo you! what are you doing, pray, you fellow on the roof?

Strep. I am walking on air, and speculating about the sun.

Soc. Ah me, unhappy! I shall be suffocated, wretched man!

Chær. And I, miserable man, shall be burnt to death!

Strep. For what has come into your heads that you acted insolently toward the gods, and pried into the seat of the moon? Chase, pelt, smite them, for many reasons, but especially because you know that they offended against the gods!   [*The thinking-shop is burned down.*

Cho. Lead the way out; for we have sufficiently acted as chorus for to-day.   [*Exeunt omnes.*

THE PLUTUS OF ARISTOPHANES

TRANSLATED BY

WILLIAM JAMES HICKIE

DRAMATIS PERSONÆ

CHREMYLUS.
CARIO, Servant of Chremylus.
CHORUS OF COUNTRY-PEOPLE.
PLUTUS, the God of Riches.
BLEPSIDEMUS.
POVERTY.
WIFE OF CHREMYLUS.
JUST MAN.
INFORMER.
OLD WOMAN.
YOUNG MAN.
MERCURY.
PRIEST OF JUPITER.

SCENE: The front of a farm-house with a road leading to it. A blind old man is seen followed at some distance by CHREMYLUS and his servant CARIO.

PLUTUS

CARIO. How troublesome a thing it is, O Jupiter and ye gods, to be the slave of a crazy master! For if the servant should happen to have given the best advice, and it should seem fit to his master not to do this, it must be that the servant share the evils; for fortune suffers not the natural owner to be master of his person, but the purchaser. And so much for this. But Loxias, who prophesies from his tripod of beaten gold, I censure with this just censure, because being a physician and a clever soothsayer, as they say, he has sent away my master melancholy-mad, who is following behind a blind man, acting contrary to what it became him to do; for we who see lead the blind; whereas he follows him, and compels me besides; and that too without even answering a syllable at all. Therefore it is not possible for me to hold my tongue, unless you tell me, master, for what in the world we are following this man, but I will give you trouble; for you will not beat me while I wear the chaplet.

Chremylus. No, by Jove! but if you trouble me in any way, I'll do it when I have taken away your chaplet, that you may grieve the more.

Ca. Nonsense! for I will not cease until you tell me who in the world this is; for I ask it, being exceedingly well disposed to you.

Chr. Well, then, I will not hide it from you, for I do

349

believe you to be the most faithful of my domestics, and
—the arrantest thief.   I, though a religious and just man,
was unprosperous and poor.

Ca. In truth I know it.

Chr. While others, sacrilegious persons, demagogues,
and informers, and villains, were rich.

Ca. I believe you.

Chr. So I went to the god to consult him, thinking
that my own life, unhappy man, had now nearly been
wasted away, but to ask about my son, who is my only
one, if he ought to change his habits and be knavish, unjust, nothing good ; since I thought this very thing to be
advantageous for life.

Ca. What then did Phœbus proclaim from among his
chaplets?

Chr. You shall hear; for the god told me this plainly :
whomsoever I should first meet with on going out, him
he bid me never let go, but prevail on him to accompany
me home.

Ca. And whom then did you first meet with?

Chr. With this man.

Ca. Then did you not understand the meaning of the
god, when it directed you, O most stupid, in the plainest
terms, to educate your son after the fashion of the country?

Chr. By what do you judge of this?

Ca. It is evident that even a blind man fancies he
knows this, that it is very advantageous to practise no
virtue in these times.

Chr. It is not possible that the oracle inclines to this,
but to something else of greater moment.   But if this fellow tell us who in the world he is, and on account of what,
and in want of what he came hither with us, we might
understand what our oracle means.

Ca. (*to* PLUTUS).   Come now, do you declare yourself
who you are, before I do what comes next?   You must
be very quick about speaking.

Plutus. A plague take you !

Ca. (*to* CHREMYLUS). Do you understand whom he professes himself to be?

Chr. He says this to you, not to me; for you inquire of him uncouthly and roughly. But [*to* PLUTUS] if you take any pleasure in the manners of a man of honour, tell me!

Plu. Go, hang yourself!

Ca. Take the man, and omen of the god.

Chr. By Ceres, you certainly shall not any longer escape unpunished!

Ca. For unless you will tell us, I will kill you, you wretch, in a wretched way.

Plu. Good sirs, depart from me.

Chr. Not a whit.

Ca. Well, now, what I say is best, master: I'll kill this fellow in a most wretched way; for I will set him up on some precipice and leave him and go away, that he may fall and break his neck.

Chr. Well, up with him quickly.

Plu. By no means.

Chr. Will you not tell us then?

Plu. But if you learn who I am, I well know that you will do me some mischief, and not let me go.

Chr. By the gods will we, if you wish it.

Plu. Then first let me go.

Chr. Lo! we let you go.

Plu. Hear now; for, as it seems, I must speak what I was prepared to conceal: I am Plutus.

Chr. O most abominable of all men! did you hold your tongue then, you Plutus?

Ca. You Plutus, so wretchedly circumstanced?

Chr. O Phœbus Apollo, and ye gods and demons, and Jove, what do you say? Are you really he?

Plu. Yes.

Chr. He himself?

Plu. His very self.

Chr. Whence then, tell us, come you so squalid?

Plu. I come from the house of Patrocles, who has not washed himself since he was born.

Chr. But how did you suffer this mishap? Declare it to me.

Plu. Jupiter treated me in this manner through envy toward mankind. For when I was a boy, I threatened that I would go to the just, and wise, and well-behaved alone. So he made me blind, that I might not distinguish any of these. So much does he envy the good.

Chr. And yet he is honoured by the good and the just alone.

Plu. I grant you.

Chr. Come, what then? if you were to recover your sight again, just as formerly, would you now shun the wicked?

Plu. Certainly.

Chr. But would you go to the just?

Plu. Most assuredly; for I have not seen them for a long time.

Chr. And no wonder too; for neither have I, who see.

Plu. Now let me go; for now you know all about me.

Chr. No, by Jove! but so much the more will we keep hold of you.

Plu. Did I not say that you would cause me trouble?

Chr. And do you, I beseech you, comply, and do not abandon me; for you will never find a man better in his morals than I, if you search. No, by Jove! for there is no other save me.

Plu. They all say this: but when they actually get possession of me, and become wealthy, they absolutely exceed all bounds in their wickedness.

Chr. So it is; yet all are not wicked.

Plu. No, by Jove! not all, but all without exception.

Ca. You shall suffer for it severely.

Chr. And that you may know how many blessings you will have, if you stay with us, give your attention, that you may hear. For I think, I think—with God's permission it shall be spoken—that I shall free you from this blindness, having made you see.

Plu. By no means do this; for I do not wish to recover my sight again.

Chr. What do you say?

Ca. This fellow is a born miserable.

Plu. I know indeed that Jupiter would destroy me, if he were to hear of the follies of these men.

Chr. But does he not do this now, who suffers you to go about stumbling?

Plu. I know not; but I dread him exceedingly.

Chr. What really, O you most cowardly of all deities? For do you suppose the sovereignty of Jove and his thunderbolts would be worth a three-obol piece, if you should recover your sight, if it were but for a short time?

Plu. Ah! say not so, you wretch!

Chr. Be quiet; for I will demonstrate you to be far more powerful than Jupiter.

Plu. Me?

Chr. Ay, by Heaven! For, for example, through whom does Jupiter rule the gods?

Ca. Through money, for he has most of it.

Chr. Come, who then is it that supplies him with this?

Ca. This person here.

Chr. And through whom do men sacrifice to him? is it not through him?

Ca. And, by Jupiter! they pray openly to be rich.

Chr. Is not he then the cause, and might he not easily put an end to this, if he wished?

Plu. Why so? why, pray?

Chr. Because no man would any longer sacrifice, either ox or barley-cake, or anything else whatever, if you were not willing.

Plu. How?

Chr. How? it is not possible for him to purchase it, I ween, unless you yourself be present and give him the

23

money; so that you alone will put down the power of Jove, if he annoy you in any way.

Plu. What do you say? do they sacrifice to him through me?

Chr. Certainly. And, by Jupiter! if there be anything magnificent and beautiful or agreeable to men, it is through you: for all things are subservient to riches.

Ca. I, in truth, have become a slave on account of a trifling sum of money, because I was not equally rich as others.

Chr. And they say that the Corinthian courtesans, when any poor man tries them, do not even pay any attention to him, but if a rich man try, that they immediately turn anything to him.

Ca. And they say that the boys do this very thing, not for their lovers', but the money's sake.

Chr. Not the better sort, but the catamites; for the better sort do not ask for money.

Ca. What then?

Chr. One asks for a good horse, another hunting dogs.

Ca. For, perhaps, being ashamed to ask for money, they gloss over their wickedness by a false name.

Chr. And all arts and clever contrivances among men have been invented through you. For one of them sits and makes shoes; and some other one is a smith, and another a carpenter; another is a goldsmith, having received gold from you; another, by Jove! steals clothes; another is a house-breaker; another is a fuller; another washes fleeces; another is a tanner; another sells onions; another, having been detected as an adulterer, is depillated through you.

Plu. Ah me, miserable! this has been unknown to me this long while.

Ca. And does not the Great King pride himself through him? And is not the Assembly held through him? But how?—do you not man the triremes? tell me. And does not he support the mercenaries in Corinth?

And will not Pamphilus suffer through him? And will not the "Needle-seller" along with Pamphilus? And does not Agyrrhius spout through him? And [*to* PLUTUS] does not Philepsius relate fables on account of you? And is not the alliance with the Egyptians through you? And does not Lais, through you, love Philonides? And the tower of Timotheus——

Chr. —— May it fall upon you. And [*to* PLUTUS] are not all our affairs transacted through you? For you alone are the cause of all, both of our miseries and our blessings, be well assured.

Ca. At any rate, in wars also, they always conquer, upon whom he only sits down.

Plu. Am I able, single as I am, to effect so many things?

Chr. And, by Jupiter! far more than these; so that no one has ever at any time been sated of you. For of all the rest there is a satiety. Of love,

Ca. Of bread,

Chr. Of music,

Ca. Of sweetmeats,

Chr. Of honour,

Ca. Of cheese-cakes,

Chr. Of manly virtue,

Ca. Of dried figs,

Chr. Of ambition,

Ca. Of barley-cakes,

Chr. Of military command,

Ca. Of lentil-broth.

Chr. But of you no one has ever at any time been sated. But if any one get thirteen talents, so much the more does he desire to get sixteen. And if he accomplish this, he wishes for forty, or he says his life is not worth living.

Plu. In truth you appear to me to speak exceedingly well; but one thing only I fear.

Chr. Tell us, what about.

Plu. How I shall become master of this power which you say I have.

Chr. Yes, by Jove, you shall! But even all say that wealth is a most timid thing.

Plu. By no means; but some housebreaker has calumniated me. For having once crept into the house, he was not able to get anything, having found everything locked up; so then he called my forethought cowardice.

Chr. Let nothing trouble you now; for if you be a zealous man yourself in the business, I'll make you more sharp-sighted than Lynceus.

Plu. How then will you be able to do this, mortal as you are?

Chr. I have some good hope from what Phœbus himself told me, having shaken the Pythian laurel.

Plu. And was he then privy to this?

Chr. Certainly.

Plu. Take care!

Chr. Do not be at all concerned, my good sir; for I, be well assured of this, will accomplish this myself, even if I must die for it.

Ca. And I too, if you wish it.

Chr. And many others will be our allies, as many as had no bread, though they were just.

Plu. Deary me! you tell us of miserable allies.

Chr. Not so, if they become rich again as before. But do you [*to* Cario] go and run quickly——

Ca. What am I to do? Tell me.

Chr. Call my fellow-labourers—and you will probably find them working hard in the fields—that each, being present here, may share an equal portion with us of this Plutus.

Ca. Well now, I am going. But let some one of the servants from within take and carry in this small bit of meat.

Chr. (*taking the meat*). This shall be my care: but run quickly. [*Exit* Cario.] And do you, O Plutus, most excellent of all gods, go in this way with me; for this is the house which you must to-day fill with riches, by fair means or by foul.

Plu. But, by the gods, I am exceedingly loath to be always going into other people's houses. For I never at any time got any good from it. For if I chance to go into the house of a miser, he immediately buries me deep in the earth: and if any good man, his friend, come to him asking to get some small sum of money, he denies that he has ever at any time even seen me. But if I chance to go into the house of a mad fellow, I am exposed to harlots and dice and driven out of doors naked in a moment of time.

Chr. Yes; for you never at any time met with a moderate man. But I am somehow always of this character. For I both take pleasure in saving, as never man did, and again in spending, whenever there is occasion for it. But let us go in; for I wish both my wife to see you and my only son, whom I love most of all—next to you.

Plu. I believe you.

Chr. For why should one not tell the truth to you?
[*Exeunt* CHREMYLUS *and* PLUTUS.

Ca. Oh, you who have often eaten of the same thyme with my master, his friends, and fellow-tribesmen, and lovers of labour, come, make haste, hurry, since the time does not admit delay, but it is at the very crisis at which you ought to be present and lend your aid.

Chorus of Country-people. Don't you see then that we have been actively hastening this long while, as is reasonable those should who are now feeble old men? But you, perhaps, expect that I should run, before you even tell me this, on what account your master has called me hither.

Ca. Have I not then, I ween, been telling you this long while? It is you yourself that don't hear. For my master says that you shall all of you live pleasantly, freed from your dreary and unpleasant mode of life.

Cho. But what, pray, and whence, is this thing which he speaks of?

Ca. He has come hither with a certain old man, ye wretches, who is filthy, crooked, miserable, wrinkled, bald, and toothless; and, by Heaven! I think he is circumcised, too.

Cho. O you who have announced golden tidings, how say you? tell me again! For you plainly show that he is come with a heap of money.

Ca. Nay, rather, with a heap of the ills of age.

Cho. Do you expect, after humbugging us, to get off unpunished, and that, too, when I have a staff?

Ca. Why, do you consider me to be altogether such a man by nature in all respects, and do you think that I would say nothing true?

Cho. How haughty the rascal is! Your legs are crying out, "Oh! oh!" longing for the stocks and fetters.

Ca. But are you not for going, when now your letter has assigned you to administer justice in the tomb, and Charon gives you your ticket?

Cho. Split you! What an impudent fellow you are, and arrant knave by nature, who humbug us, and have not yet had the patience to tell us on what account your master has called us hither, who, after labouring much, have come hither readily, though we had no leisure, passing over many roots of thyme!

Ca. Well, then, I will not conceal it any longer; for, sirs, my master has come with Plutus, who will make you rich.

Cho. Why, is it really possible for us all to be rich?

Ca. Nay, rather, by the gods, all Midases, if you get ass's ears.

Cho. How I am delighted and gladdened, and wish to dance for joy, if you are really speaking this truly!

Ca. Well, now, I should like to lead you, imitating the Cyclops, threttanelo! and moving thus to and fro with my feet. But come, my children, crying out frequently, and bleating the strains of sheep and stinking goats, follow me lewdly, and you shall breakfast like goats.

Cho. And we, on the other hand, bleating, when we have caught you, this Cyclops, threttanelo! dirty, with a wallet and dewy, wild potherbs, having a drunken headache, leading your sheep, and carelessly asleep somewhere, will take a great lighted, sharp stake and try to blind you.

Ca. And I will imitate in all her ways Circe, who mixed up the drugs, who once in Corinth persuaded the companions of Philonides, as if they were boars, to eat kneaded dung; while she herself kneaded it for them. But do you, grunting for delight, follow, like swine, your mother.

Cho. Therefore we, having caught you, the Circe, who mixed up the drugs and bewitched and defiled our companions, imitating for delight the son of Laertes, will hang you up and besmear your nostrils with dung, like a goat's; while you, gaping like Aristyllus, shall say, " Follow, like swine, your mother."

Ca. But come now, do you now have done with your jests and turn yourselves into another shape; while I should like now to go unknown to my master and take some bread and meat and eat it, and so afterward to join in the work. [*Exit* CARIO.

Chremylus (*entering and addressing the* CHORUS). To bid you " hail," my fellow-tribesmen, is now old-fashioned and obsolete; so I "embrace you," because you have come readily and eagerly, and not tardily. But see that you be my coadjutors in the rest as well, and truly preservers of the god.

Cho. Be of good courage! for you shall think I look downright martial. For it would be absurd if we constantly jostle one another in the Assembly for the sake of three obols, while I were to yield up Plutus himself to any one to take away.

Chr. Well, now, I see also Blepsidemus here approaching: and 'tis plain from his gait and haste that he has heard something of the affair.

Enter BLEPSIDEMUS

Blepsidemus (*talking to himself*). What then can the affair be? in what way has Chremylus suddenly become rich? I don't believe it: and yet, by Hercules, there was much talk among those who sat in the barbers' shops, that the man has suddenly become wealthy. But this very thing is marvellous to me, that he, being well off, sends for his friends. In truth he does not do a thing fashionable in the country.

Chr. (*aside*). Well then, by the gods, I'll tell him, without concealing anything. O Blepsidemus, we are better off than yesterday, so that it is permitted you to share; for you are of the number of my friends.

Bl. But have you really become rich, as people say?

Chr. Nay, but I shall be very soon, if God please; for there is—there is some hazard in the affair.

Bl. Of what sort?

Chr. Such as——

Bl. Tell me quickly what in the world you mean.

Chr. —that, if we succeed, we shall be always well off; but if we be foiled, we shall be utterly undone.

Bl. This load looks bad, and does not please me. For your suddenly becoming so excessively rich, and, again, your fearing, is in character with a man who has done nothing good.

Chr. How nothing good?

Bl. If, by Jove! you have come from thence, having stolen any silver or gold from the god, and then, perhaps, repent.

Chr. O Apollo, averter of evil! not I, by Jove!

Bl. Cease talking nonsense, my good sir; for I know it for certain.

Chr. Do you suspect nothing of the kind of me.

Bl. Alas! how there is absolutely no good in any one! but all are slaves of gain.

Chr. By Ceres! you certainly do not appear to me to be in your right senses.

Bl. (*aside*). How much he has altered from the character he formerly had!

Chr. By Heaven, fellow, you are mad!

Bl. (*aside*). But not even does his glance itself keep in its place, but is like to one who has committed some villainy.

Chr. I know what you are croaking about: you seek to get a share, as if I had stolen something.

Bl. I seek to get a share? of what?

Chr. Whereas it is not of such nature, but different.

Bl. Have you not stolen, but snatched it away?

Chr. You are possessed.

Bl. But have you, in truth, not even defrauded any one?

Chr. Not I, indeed!

Bl. O Hercules, come, whither can one turn himself? for you will not tell the truth.

Chr. For you accuse me before you know my case.

Bl. My good friend, I will settle this for you at a very trifling expense, before the city hear of it, by stopping the orators' mouths with small coin.

Chr. And verily, by the gods, methinks you would in a friendly way lay out three minæ and set down twelve.

Bl. I see a certain person who will sit at the Bema, holding the suppliant's bough, with his children and his wife; and who will not differ at all, not even in any way, from the Heraclidæ of Pamphilus.

Chr. Not so, you wretch, but, on the contrary, I will cause the good alone, and the clever and discreet, to become rich.

Bl. What do you say? have you stolen so very much?

Chr. Ah me, what miseries! you will destroy me.

Bl. Nay, rather, you will destroy yourself, as it seems to me.

Chr. Certainly not; for I have got Plutus, you sorry wretch.

Bl. You, Plutus? what Plutus?

Chr. The god himself.

Bl. Why, where is he?

Chr. Within.

Bl. Where?

Chr. At my house.

Bl. At your house?

Chr. Certainly.

Bl. Go to the devil! Plutus at your house?

Chr. Yes, by the gods!

Bl. Are you speaking truth?

Chr. Yes.

Bl. By Vesta?

Chr. Yea, by Neptune!

Bl. Do you mean the sea Neptune?

Chr. Ay, and t'other Neptune, if there be any other.

Bl. Then are you not for sending him round to us also your friends?

Chr. The affair is not yet come to this point.

Bl. What do you say? not to the sharing point—eh?

Chr. No, by Jupiter! for we must first——

Bl. What?

Chr. Cause him to see.

Bl. Whom to see? tell me.

Chr. Plutus, as before, in some way or other.

Bl. Why, is he really blind?

Chr. Yes, by Heaven!

Bl. No wonder, then, he never at any time came to me.

Chr. But, if the gods please, he shall come now.

Bl. Ought you not then to call in some physician?

Chr. What physician then is there now in the city? For neither is the fee of any value, nor the profession.

Bl. Let us see.

Chr. But there is none.

Bl. Neither do I think so.

Chr. No, by Jupiter! but 'tis best to lay him on a couch in the Temple of Æsculapius, as I was intending this long while.

Bl. Nay, rather, far the best, by the gods. Do not then delay, but make haste and do something or other.

Chr. Well now, I am going.

Bl. Hasten then.

Chr. I am doing this very thing.

Enter POVERTY

Poverty. O you pitiful manikins, who dare to do a hasty and unholy and unlawful deed! whither? whither? why do you fly? will you not remain?

Bl. O Hercules!

Pov. I will destroy you, you wretches, in a wretched way; for you are venturing on a daring act not to be borne, but such as no other person even at any time, either god or man, has ventured on; therefore you are undone.

Chr. But who are you? for you appear to me to be ghastly pale.

Bl. Perhaps 'tis some Fury from tragedy: at least she certainly looks very mad and tragic.

Chr. But she has no torches.

Bl. Then she shall suffer for it.

Pov. Whom do you think me to be?

Chr. Some hostess or pulse-porridge-seller: for otherwise you would not have cried out so loud against us, having been wronged in no way.

Pov. What, really? for have you not acted most shamefully in seeking to banish me from every place?

Chr. Is not then the Barathrum left you? But you ought to tell me immediately who you are.

Pov. One who will make you to-day give satisfaction, because you seek to expel me from hence.

Bl. Is it the tavern-keeper of our neighbourhood, who is always cheating me grossly with her half-pints?

Pov. Nay, but I am Poverty, who have been dwelling with you many years.

Bl. (*running away*). O King Apollo, and ye gods! Whither must one fly?

Chr. Halloo! what are you about? O you most cowardly beast, will you not stay?

Bl. By no means.

Chr. Will you not stay? What! shall we two men fly from one woman?

Bl. Yes, for 'tis Poverty, you wretch, than whom there is no living being anywhere more ruinous.

Chr. Stand, I beseech you, stand!

Bl. No, by Jove, not I!

Chr. Well, now, I tell you, we shall do a deed by far the most shameful of all deeds, if we shall leave the god unprotected and fly any whither, through fear of her, and not fight it out.

Bl. Relying on what sort of arms or strength? For what sort of breastplate and what sort of shield does not the most abominable wretch put in pawn?

Chr. Be of good courage; for this god alone, I well know, can set up a trophy over her ways.

Pov. And do you also dare to mutter, you scoundrels, when you have been detected in the very act of doing shameful things?

Chr. But why do you, the devil take you, come against us and revile us, being wronged not even in any way?

Pov. For do you think, oh, by the gods! that you wrong me in no way in endeavouring to make Plutus see again?

Chr. What wrong then do we do you in this, if we contrive good for all men?

Pov. But what good could you devise?

Cho. What? by banishing you from Greece, in the first place.

Pov. By banishing me? and what greater evil do you suppose you could do to men?

Chr. What, if we were to delay to do this and forget it?

Pov. Well, now, I wish first to render you an account of this very matter. And if I prove that I am the sole cause of all blessings to you, and that you live through me, it is well; but if not, now do this, whatever seems good to you.

Chr. Do you dare to say this, O most abominable?

Pov. Ay, and do you suffer yourself to be taught. For I think I shall very easily prove that you are altogether in the wrong, if you say you will make the just wealthy.

 Chr. O cudgels and pillories, will you not aid me?

Pov. You ought not to complain angrily and cry out before you know.

Bl. Why, who would be able not to cry out "Oh! oh!" at hearing such things?

Pov. He who is in his right senses.

Chr. What penalty, then, shall I set down in the title of the suit for you, if you be cast?

Pov. Whatever seems good to you.

Chr. You say well.

Pov. For you also must suffer the same if you lose your cause.

Bl. Do you think then twenty deaths sufficient?

Chr. Yes, for her; but two only will suffice for us.

Pov. You can not be too quick in doing this: for what just plea could any one any longer bring against me?

Cho. Well, you ought now to say something clever, by which you shall conquer her, opposing her in argument, and not effeminately give in.

Chr. I think that this is plain for all alike to understand, that it is just that the good men should be prosperous, but the wicked and the ungodly, I ween, the contrary of this. We therefore desiring that this should take place, have with difficulty found out a plan, excellent, and noble, and useful for every enterprise. For if Plutus now should have the use of his eyes, and not go about blind, he will go to the good men, and not leave them, but will fly from the wicked and the ungodly; and then he will make all to be good and rich, I ween, and to reverence things divine. And yet, who could ever devise a better thing than this for men?

Bl. No one; I am your witness in this; don't ask her.

Chr. For as life is at present circumstanced for us men, who would not think it to be madness, or rather still a demoniacal possession? For many men who are wicked are rich, having accumulated them unjustly; while many who are very good, are badly off, and suffer hunger, and live with you [*to* POVERTY] for the most part. I say, then, that there is a way, proceeding upon which a person might procure greater benefits for men, namely, if Plutus were ever to have the use of his eyes and put a stop to her.

Pov. Nay, O you two old dotards, partners in nonsense and folly, of all men the most easily persuaded not to be in your right senses, if this were to happen, which you desire, I deny that it would profit you. For if Plutus were to have the use of his eyes again and portion himself out equally, no man would practise either art or science; and when both these have disappeared through you, who will be willing to be a smith, or to build ships, or to sew, or to make wheels, or to make shoes, or to make bricks, or to wash, or to tan hides, or who will be willing to break up the soil of the earth with ploughings and reap the fruits of Ceres, if it be possible for you to live in idleness, neglecting all these?

Chr. You talk nonsense; for our servants shall toil at all these things for us, as many as you have now enumerated.

Pov. Whence then will you have servants?

Chr. We will buy them for money, to be sure.

Pov. But first, who will be the seller, when he too has money?

Chr. Some one wishing to make gain, having come as a merchant from Thessaly, from among very many kidnappers.

Pov. But first of all, there will not even be any one, not even a kidnapper, according to the statement, I ween, which you mention. For who that is wealthy will be willing to do this at the hazard of his own life? So that, having been compelled to plough, and dig, and toil at the other labours yourself, you will spend a much more painful life than the present one.

Chr. May it fall on your own head!

Pov. Moreover, you will not be able to sleep either in a bed—for there will be none—or in carpets; for who will be willing to weave them when he has gold? Nor, when you lead home a bride, to anoint her with dropping unguents; nor to adorn her with sumptuous garments, dyed, and variegated. And yet, what advantage will it be to you to be rich, when in want of all these? But from me all these which you stand in need of are easily obtained; for I sit, compelling the artisan, like a mistress, through his want and his poverty, to seek whence he shall have subsistence.

Chr. Why, what good could you procure, except a swarm of blisters from the bath, and of children beginning to be hungry, and of old women? and the quantity of lice, and gnats, and fleas, I don't even mention to you, by reason of their multitude, which buzz about my head and torment me, wakening me and saying: "You will suffer hunger; come, get up." Moreover, to have a rag instead of a garment; and instead of a bed, a mattress of rushes, full of bugs, which wakens the sleepers; and to have a rotten mat instead of a carpet; and a good-sized stone against one's head instead of a pillow; and to eat shoots of mallow instead of bread; and leaves of withered radish instead of barley-cake; and to have the head of a broken jar instead of a bench; and the side of a cask, and that too broken, instead of a kneading-trough. Do

I not demonstrate you to be the cause of many blessings to all men?

Pov. You have not mentioned my way of life, but have attacked that of beggars.

Chr. Therefore we say, I ween, that poverty is sister of beggary.

Pov. Ay, you who also say that Dionysus is like Thrasybulus. But my mode of life is not thus circumstanced, no, by Jove! nor will it. For a beggar's mode of life, which you describe, is to live possessed of nothing; but that of a poor man to live sparingly, and attentive to his work; and not to have any superfluity, nor yet, however, to have a deficiency.

Chr. O Ceres! how blessed is his life which you have set forth, if after sparing and toiling he shall leave behind him not even wherewith to be buried.

Pov. You are trying to scoff at and ridicule me, heedless of being earnest, not knowing that I render men better both in mind and body than Plutus does. For with him they are gouty in their feet, and pot-bellied, and thick-legged, and extravagantly fat; but with me they are thin and slender, and grievous to their foes.

Chr. For, no doubt, you bring about the slenderness for them by hunger.

Pov. Now therefore I will discourse to you respecting sobriety, and will demonstrate that orderly behaviour dwells with me, but that riotousness belongs to Plutus.

Chr. In sooth it is very orderly to steal and to dig through walls.

Bl. Yes, by Jove! how is it not orderly, if he must escape notice?

Pov. Consider therefore the orators in the states, how, when they are poor, they are just toward the people and the state; but when they have become rich out of the public purse, they immediately become unjust, and plot against the commons, and make war upon the democracy.

Chr. Well, you don't speak falsely in any of these

things, although you are exceedingly slanderous. But you shall suffer none the less—don't pride yourself on this—because you seek to convince us of this, that poverty is better than riches.

Pov. And you too are not yet able to refute me about this, but talk nonsense and flap your wings.

Chr. Why, how is it that all shun you?

Pov. Because I make them better. But you may see it best in children; for they shun their fathers who are very well-disposed toward them. So difficult a matter is it to distinguish what is right.

Chr. You will say, then, that Jupiter does not correctly distinguish what is best; for he too has wealth.

Bl. And despatches her to us.

Pov. Nay, O you who are both of you purblind in your minds with old-fashioned prejudices, Jupiter is certainly poor; and I will now teach you this clearly. For if he was rich, how would he, when celebrating the Olympic games himself, where he assembles all the Greeks every fifth year, have proclaimed as conquerors the victorious athletes, having crowned them with a chaplet of wild olive? And yet he ought rather to crown them with gold, if he was rich?

Chr. By this therefore he certainly shows that he honours riches. For through parsimony and a wish to spend none of it, he crowns the victors with trifles and lets his wealth remain by him.

Pov. You seek to fix upon him a much more disgraceful thing than poverty, if he, though rich, be so stingy and avaricious.

Chr. Well, may Jupiter utterly destroy you, having crowned you with a chaplet of wild olive!

Pov. To think of your daring to contradict me, that all your blessings are not through poverty!

Chr. One may learn this from Hecate, whether to be rich or to suffer hunger is better. For she says that those who have property and are wealthy send a dinner every

24

month, while the poor people snatch it away before one
has set it down. But go and be hanged, and don't mutter
anything more whatever. For you shall not convince me,
even if you should convince me.

Pov. "O city of Argos, you hear what he says!"

Chr. Call Pauson, your messmate.

Pov. What shall I do, unhappy woman?

Chr. Go to the devil quickly from us!

Pov. But whither on earth shall I go?

Chr. To the pillory; you ought not to delay, but to
make haste.

Pov. Assuredly you will have to send for me hither
some time.

Chr. Then you shall return; but now go and be hanged!
For it is better for me to be rich, and to leave you to wail
loudly in your head.   [*Exit* POVERTY.

Bl. By Jove! then I wish, when I am rich, to feast
along with my children and my wife; and going sleek
from the bath, after I have bathed, to hoot at the artisans
and Poverty.

Chr. This cursed wretch is gone. But let you and me
convey the god as soon as possible to the Temple of Æsculapius to put him to bed in it.

Bl. And let us not delay, lest again some one come and
hinder us from doing something useful.

Chr. Boy Cario, you must bring out the bedclothes,
and convey Plutus himself, as is customary, and the other
things, as many as are ready prepared in the house.

                    [*Exeunt* CHREMYLUS *and* BLEPSIDEMUS.

Cario (*returning from the temple*). O you old men, who
very often at the festival of Theseus had sopped up soup
to very little bread, how prosperous you are, how happily
you are circumstanced, and the rest of you, as many as
have any claim to a good character!

Cho. But what news is there, O good sir, about your
friends? for you appear to have come as a messenger of
some good news.

Ca. My master is most prosperously circumstanced—
or rather Plutus himself; for instead of being blind, he
has been restored to sight, and has been made clear-
sighted in the pupils of his eyes, having found Æsculapius
a friendly physician.

Cho. You tell me a matter for joy, you tell me a matter
for shouting.

Ca. 'Tis your lot to rejoice, whether you wish it or no.

Cho. I will loudly praise Æsculapius blessed in his children, and a great light to mortals.

Enter WIFE OF CHREMYLUS

Wife. What in the world means the shout? Is some
good news announced? for, longing for this, I have
been sitting in the house this long while, waiting for this
fellow.

Ca. Quickly, quickly, bring wine, mistress, in order
that you yourself also may drink—and you are very fond
of doing it—for I bring you all blessings in a lump.

Wife. Why, where are they?

Ca. You will soon learn by what is said.

Wife. Be quick and finish then some time or other
what you are for saying.

Ca. Hear, then; for I will tell you the whole affair from
the foot to the head.

Wife. Nay, not on my head, pray.

Ca. Not the blessings which have now taken place?

Wife. Nay, rather, not the troubles.

Ca. As soon as we came to the god, conveying a man,
at that time most miserable, but now blessed and fortunate, if there ever was one, we first conveyed him to the
sea, and then washed him.

Wife. By Jupiter, then he was fortunate, an old man
washed in the cold sea!

Ca. Then we went to the temple of the god. And
when our wafers and preparatory sacrifices were offered
on the altar, and our cake in the flame of Vulcan, we laid

Plutus on a couch, as was proper, while each of us began putting his mattress in order.

Wife. And were there any others also in need of the god?

Ca. Yes, there was one Neoclides, who is indeed blind, but outdoes in stealing those who see: and many others having all sorts of diseases. But when the sacrist of the god put out the lamps and ordered us to sleep, telling us if any one should hear a noise, he must be silent, we all lay down in an orderly manner. And I could not sleep; but a pot of porridge which was lying a little way off from the head of an old woman strongly affected me, toward which I desired exceedingly to creep. Then on looking up I saw the priest snatching away the cakes and dried figs from the sacred table. And after this he went round to all the altars round about, if anywhere a cake might be left; and then he consecrated these—into a sack. And I, supposing there was great piety in the thing, got up toward the pot of porridge.

Wife. O most daring of men, were you not afraid of the god?

Ca. Yes, by the gods, lest he might get to the pot before me, with his garlands on; for his priest taught me that beforehand. But the old woman, when she heard my noise, stretched forth her hand; and then I hissed and seized it with my teeth, as if I were an Æsculapian snake. But she immediately drew back her hand again, and lay down, having wrapped herself up quietly, trembling with fear. And then I swallowed greedily the greater part of the porridge: and then, when I was full, I rested.

Wife. But did not the god come to you?

Ca. Not yet.

Wife. Doubtless he was immediately disgusted at you on account of this.

Ca. After this I immediately covered myself up for fear; while he went round in a circuit inspecting all the maladies very regularly. Then a servant set before him a small stone mortar and a pestle and a small chest.

Wife. Of stone?

Ca. No, by Jove, certainly not, not the little chest.

Wife. But how did you see, the devil take you! who say you were wrapped up?

Ca. Through my little threadbare cloak; for, by Jupiter! it has no few holes. First of all he began to pound up a plaster for Neoclides, having thrown in three heads of Tenian garlic. Then he beat them up in the mortar, mixing along with them gum and squill; and then he moistened it with Sphettian vinegar, and spread it over, having turned his eyelids inside out, that he might be pained the more. And he crying out and bawling, jumped up and ran away, while the god laughed and said, "Sit there now, plastered over, that I may stop your excusing yourself on oath from the Assembly."

Wife. How very patriotic and wise the god is!

Ca. After this he sat down beside Plutus; and first he handled his head, and then he took a clean napkin and wiped his eyelids all round: and Panacea covered his head and the whole of his face with a purple cloth. Then the god whistled; then two snakes rushed forth from the temple, prodigious in size.

Wife. O ye friendly gods!

Ca. And these two gently crept under the purple cloth and began to lick his eyelids all round, as it appeared to me. And before you could have drunk up ten half-pints of wine, mistress, Plutus was standing up, having the use of his eyes: and I clapped my hands for joy, and began to wake my master. But the god immediately took himself out of sight, and the snakes took themselves into the temple; while those who were lying in bed near him, you can't think how they began embracing Plutus, and kept awake the whole night, until day dawned. But I praised the god very much, because he had quickly caused Plutus to see, while he made Neoclides more blind than before.

Wife. How much power you possess, O king and master! But [*to* CARIO] tell me, where is Plutus!

Ca. He is coming. But there was a prodigious crowd about him. For all those who were formerly just, and had a scanty subsistence, were embracing him and shaking hands with him for joy; but as many as were rich, and had much property, not having acquired their subsistence justly, were contracting their brows, and at the same time looking angry. But the others were following behind with garlands on, laughing and shouting in triumph; and the shoe of the old men was resounding with their steps in good time. But come, do you all together with one accord dance, and leap, and form a chorus; for no one will announce to you when you go in that there is no meal in the bag.

Wife. And I, by Hecate, wish to crown you for your good news with a string of cracknels, who have announced such tidings.

Ca. Do not then delay any longer, for the men are now near to the door.

Wife. Come, then, let me go in and fetch some sweetmeats to be showered as it were over his newly purchased eyes. [*Exit* WIFE OF CHREMYLUS.

Ca. But I wish to go to meet them. [*Exit* CARIO.

Enter PLUTUS, *accompanied by* CHREMYLUS *and a great crowd of people*

Plutus. And first I salute the sun, and then the illustrious soil of the august Pallas, and the whole land of Cecrops, which received me. I am ashamed of my misfortunes, because I associated with such men without my knowing it, but shunned those who were worthy of my society, knowing nothing, oh, unhappy me! How wrongly I acted both in that case and in this! But I will reverse them all again, and henceforth show to all men that I unwillingly gave myself up to the wicked.

Chr. (*to some bystander*). Go to the devil! How

troublesome a thing are the friends who appear immediately, when one is prosperous! For they nudge me with their elbows, and bruise my shins, each of them exhibiting some good-will. For who did not address me? What a crowd of old men was there not around me in the market-place?

Enter WIFE OF CHREMYLUS

Wife. O dearest of men! Welcome, both you, and you! Come now, for it is the custom, let me take and pour these sweetmeats over you.

Plu. By no means; for on my first entry into the house, and when I have recovered my eyesight, it is in no wise becoming to carry out anything, but rather to carry in.

Wife. Then, pray, will you not accept my sweetmeats?

Plu. Yes, in the house, by the fireside, as is the custom. Then also we may avoid the vulgarity of the thing; for it is not becoming for the dramatic poet to throw dried figs and sweetmeats to the spectators and then force them to laugh at this.

Wife. You say very well; for see! there's Dexinicus standing up, with the intention of snatching at the dried figs! [*Exeunt* PLUTUS, CHREMYLUS, WIFE, *and attendants.*

Cario (*coming out of the house*). How delightful it is, sirs, to fare prosperously! especially if one has brought out nothing from home. For a heap of blessings has rushed into our house, without our committing any injustice. Under these circumstances wealth is a very delightful thing. Our meal-chest is full of wheaten flour, and our wine-jars of dark wine with a high perfume. And all our vessels are full of silver and gold, so that I wonder. And our oil-jar is full of oil; and our flasks are full of unguents, and our garret of dried figs. And every vinegar-cruet, and platter, and pot has become of brass; and our rotten, fishy chargers you may see of silver. And our lantern has suddenly become of ivory.

And we servants play at even and odd with golden staters; and we no longer wipe ourselves with stones, but always with garlic, through luxury. And at present my master is sacrificing within a pig, and a goat, and a ram, with a chaplet on: but the smoke drove me out; for I was not able to remain within; for it stung my eyelids.

Enter a JUST MAN *attended by his servant*

Just Man. Follow with me, my little boy, that we may go to the god.

Enter CHREMYLUS

Chr. Ha! who is this who approaches?

J. M. A man, formerly wretched, but now prosperous.

Chr. It is evident that you are one of the good, as it appears.

J. M. Most certainly.

Chr. Then, what do you want?

J. M. I have come to the god: for he is the author of great blessings to me. For having received a considerable property from my father, I used to assist those of my friends who were in want, thinking it to be useful for life.

Chr. Doubtless your money soon failed you.

J. M. Just so.

Chr. Therefore after this you were wretched.

J. M. Just so. And I thought I should have as really firm friends, if ever I might want them, those whom I had before done kindness to when they were in want: but they began to avoid me, and pretended not to see me any longer.

Chr. And also laughed at you, I well know.

J. M. Just so. For the dearth which was in my vessels ruined me.

Chr. But not now.

J. M. Wherefore with good reason I have come hither to the god, to offer up my vows.

Chr. But what has the threadbare cloak to do with the god, which this servant is carrying in your retinue? tell me.

J. M. This also I am coming to the god to dedicate.

Chr. Were you initiated, then, in the Great Mysteries in it?

J. M. No; but I shivered in it for thirteen years.

Chr. But your shoes?

J. M. These also have weathered the storm along with me.

Chr. Then were you bringing these also to dedicate them?

J. M. Yes, by Jupiter!

Chr. You have come with very pretty presents for the god.

Enter an INFORMER *attended by his witness*

Informer. Ah me, unhappy! How I am undone, miserable man, and thrice unhappy, and four times, and five times, and twelve times, and ten thousand times! alas! alas! with so powerful a fate have I been mingled.

Chr. O Apollo, averter of evil, and ye friendly gods! what in the world is the misfortune which the man has suffered?

Inf. Why, have I not now suffered shocking things, who have lost everything out of my house through this god, who shall be blind again, unless lawsuits be wanting?

J. M. I imagine I pretty nearly see into the matter; for a man is approaching who is badly off; and he seems to be of the bad stamp.

Chr. By Jupiter, then, he is rightly ruined!

Inf. Where, where is this fellow who singly promised he would immediately make us all rich, if he were to recover his sight again as before? On the contrary, he has ruined some much more.

Chr. And whom, pray, has he treated thus?

Inf. Me here.

Chr. Were you of the number of the wicked ones and house-breakers?

Inf. By Jove! there is certainly no good in any of you; and it must be that you have my money.

Ca. O Ceres, how insolently the informer has come in! It is evident that he is ravenously hungry.

Inf. You can not be too quick in going speedily to the market-place; for you must there be racked upon the wheel and declare your villainies.

Ca. Then you'll suffer for it.

J. M. By Jupiter the Preserver! this god is of great value to all the Greeks, if he shall utterly destroy the informers, the wretches, in a wretched way.

Inf. Ah me, miserable! Are you also laughing at me, who are an accomplice? for whence have you got this garment? But yesterday I saw you with a threadbare cloak on.

J. M. I care nothing for you: for see! I wear this ring, having purchased it from Eudemus for a drachma.

Chr. But it is not possible to wear one against an informer's bite.

Inf. Is not this great insolence? You mock me, but you have not stated what you are doing here. For you are here for no good.

Chr. Certainly not, by Jove! for your good; be well assured.

Inf. For, by Jove! you will dine at my cost.

Chr. For the sake of truth may you burst, together with your witness, filled with nothing.

Inf. Do you deny it? There is a great quantity of slices of salt-fish and roast meat within, you most abominable fellows. [*Sniffs*] uhu, uhu, uhu, uhu, uhu, uhu.

Chr. Do you smell anything, you poor wretch?

J. M. The cold, perhaps; since he has on such a threadbare cloak.

Inf. Is this bearable then, O Jupiter and ye gods, that these should commit outrages upon me? Ah me! how grieved I am that, good and patriotic as I am, I fare badly.

Chr. You patriotic and good?

Inf. As never man was.

Chr. Well, now, answer me when asked——

Inf. What?

Chr. Are you a husbandman?

Inf. Do you suppose me to be so mad?

Chr. Or a merchant?

Inf. Yes, I pretend to be, upon occasion.

Chr. Well, then, did you learn any trade?

Inf. No, by Jove!

Chr. How then, or whence, did you live, if you do nothing?

Inf. I am manager of all the affairs of the state and private affairs.

Chr. You? Wherefore?

Inf. I please to do so.

Chr. How then, you house-breaker, can you be good, if, when it in no wise concerns you, you are then hated?

Inf. Why, does it not concern me, you booby, to benefit my own city as far as I be able?

Chr. Then is to be a meddling busybody to benefit it?

Inf. Nay, rather, to aid the established laws, and, if any one do wrong, not to permit it.

Chr. Does not the state, then, purposely appoint judges to preside?

Inf. But who is the accuser?

Chr. Any one who pleases.

Inf. Then I am he; so that the affairs of the state have devolved on me.

Chr. Then, by Jove! it has a sorry patron. But would you not prefer that, to keep quiet and live idle?

Inf. Nay, you are describing the life of a sheep, if there shall appear no amusement in life.

Chr. And would you not learn better?

Inf. Not even if you were to give me Plutus himself, and the silphium of Battus.

Chr. Quickly lay down your cloak.

Ca. (*to the* INFORMER). Ho you! he is speaking to you.

Chr. Next take off your shoes.

Ca. (to the INFORMER). He says all this to you.

Inf. Well, now, let any of you that pleases come hither against me.

Ca. " Then I am he." [*Seizes the* INFORMER *and strips him of his cloak and shoes.*

Inf. Ah me, miserable! I am stripped in the day-time.

Ca. For you do not hesitate to get a livelihood by meddling with other people's business.

Inf. (to his witness). Do you see what he is doing? I call you to witness this. [*His witness runs off.*

Chr. But the witness whom you brought is running away.

Inf. Ah me, I have been caught alone.

Ca. Do you bawl now?

Inf. Ah me, again and again!

Ca. Do you (*to the* JUST MAN) give me your thread-bare cloak, that I may put it on this informer.

J. M. Certainly not; for it has been this long while consecrated to Plutus.

Ca. Where, then, will it be better dedicated than around a knavish man and house-breaker? But Plutus it is fitting to adorn with grand dresses.

J. M. But what shall one make of the shoes? tell me.

Ca. These also I will instantly nail fast to this man's forehead, as if to a wild olive.

Inf. I'll begone; for I perceive I am much weaker than you. But if I find a comrade, even of fig-tree wood, I will to-day make this powerful god give me satisfaction, because he singly and alone is manifestly putting down the democracy, having neither prevailed upon the Senate of the citizens nor the Assembly.

J. M. Well, now, since you are marching with my panoply on, run to the bath, and then stand there in front and warm yourself. For I also once held this post.

[*Exit* INFORMER.

Chr. But the bath-man will take and drag him out of doors; for when he has seen him he will perceive that he is of that bad stamp. But let us two go in, that you may offer up your vows to the god.

[*Exeunt* CHREMYLUS *and* JUST MAN.

Old Woman (entering and bearing some cakes on a platter). O dear old men, have we really come to the house of this new god, or have we altogether missed the road?

Cho. Nay, know that you have come to the very door, my little girl; for you ask seasonably.

Old Wom. Come, then, let me summon some one of those within.

Enter CHREMYLUS

Chr. Certainly not; for I myself have come out. But you must tell me for what in particular you have come.

Old Wom. O dearest sir, I have suffered dreadful and unjust things: for since what time this god began to have the use of his eyes, he has made my life to be insupportable.

Chr. What's the matter? I suppose you also were an informeress among women?

Old Wom. No, by Jupiter, not I!

Chr. Or did you not drink in your letter, having obtained it by lot?

Old Wom. You are mocking me; but I burn with love, unhappy woman.

Chr. Will you not then quickly tell me what is your love?

Old Wom. Hear then! I had a dear youth, poor, indeed, but, for the rest, good-looking, and handsome, and good. For if I wanted anything, he used to perform everything for me decently and well, while I assisted him in all his wants in the same manner.

Chr. But what was it he especially wanted of you, on each occasion?

Old Wom. Not much; for he was marvellously respectful to me. But he used to ask for twenty drachmæ of silver for a mantle, and eight for shoes ; and he used to entreat me to purchase a tunic for his sisters, and a little mantle for his mother ; and he used to beg for four medimni of wheat.

Chr. Certainly, by Apollo! this is not much which you have mentioned ; but it is evident that he respected you.

Old Wom. And these, moreover, he said he asked of me, not on account of lewdness, but for affection, that while wearing my mantle he might think on me.

Chr. You describe a man most marvellously in love with you.

Old Wom. But the abominable fellow now no longer has the same mind, but has changed very much. For when I sent him this cheese-cake here and the other sweetmeats which are upon the plate, and whispered that I would come in the evening——

Chr. What did he do to you? tell me.

Old Wom. He sent back to us besides this milk-cake here, on condition that I never came thither any more ; and besides, in addition to this, when sending it off he said, " Once in olden time the Milesians were brave."

Chr. It is evident that he was not very bad in his character.   So then, being rich, he no longer takes pleasure in lentil-porridge ; but formerly, through his poverty, he used to eat everything as a relish.

Old Wom. And yet formerly, by the two goddesses, he used always to come to my door every day.

Chr. For your burial?

Old Wom. No, by Jupiter! but merely through a desire to hear my voice.

Chr. Nay, rather, for the sake of getting something.

Old Wom. And, by Jove! if he perceived me afflicted, he used to call me coaxingly his little duck and little dove.

Chr. And then, perhaps, he used to ask you for money for shoes.

Old Wom. And when any one looked at me when riding in my carriage at the Great Mysteries, I was beaten on account of this the whole day; so very jealous was the young man.

Chr. For he took pleasure, as it seems, in eating alone.

Old Wom. And he said I had very beautiful hands.

Chr. Ay, whenever they offered twenty drachmæ.

Old Wom. And he said I smelt sweet in my skin——

Chr. Ay, like enough, by Jove! if you poured in Thasian wine for him.

Old Wom. And that I had a gentle and beautiful look.

Chr. The man was no fool, but knew how to devour the substance of a lustful old woman.

Old Wom. In this therefore, O dear sir, the god does not act rightly, who professes to succour whoever happen to be wronged.

Chr. Why, what must he do? speak, and it shall be done immediately.

Old Wom. It is just, by Jove! to compel him who has been benefited by me to benefit me in turn, for he deserves to possess no blessing whatever.

Chr. Did he not then repay you every night?

Old Wom. But he said he would never desert me while I lived.

Chr. Ay, rightly; but now he thinks you no longer alive.

Old Wom. For I am wasting away through grief, O dearest friend.

Chr. No, but you have rotted away, as it appears to me.

Old Wom. Indeed, then, you might draw me through a ring.

Chr. Yes, if the ring were the hoop of a sieve.

Old Wom. Well, now, see! here's the youth approaching, whom I have been accusing this long while; and he seems to be going to a revel.

Chr. He appears so: at least he is certainly coming with a chaplet and a torch.

Enter a YOUNG MAN *with a lighted torch in his hand,
followed by a band of revellers.*

Young Man. I salute you.

Old Wom. (*to* CHREMYLUS). What says he?

You. My ancient sweetheart, by Heaven! you have
quickly become gray.

Old Wom. Unhappy me, for the insult with which I am
insulted!

Chr. He seems to have seen you after a long time.

Old Wom. Since what time, O most audacious, who
was at my house yesterday?

Chr. Then he is affected in a manner opposite to most
people; for, as it seems, he sees sharper when he's drunk.

Old Wom. No, but he is always saucy in his manners.

You. (*holding the torch close to her face*). O Sea-Posei-
don and ye elderly gods, how many wrinkles she has in
her face!

Old Wom. Ah! ah! don't bring the torch near me!

Chr. Upon my word, she says rightly; for if only a
single spark catch her, it will burn her like an old harvest-
wreath.

You. Will you play with me for a while?

Old Wom. Where, wretch?

You. Here, having taken some nuts.

Old Wom. What game?

You. How many teeth you have.

Chr. Come, I also will have a guess; for she has three,
perhaps, or four.

You. Pay up! for she carries only one grinder.

Old Wom. Most audacious of men, you don't appear
to me to be in your right senses, who make a wash-pot of
me in the presence of so many men.

You. Upon my word, you'd be the better for it, if one
were to wash you clean.

Chr. Certainly not, for now she is playing the cheat;
but if this white-lead shall be washed off, you'll see the
wrinkles in her face quite plain.

Old Wom. You don't appear to me to be in your right senses, old man as you are.

You. Perhaps, indeed, he is tempting you, and is touching your breasts, fancying that he escapes my notice.

Old Wom. No, by Venus, not mine, you abominable fellow!

Chr. No, by Hecate! certainly not! for I should be mad. But, young man, I won't suffer you to hate this girl.

You. Nay, I love her beyond measure.

Chr. And yet she accuses you.

You. What does she accuse me of?

Chr. She says that you are an insolent person, and that you tell her, "Once in olden time the Milesians were brave."

You. I will not quarrel with you about her.

Chr. Why so?

You. Out of respect for your age; for I would never have suffered another to do so; but now go in peace, having taken the girl along with you.

Chr. I know, I know your meaning; perhaps you no longer deign to be with her.

Old Wom. But who is there to permit him?

You. I would not have to do with one who has been embraced by thirteen thousand years.

Chr. But yet, since you thought proper to drink the wine, you must also drink up the dregs.

You. But the dregs are altogether old and fusty.

Chr. Then a straining-cloth will cure all this.

You. Come, go within! for I wish to go and dedicate to the god these chaplets which I have on.

Old Wom. And I also wish to say something to him.

You. But I will not go in.

Chr. Be of good courage, don't be afraid! for she sha'n't ravish you.

You. Now you say very well; for I have been pitching her up long enough already.

25

Old Wom. Go in, and I'll enter after you.

[*Exeunt* OLD WOMAN *and* YOUNG MAN.

Chr. How forcibly, O King Jove, the old woman sticks to the youth like a limpet!   [*Exit* CHREMYLUS.

Enter MERCURY, *who knocks at the door and then runs away, frightened at the noise he has made*

Cario (*from within*). Who's that knocking at the door? [*Comes out and looks about.*] What's this? It appears to be nobody. Then certainly the door shall suffer for creaking without cause.   [*Retires again.*

Mer. (*running out of his hiding-place*). Cario! You, I say! stop!

Ca (*coming out again*). Hallo, you! Tell me, did you knock at the door so violently?

Mer. No, by Jove! but I was going to; and then you anticipated me by opening it. Come, run quickly and call out your master, then his wife and children, then his servants, then the dog, then yourself, then the sow.

Ca. Tell me, what's the matter?

Mer. Jupiter, you rascal, intends to mix you up in the same bowl and cast you all together into the Barathrum.

Ca. The tongue is given to the herald of these tidings. But on what account, pray, does he purpose to do this to us?

Mer. Because you have done the most dreadful of all deeds. For since what time Plutus began to have the use of his eyes as before, no one any longer offers to us gods either frankincense, or laurel, or barley-cake, or victim, or anything else.

Ca. No, by Jupiter! nor will he offer them. For you took bad care of us aforetime.

Mer. And for the other gods I care less; but I am undone, and am ruined.

Ca. You're wise.

Mer. For formerly I used to enjoy all good things in the female innkeepers' shops as soon as it was morning,

wine-cake, honey, dried figs, as many as 'tis fitting that
Mercury should eat; but now I go to bed hungry with
my legs lying up.

Ca. Is it not then with justice, who sometimes caused
their loss, although you enjoyed such good things?

Mer. Ah me, miserable! Ah me, for the cheese-cake
that was baked on the fourth day!

Ca. "You long for the absent, and call in vain."

Mer. Ah me for the ham which I used to devour!

Ca. Leap upon the bottle there in the open.

Mer. And for the warm entrails which I used to
devour!

Ca. A pain about your entrails seems to torture you.

Mer. Ah me, for the cup that was mixed half-and-half!

Ca. You can not be too quick in drinking this besides
and running away.

Mer. Would you assist your own friend in any way?

Ca. Yes; if you want any of those things in which I
am able to assist you.

Mer. If you were to procure me a well-baked loaf and
give it me to eat, and a huge piece of meat from the sacrifices you are offering within.

Ca. But there is no carrying out.

Mer. And yet whenever you stole any little vessel from
your master, I always used to cause you to be undetected.

Ca. On condition that you also shared yourself, you
house-breaker. For a well-baked cake used to come to you.

Mer. And then you used to devour this yourself.

Ca. For you had not an equal share of the blows with
me, whenever I was caught in any knavery.

Mer. Don't bear malice, if you have got possession of
Phyle; but, by the gods, receive me as a fellow-inmate!

Ca. Then will you abandon the gods and stay here?

Mer. Yes; for your condition is much better.

Ca. How then? do you think desertion a fine thing?

Mer. Yes; "for his country is every country, wherever
a man is well off."

Ca. What use then would you be to us, if you were here?

Mer. Post me beside the door as turnkey.

Ca. As turnkey? but we have no need of turns.

Mer. As merchant, then.

Ca. But we are rich; what need then for us to maintain a huckstering Mercury?

Mer. Well, as deceiver, then.

Ca. As deceiver? By no means. For we have no need of deception now, but of simple manners.

Mer. As conductor, then.

Ca. But the god now has the use of his eyes; so we shall no longer want a conductor.

Mer. Then I will be president of the games. And what further will you say? For this is most convenient for Plutus, to celebrate musical and gymnastic contests.

Ca. What a good thing it is to have many surnames! for this fellow has found out a scant living for himself by this means. No wonder all the judges often seek eagerly to be inscribed in many letters.

Mer. Then shall I go in upon these terms?

Ca. Ay, and go yourself to the well and wash the puddings, that you may immediately be thought to be serviceable. [*Exeunt* MERCURY *and* CARIO.

Priest of Jupiter (*entering hastily*). Who can tell me for certain where Chremylus is?

Enter CHREMYLUS

Chr. What is the matter, my good sir?

Priest. Why, what else but bad? For since what time this Plutus began to have the use of his eyes, I perish with hunger. For I have nothing to eat; and that, too, though I am the priest of Jupiter the Preserver.

Chr. Oh! by the gods, what is the cause?

Priest. No one deigns to sacrifice any longer.

Chr. On what account?

Priest. Because they are all rich. And yet, at that

time, when they had nothing, the one, a merchant, used to come and sacrifice some victim for his safety; and some other one, because he had been acquitted on his trial; and some other one used to sacrifice with favourable omens, and invite me too, the priest. But now not even a single person sacrifices anything at all, or enters the temple, except it be more than a myriad to ease themselves.

Chr. Do you not, then, receive your lawful share of these?

Priest. Therefore I also am resolved to bid farewell to Jupiter the Preserver and stay here in this place.

Chr. Be of good courage! for it will be well, if the god please. For Jupiter the Preserver is present here, having come of his own accord.

Priest. Then you tell me all good news.

Chr. We will therefore immediately establish — but stay here—Plutus where he was before established, always guarding the inner cell of the goddess. But let some one give me out here lighted torches, that you may hold them and go before the god.

Priest. Yes, by all means we must do this.

Chr. Call Plutus out, some of you.

Enter OLD WOMAN

Old Wom. But what am I to do?

Chr. Take the pots with which we are to establish the god, and carry them on your head in a stately manner, for you came yourself with a party-coloured dress on.

Old Wom. But on what account I came?

Chr. All shall be immediately done for you. For the young man shall come to you in the evening.

Old Wom. Well, by Jove! if indeed you promise me that he shall come to me, I'll carry the pots. [*Takes up the pots and puts them on her head.*

Chr. (*to the spectators*). Well, now, these pots act very differently from the other pots. For in the other pots the scum is on the top; but now the pots are on the top of this old woman.

Cho. Therefore 'tis fitting that we delay no longer, but go back to the rear; for we must follow after these, singing. [*Exeunt omnes.*

THE END